HESTON'S FANTASTICAL FEASTS

HESTON BLUMENTHAL

HESTON'S FANTASTICAL FEASTS

PHOTOGRAPHY BY ANDY SEWELL

ILLUSTRATIONS BY TOM LANE

optomen

BLOOMSBURY

Contents

Introduction

EATING'S PLEASURE depends on more than just taste. Sights, smells, sounds and textures have a huge influence on our enjoyment of food, as do all the memories and associations that we bring to the table, and the context in which a dish is served.

Soon after I opened the Fat Duck I began trying to create recipes that drew on as many of the senses as possible, and that triggered not just the tastebuds but also memories—an ice-cold sorbet, for example, surrounded by flames and the aromas of an old-fashioned study: leather, wood fires and tobacco. Or a dish of sea urchins, baby anchovies, foam and samphire that, with the help of headphones relaying the crash of surf and the keening of gulls, transports each diner to his or her own seascape.

There are, however, limits to what you can do in a restaurant environment. Whatever's going on at one table mustn't be allowed to disrupt the experience of those on neighbouring tables. Special culinary effects have to be modest and contained—chamber music rather than the full orchestra. (Even those headphones didn't get introduced until I had found a way of doing it that didn't distract other diners.)

So when I got the opportunity to dream up six historical feasts inspired by books, legends and fairy tales, and then serve them up to guests, I jumped at the chance. For my historical cornerstones I chose the Regency and Edwardian periods, the Gothic Revival and the 1960s, 1970s and 1980s, and then began my research and development, delving into *Grimm's Fairy Tales* and memories of my schooldays, re-reading *Dracula* and *Charlie and the Chocolate Factory*, checking out Slush Puppie machines and microwaves and menus from the *Titanic*.

I wanted to create feasts that captured the spirit of their times. They had to be theatrical and fantastical, stimulating all the senses and conjuring up for my guests all sorts of memories and allusions and associations, as though I had waved a magic wand. To that end, I explored some strange places and some even stranger ideas. I ate boar's eyes, Play-Doh and a lot of Spam. I went to the walled city in Fes to get tips on cooking camel meat and to snowy Transylvania to find out about a legendary recipe for leeches fed on goose blood. I tried to make edible bones, lickable wallpaper, floating food, superstringy cheese, a savoury Zoom lolly and fake Champagne using a SodaStream. It was a mad, invigorating, informative, frustrating, funny, shocking and surprising journey—and it's all here in the pages of this book.

This, then, is not so much a cookbook as a culinary adventure story, with recipes. Each chapter finishes with a selection of the recipes for that Feast—this is where you'll learn the secrets of how it was done on the night. The recipes are long (if I'd included all of them, the book would have been the size and weight of a telephone directory) and very complicated because they detail every stage of the process for a large team of highly trained professional chefs. If you're going to undertake them, then, as in all good fairy tales, you'll need skill and a certain determination. But if you do so, I believe that, again as in fairy tales, you will get your reward.

Heston Blumenthal,
Bray, May 2010

A Fairy Tale Feast

THE Regency era extended from 1812—when the porphyria-induced "madness" of King George III meant control of the country passed to his son, George, as Prince Regent—to the death of George IV in 1830. It was a time of great unrest, division and contradictions: the victory over Napoleon at Waterloo in 1815 was followed four years later by the Peterloo Massacre, in which troops opened fire on a parliamentary reform rally in Manchester, killing eleven people and wounding hundreds more.

Symbolic of his time, the Prince Regent was equally contradictory. George incurred colossal debts, had a series of affairs, and drank and ate to such an extent that he ballooned to twenty stone and was given the nickname "The Prince of Whales". (Uncorseted, his belly is said to have reached to his knees.) His self-indulgence overshadowed the wit, intelligence and artistic sensitivity that were also parts of his character. Even his detractors, such as the Duke of Wellington, admitted that he was "a most magnificent patron of the arts", commissioning works from Gainsborough, Stubbs and Nash, who designed Brighton Pavilion and began the remodelling of Buckingham House into a palace. George was also largely responsible for the transformation of dilapidated Windsor Castle into the imposing Gothic edifice we know today. Indeed the so-called Regency style is in part due to George's taste for ceremony and presentation. According to Antonia Fraser's *The Lives of the Kings and Queens of England,* his coronation was "probably the most elaborate of all time, the ultimate in regal splendour, with the new King looking like some gorgeous bird of paradise".

I wanted my Feast to capture the fantasy and extravagance of the Regency era, and also a little of its flipside: the greed, selfishness and cruelty. I was looking for something from the period that would still have resonance nowadays, and found it via the German roots of the Georgian kings. The first volume of Jacob and Wilhelm Grimm's *Fairy Tales* was published in 1812, the same year as George became Prince Regent. Its stories of *Rapunzel, Cinderella, Sleeping Beauty* and *Snow White* had fantastical palaces and bird-of-paradise princes, but also brutal deaths and suffering ragamuffin children. I wouldn't necessarily confine myself to works of the Brothers Grimm, I decided, but fairy tales would provide the main inspiration for my Feast.

THE ABANDONED KITCHEN BOY

I found myself in Syon House, west London (which got a makeover by Robert Adam around the time George IV's father acceded to the throne), offering vol-au-vents containing minced chicken's testicles to little old ladies. Why was I doing this? Partly because the film crew loves a controversial ingredient, and the prospect of catching me on film delivering the line "Have you ever had a couple of testicles in your mouth before?", like some latterday Sid James, was impossible for them to resist. But beyond the innuendo there was a serious purpose. I was trying out a recipe invented by the most influential and celebrated chef of the Regency era—Antonin Carême.

Like a character in *Grimm's Fairy Tales,* Carême (1783—1833) was abandoned by his impoverished family, went to work as a kitchen boy in a Paris chophouse and rose to become the most famous chef of the nineteenth century. Unfortunately, his demise, too, had some of the Grimms' grimness about it. He died from overwork and the toxic effects of the fuel used for cooking—"burnt out by the fire of his genius and the charcoal of the rotisserie", as the poet Laurent Tailhade put it.

Although for a time he owned a patisserie on rue de la Paix, Carême worked mainly for high-profile clients. From 1804 he was employed by Talleyrand to cook for the official banquets that formed a key part of the French diplomat's international politicking. Over the next ten years Carême produced food for visiting dignitaries, deposed Spanish princes and members of Napoleon's family. He worked on the wedding banquet of Napoleon's brother, Jérôme, and made the wedding cake for Napoleon's wedding to Marie-Louise of Austria in 1810. At the ball thrown for the Emperor on the eve of his departure for Germany, he created thirty impossibly tall suédoises (layered fruit and jelly desserts) that were—according to Carême at least—the talk of the town.

At one of their daily meetings at Valençay to discuss dinner, Talleyrand challenged Carême to create a different menu for every day of the year, using seasonal produce where possible. The results were later to form the backbone of Carême's book *Le Maître d'Hôtel Français* (1822), which is a key text in the development of *haute cuisine*. By presenting the new style of cooking in the context of royal dinners, Câreme gave it a legitimacy; and by setting out sauces and suchlike in logical groups he made it more accessible and practicable.

After the Battle for Paris (1814) when troops led by Alexander I forced Napoleon's abdication, Talleyrand's table was no longer centre-stage. Although the Tsar invited Carême to work for him in Russia, Antonin chose instead to come to Britain to cook for the Prince Regent. It was the start of a frustrating period in his career. Although "every modern improvement to facilitate the process of the culinary art" had been introduced in the kitchen of the Brighton Pavilion (including clockwork roasting spits, a steam table to keep dishes hot and a giant ice house) and his food budget appeared to have no limits, Carême stayed only two years, driven away by the British weather and his employer's undiscerning gluttony. He then spent a disappointing time in St Petersburg where he never got to cook for his employer, Tsar Alexander, who left for Arkangel at the time Carême arrived, requesting that the chef wait indefinitely for his return. After a few months Antonin "decided to put honour before interest, and quit Russia".

Eventually Carême's life came full circle and he ended up in Paris cooking for the Rothschilds, who used the table to entertain, impress and influence powerful people, although this time the diners were not diplomats so much as key figures of French high society. The Rothschilds wanted to have the pre-eminent salon in Paris and Carême helped them to achieve this. He worked for them from 1823 until his retirement due to ill health in 1830. He died three years later, still trying to finish his encyclopaedic *L'Art de la Cuisine Française au XIXe Siècle*.

Carême's influence on *haute cuisine* is in part due to the fact that he came to prominence at a pivotal moment in French cooking. In the eighteenth century, the restaurant was simply a place to get a restorative bowl of soup (hence the name). Eating out was done in taverns, inns and cafés that generally served very basic fare, designed to fuel long journeys or soak up the booze rather than provide a gastronomic experience. However, the French Revolution (1789—99) led to many wealthy families of the *ancien régime* losing their positions and their prestige, and the chefs they had once employed had to find work elsewhere, often in restaurants. According to Ian Kelly in *Cooking for Kings*, before the revolution there were fewer than fifty restaurants in Paris, but by 1814 there were more than three thousand. At first, these had little in the way of culinary tradition to draw on, and so they relied on recipes developed and written down by Carême.

At the same time, Antonin's curiosity and creativity would probably have helped shape cuisine whatever century he was born into. Though he's perhaps best known for popularising the soufflé and inventing the vol-au-vent, Nesselrode pudding and large meringues, his innovations extend into impressively diverse areas of cuisine, from changing the shape of the saucepans used to pour sugar and introducing borscht and koulibiac to France, to establishing a set of terms and tests for the stages of boiling sugar—still in use today—and designing the tall white chef's hat known as a toque.

So my Fairy Tale Feast wouldn't be complete without some reference to Carême's cuisine. Were chicken's testicles the way to do this—or was I ballsing it up? I wasn't sure.

THE HOUSE THAT HESTON BUILT

They are the first edible houses and beauty shall be nothing if
not edible!

SALVADOR DALÍ, *Minotaure*

Once upon a time there was a humble baker's shop, run by a man named
Tom Slatter. Eventually the shop was passed on to his son, Ken, who
studied hard and became a skilled and ambitious baker, winning many
awards for his confectionery. Soon Slatter's bakeries could be found
up and down the high streets of southeast London—enticing customers
with their jauntily striped walls, quaint latticed bottle-glass windows
and promises of CHOCOLATE and FRESH CREAM CAKES within.

Then giants took over the city. Huge supermarkets lured customers
away with their cheaper goods. Soon butchers and bakers everywhere
(the candlestick maker having long gone) began to close down. Ken's
sons, Tim and Kevin, had to find a way to protect themselves…

✳

With his gentle manner, Steve Howard might seem like an unlikely
white knight. But, ten years ago, when the Slatter brothers saw what
Steve could do with a cake, they realised they had found the answer to
their struggle with the commercial giants. They renamed their business
The Cake Store, began specialising in "celebration cakes" and set up
a website. The site offers a spectacular range, from wedding cakes and
children's cakes to corporate cakes and even saucy cakes.

On the upper floor of the shop, I marvelled at the handiwork of
Steve and his team. Shelves housed a pink fairy-tale castle with tall
turrets; a stockade topped by a pink elephant surrounded by stars;
Homer Simpson and his family sitting on the sofa. There was even a
lovingly reproduced builder's bum, the icing jeans faithfully sagging
to reveal more than they should. They were skilful, technically intricate
pieces of work, which was just as well because I had a tough task for
Steve and Tim.

Trying in vain to construct scaffolding from peppermint rock.

"I'm preparing a feast based on *Grimm's Fairy Tales* and my idea for the dessert comes from *Hansel and Gretel*. D'you remember the story? A woodcutter and his wife are so poor they abandon their children in the forest. The kids find a house built of bread and start to eat it. The owner is a witch who imprisons Hansel and gets Gretel to feed him up so she can devour him. In the end Gretel tricks the witch into the oven, bolts the door shut, and the children escape back to their parents, taking with them the witch's treasure. As with many of the Grimms' stories, it's a savage tale and I'm not sure what we're supposed to learn from it, but the point is, I want to build a house you can eat."

There was a pause as Tim and Steve mulled over my project. Eventually Steve offered warily, "Any idea what ingredients?"

"The story just says the roof was made of cake and the windows were clear sugar. So we've got a lot of freedom," I offered.

They both still looked sceptical, but as we began drawing ideas, Steve's technical curiosity fired up and he started thinking through the structural problems. "The windows could be cracked sugar. We'd need to make the roof lighter than the walls because they've got to hold it up. Some kind of chocolate layers, perhaps, arranged in tiles...?"

"Yes," I agreed. "Though there's also the problem of sitting under studio lights. I don't want to end up with something like the melted palace of Prince Pondicherry in *Charlie and the Chocolate Factory*."

"Structurally," Tim said, "the corners are the most important. The middle could be light sponge as long as the corners are made of a solid material like gingerbread or sugar. Rock's certainly strong enough."

"I could give the guests little chisels so they could break off bits of the hard stuff." Ideas were beginning to take shape and I was keen to get going. "Let's try it out. What've you got that we can build with?"

Tim disappeared into another room and returned wheeling a trolley with shelves piled high with fruit cake, gingerbread, slabs of sponge, chocolate fingers, candy canes and sticks of rock. I noticed a stack of brownies topped with chocolate sprinkles that looked a lot like thatch and earmarked them for the roof—if we got that far. We began cutting brick-shaped pieces of cake, trowelling on buttercream with a palette knife, and building them up in rows, as you would a real brick wall. The buttercream looked convincingly like mortar. We were about to congratulate ourselves when the whole thing gently keeled over.

It was—literally—back to the drawing board. I sketched out the front and back faces of a house, and used them as a template to cut panels of gingerbread. The whole process took me back to woodwork lessons at school. "They actually look like MDF!" said Steve.

"I thought the gingerbread might shatter as I sawed through it with this serrated knife, but it has stayed intact." The fact that an ingredient actually responded like a real building material made me feel optimistic. Maybe this time we were on the right track.

Clearly, Steve and Tim felt the same. There was a renewed sense of purpose in the air. While I'd been cutting out the panels, they had worked on making the whole structure look more realistic. The cakeboard was now covered in a sheet of grass-green icing, and they had a batch of fondant ready to use as mastic. I held an endpiece and a sidepiece at right angles to one another and Steve ran the piping bag along the join, gluing them together. We repeated the process with the other pieces. Suddenly we had the basic shell of a roofless house.

I still wanted to give the illusion of brick, so we had recessed the sidepieces slightly and covered them with jam "glue". Tim began laying a wall of cake breeze-blocks up against the sidepieces, tapping the tops into place with the palette knife. Now that we had a structure, it was obvious that the roof would need more support than the endpieces could provide: we had to cut another gingerbread panel to fit neatly between the sides and with exactly the same pointy top as the endpieces, otherwise the roof wouldn't sit properly. We knew the test would be whether the structure would hold up when the roof was positioned.

It was feeling like an architectural challenge now. "Anyone got a spirit level?" Tim bantered as he finished off the walls with thick strips of sponge. One of his colleagues handed over a six-footer as a joke, but we ended up using it to verify that the pitch of the mid-section aligned with the endpieces. Columns of seaside-style rock were jam-glued into the four corners to increase the load-bearing capacity.

A sugar stained-glass window and a cake brick.

Making the chocolate doormat for the edible house.

"Right," announced Tim, picking up a large slab of sponge. "It's the moment of truth." We laid the sponge gently on top of our efforts and let go nervously. This time there was no keeling over. I started laying chocolate-sprinkle brownies as tiles, and gradually it began to look quite realistic—more of a barn than a house perhaps, but a credible construction none the less. There was just one finishing touch to add, inspired by one of the cakes that I'd noticed when I first walked in.

"This is great. Thanks for your help, gentleman. I've learned a lot," I said, beckoning to one of Steve's assistants who I'd asked to knock up something on the sly. "In the Regency period, most people didn't have an oven, so they'd get the baker to bake their bread. To identify their loaf, they'd fashion some kind of mark on it. So I thought I'd do so on this house." I picked up the icing figure and made him cling to the roof—a miniature builder with his bum hanging out of his trousers.

"As it happens," Steve replied, "we've also got something for you, Heston." One of his team appeared carrying what looked like a plain sheet of white icing until I got up close and saw my own face looking back at me. "You said that in *Hansel and Gretel* the witch intends to eat Hansel. Well, we've given you the opportunity to eat yourself!"

CARÊME'S EXTRAORDINAIRES

You might think that the ambition to build an edible house was just a typical example of my approach to cuisine. But in fact there's a great tradition of such architectural antics. In medieval times so called "subtleties"—ships, statues and dragons— were carved out of sugar. But the practice reached its pinnacle with Carême's creations.

Carême saw cuisine essentially as an art form, and the highest expressions of this were his *pièces montées* or *extraordinaires*: models of classic temples, rotundas and bridges rendered in fastidious detail in marzipan, pork fat and pastry, decorated with spun sugar or fruits. Some of these were purely visual treats but others were designed to be eaten. They would be brought to the table as spectacular set pieces, to be placed alongside more conventional dishes. At one dinner for forty people given by the Prince Regent in Brighton Pavilion, a first course of forty-eight dishes was followed by eight Carême creations, including a "Chinese Hermitage" and "The Ruin of the Turkish Mosque".

THE CONFECTIONER'S SHOP

Nostalgia often influences my development of recipes for the Fat Duck—the tasting menu features, among other things, versions of the sherbet dab and coconut baccy—so I'm thrilled to see new versions of old sweet shops popping up all over the country, such as Suck It and Sea in Brighton and the chain of Mr Simms Old Sweet Shoppes.

One of my favourites is Hope and Greenwood in Covent Garden. The floor-to-ceiling shelves are stacked with glass jars full of sweets with evocative names: Lime Juice & Soda, Lemon Bon Bons, Magic Millions, Cough Candy, Rhubarb & Custard. Fragile glass-fronted display cases house the owners' personal selections—Miss Hope's Jolly Mixture; Best of British; Perfect Princess—packaged in imitation sweetie jars or multicoloured polka-dot boxes or beribboned cellophane bags and labelled: "Hope and Greenwood, Purveyors of Splendid Confectionery". This devotion to the period and attention to detail is invested in every aspect of the shop. Old biscuit tins adorn the shelves and a set of three ducks fly up one wall. Mr Greenwood sports a dandy waxed tache and beard, while Miss Hope wears a fifties floral-print dress and a cardie. They refer to one another formally as "Miss Hope" and "Mr Greenwood", though with a mischievous glint in the eye.

I'd come to their shop because even I realised that a dish of chicken's testicles might encounter some resistance from my Feast guests, and so I'd decided the best way to overcome this was to present them in a format that was especially comforting and approachable. The testicles had a kidney shape that reminded me of jelly beans, so I wanted to find out if there was a way to capitalise on that appearance. I pushed open the door and demanded, "Can I make my testicles look like jelly beans?"

Miss Hope stood behind the counter with her arms folded. She was wearing rollers, which somehow emphasised the *Carry-On* flavour of our encounter. "Well, I can see why you might need to, Heston. They do look grim," she replied, prodding the plastic pouch of chicken's testicles that I'd put on the counter. "Rather like giant butterbeans. But with veins. Ugh."

"Actually, they taste delicious." I felt the need to defend my poor misunderstood foodstuff. "They're highly regarded in France, where they're known as *rognons blanc*—white kidneys. I'm hoping to cover them in something that makes them less offputting for people…"

"… Who've less experience than you of putting testicles in their mouths? I think I understand your problem, Heston." She began

Miss Hope helps transform a chicken's testicle into a jelly bean.

ransacking store cupboards and soon the countertop was crowded with packets and tubes of Wilton sprinkles, crystallised violets, hundreds and thousands, rainbow pearls, Dr Oetker chocolate stars, mini cupcakes, violet-flavoured drops, edible wafer paper.

Not to be outdone, I brought out some sugar syrup, icing sugar and a hairdryer and placed them beside the unseemly bag o' balls. "What I thought we'd try first is coating the *rognons* in much the same way as you would sugared almonds. That's why I've brought the hairdryer."

"Well, I didn't think it was for your own personal use."

"Have you got any shellac? We can mix up a solution of that plus a little sugar to make it sweeter and thicker. Dip the chicken ball into it. Dry it off with the hairdryer. Dip it in again. Build up the layers." I prepared a cup of shellac-and-sugar mix, stabbed a toothpick into one of the testicles (to a slight wince from Miss Hope), dunked it in the solution, then lifted it and twizzled as she trained the dryer on it.

"Reheating cooked meat like this is poor practice from a food safety point of view," I cautioned. "This is just to see if we can get the effect I want. If so, then I'll have to find a safer way of doing it."

In fact, after only a couple of rounds of dunk-lift-twizzle-dry, the effect began to look very promising. "It's got a real sheen to it," declared Miss Hope. "You could add a pickled silverskin onion and serve it at a cocktail party as a sausage-on-a-stick."

It wasn't quite the look I was after. "Have you any food colouring?" Another rummage in store cupboards produced some red, which I added to the shellac and began dunking again. My *rognon blanc* turned an angry scarlet. It now looked like the kind of thing that surgeons grappled with in TV hospital dramas.

"Chicken's testicles in blood. Very *Wicker Man*. That's *nasty*," Miss Hope said, encouragingly, but I continued and gradually, as the coats of colour built up, it came to resemble a jelly bean perfectly—exceeding all my expectations. I packed away my sugars and hairdryer, and Miss Hope regretfully returned her packets and tubes to the store cupboard. Obviously I'd have to refine the technique, but I was definitely going to serve my guests *rognon blanc* jelly beans in some form or other.

THE BLACK FOREST

Wild boar was one of Carême's performance pieces. For the wedding breakfast of the (somewhat shotgun) marriage of Napoleon's brother Jérôme to Princess Catharina of Württemberg in 1807, he served two stuffed boar's heads, garlanded with yew branches and roses made of wax. Decorated skewers of meat balls bristled from the boar's brow.

I thought I might make a boar's head the centrepiece of my Feast, too, so I contacted the chef Karl-Josef Fuchs, whose family has run the Spielweg hotel in Münstertal since 1861. His cookbooks, *Wild* and

Wild & Mehr (*Wild* and *Wild & More*), show a true enthusiasm for both wild produce and culinary history—an ideal combination for my project. When I outlined my plan to cook Carême's recipe, he told me he knew of an earlier recipe in *Rottenhöfers Kochbuch* that must have been the inspiration for Antonin's version. I was very interested to try it out, and booked a flight to Basel straight away. Karl-Josef was waiting at the airport. Broad-shouldered, solid and dressed in a loden jacket, he seemed at first a little formal (though I later realised this just hid his shyness). "Come, Heston. Let's go hunting."

We drove in convoy with the other hunters up into the hills, the bends in the road becoming ever tighter and the drop steeper. Battalions of pine and fir trees marched up the slopes. The icing-sugar sprinkle of snow on the ground gradually gave way to a thick, blindingly white crust. Eventually we parked at a passing point and the hunters stood attentively in a semi-circle as Karl-Josef outlined the rules of the hunt. There was a timeless, ritualistic quality to all this. Dressed in polished brown leather boots, khaki-coloured gaiters, waxed jackets and flat caps or green felt trilbies, the hunters would have looked like country squires but for the bright orange over-jackets most of them wore to make sure they weren't shot at by mistake. Before we finally set off, two men played a rousing bugle call on curly instruments that looked like ram's horns. The notes echoed round the valley and it was easy to imagine that the inhabitants of the Black Forest had heard much the same call for centuries.

"So, Heston, to be dressed right, you must wear these," said Karl-Josef, handing me a trilby and furry green fleece. "I've sent groups of hunters to strategic points along this ridge. I will go lower down the valley and try to disturb the animals into heading up towards you. You will go to a hide with my friend Lutz." He gestured towards a man who looked disconcertingly like Hugh Fearnley-Whittingstall. I noticed Lutz had foregone the over-jacket in favour of an orange scarf knotted at the throat, giving him a raffish air. "He will look after you."

"I'm from the North," Lutz confided in a stage whisper as we crunched off down a wide, sloping path off the main road. "I'm invited

because these Southerners couldn't hit an elephant, let alone a boar." After ten minutes' walk we left the path and inched our way sideways down the steep valley side to a tiny cabin. A roof and rear wall of logs offered scant shelter from the wind. The rest was largely open, giving a view out over the clustered pines and valley below, and allowing Lutz a good chance of spotting any passing wild boar. We sat inside on a small log bench. Occasionally Lutz would tell me a bit about the boar's habits but for the most part we waited in silence, concentrating intently, hoping to be the first to spot something. The calls of Karl-Josef, trying to flush out the animals, came up faintly from below.

BOOM! The sound was deafening. It took me a second to realise that Lutz had loosed off a shot. I squinted in the direction of the gun barrel and saw not a wild boar but a deer a few hundred feet away.

"We've been lucky to get that one on a day like this," observed Lutz. "Let's go down and see." We edged our way slowly along and found the deer lying on its side. Above it a few small pools of blood smeared the snow, like evidence at a crime scene. "This one's an old lady," Lutz said, inspecting the deer. "Five or six years old." He grabbed the front legs and I took the back and we began the trudge back up the hill. "I hope we can get a boar, too, before the day is done."

Like many chefs, Karl-Josef was happiest letting his cooking do the talking, and when we discussed or worked with food, his shyness evaporated. "Come, Heston," he said, a smile on his face, when we got back to the Spielweg hotel after the hunting was over. "The hunters have had a good day and we have some heavy work to do."

He led me through a warren of corridors to a small cobbled courtyard where two wild boars lay in a steel wheelbarrow, their heads lolling over the sides. They were large, brown and bristly, and looked almost peaceful, giving little sense of their power and speed (over short distances they can run at 30mph). "You can push the barrow," Karl-Josef said, striding off towards a wooden barn at the top of a hill behind the hotel. I began to shove my burden up the path.

The raw ingredient for the signature dish of the first celebrity chef, Antonin Carême.

From the barn's ceiling hung two lengths of nylon cord that ended in sharp S-shaped butcher's hooks. With some effort (the average boar weighs well over 100lb) we manhandled the heads onto the hooks so that each animal dangled a foot or so above the floor. "We will take the smaller one. The other has too-tough hair," Karl-Josef decided. He handed me a hunting knife and fired up a blow-torch that looked like a flame-thrower and had a roar like an aeroplane engine.

"The boar's hair is more wiry than that of the pig. It needs rather more than a simple singeing," he explained, training the gas jet on the head and engulfing it in flames. The skin bubbled black and a burning smell filled the air. "Scrape the hair, Heston," he advised,

Boar's bristles are like wire—removal requires some serious firepower.

gesturing towards the knife in my hand. "Be careful not to pierce the skin." Despite our firepower, it was slow, laborious work. We did three rounds of burn-and-slash, then swapped places and carried on. Eventually Karl-Josef consulted *Rottenhöfer's Kochbuch*. "The recipe says that we need to clear the hair to three fingers below the shoulder." He lifted his hand towards the boar's head—now smooth and with an appearance like sculpted stone—and measured. "Okay. That's good. The last bits we can do later with a brush." He pushed a butcher's hook through the crossed back legs and upended the animal so that the feet were where the head had been, made a quick incision round the neck while advising me to steady the legs, then severed the head in an instant. "Here you are, Heston," he said, handing over what looked like a death-mask. "Let's go and stuff this."

In the kitchen, Karl-Josef put on chef's whites. "You know, boar is quite common in Germany but often it is not cooked well and so people think it is not nice," he told me as he scrubbed at the head with a brush, then placed it on a chopping board. "Here in the south of Germany we eat all parts of the boar. The liver. The head. The kidneys. In the north they don't understand this. They say, 'Are you really so poor that you must eat these things?'"

"It's the same in Britain. Many people are squeamish about that kind of stuff. In the early days at the Fat Duck I served a dish of calf's head but I had to call it *Fromage de Tête*, otherwise customers wouldn't have eaten it. It was the only dish on the menu written in French."

Karl-Josef made an incision below the boar's chin, fanned out the two flaps of flesh and began carefully running a knife between them and the skullbone. "We must still be careful not to pierce the skin. We do not want any leaks." As the meat and skull separated, he lifted out the skull and put it to one side. I trimmed and tidied the meat, removing any bloody bits that would render it bitter.

"So. *Perfekt*," he said. "Now we wash it again and start to prepare the stuffing. If you can cut the fat into cubes." He handed me a pale pink strip. "I will start up the machine."

The fat would flavour and moisten the stuffing (or *farce*), and help make it tender. We loaded it into the feeding-cone of the grinder and threw in a fistful of chopped parsley. "Rottenhöfer's book just says 'herbs' but I don't want rosemary or thyme—they are too strong." We seasoned the pale sludge that emerged and added tongue, salted rump and more seasoning. The salt would help bond the proteins, binding all the ingredients together. "I like the idea that we're using relatively cheap cuts of meat to make a very complex dish," I said.

"And I am adding another cheap ingredient—dried *trompette de mort* mushrooms," Karl-Josef replied. "Cheaper than the one-and-a-half kilograms of truffle that Carême and Rottenhöfer suggest."

"That's the Regency period for you."

"I will put in some chopped truffle, but not much. The rest will be replaced with the *trompettes*. And we must have some pistachios, too." As he mentioned each ingredient, he folded it into the *farce* mixture. "*Gut. Alles klar*," he said, clearly happy with how the recipe was working out. He put the bowl to one side and picked up a roll of twine and a thick, six-inch needle. "How good is your sewing, Heston? We must make sure that the *farce* does not get out."

My sewing isn't good at the best of times, and this was like trying to push a needle through leather. But I managed to sew together the neck and seal up the eyes, mouth, nostrils and a couple of accidental little slits. It looked more like a head again, but the crude stitching gave it a Frankenstein-like quality. Karl-Josef held it up to the light to look for gaps and gave my work the thumbs-up. "Thanks," I said. "But please don't tell my wife, or she'll have me darning socks."

"It is a deal. Now the *farce*." We scooped up small handfuls of the stuffing, rolled them between our palms and pressed them into the cavity. "We need to be careful here," he cautioned. "Do not push in too tight because the skin shrinks when it is cooking and we do not want it to split. There, it is full. The recipe tells us to stitch a piece to the back of the head but this is a lot of work for little effect." Instead he doubled up a sheet of foil, placed it on the board and sat the boar on top, snout upwards. He crimped the foil around the head, then rolled another thin strip of foil and Alice-banded it around the head to keep it all in place. We both eyed our creation sceptically.

"It doesn't look much like the picture in the book."

"No," Karl-Josef agreed. "But they would have covered the whole head with something," he added, brightening. "Perhaps they would use fat to hide the black of the skin. Or a chaud-froid that would act as a glaze. And then add carved vegetables and aspic."

"Yes. That would look better, but the flavour of that layer wouldn't be spectacular." I was beginning to have my doubts about whether this would make it to my Feast, no matter how good it might taste.

As if to hide it from view, Karl-Josef took a large square of white cloth, wrapped the head in it—the corpse in its winding sheet—and

After singeing, stuffing and sewing, the boar's head is nearly ready for the oven.

began to truss it. "Anyway. Later, my hunting friends will come to the Spielweg to taste our stuffed boar's head at a special hunters' feast. They are all very traditional and I am excited to see what they think of this old recipe. If they do not like it, you and I will eat it alone." His practised hands soon had the head neatly bound.

He picked up the trussed parcel and took it to the steam oven. "We cook it for a long time—four or five hours—so that the collagen surrounding the muscle fibres breaks down. The first hour at 100°C to get it going. Then at a lower temperature—80-90°C—so that it does not overcook and dry out." He shut the door on our creation. Would the steam oven give it life? "And while we are waiting, I have a couple of wild boar snacks to show you."

Meat sat on the board, unmistakable in shape. "So, Heston, I have here a boar's heart. This is just an aperitif—it's all about the taste." He cut it into cubes, seasoned them and flipped them onto the hot solid top. "When the heart is fresh like this, no water comes out."

"Yes. Many cuts improve with a bit of ageing, but the organs have lots of enzymes that tend to break down the flesh quickly, so they need to be cooked soon, otherwise the texture turns to cotton wool."

"Two minutes. That is all it takes. They are still nicely rosé in the middle." He moved the fried cubes to one side of the solid top and put strips of liver in their place. "These too need to cook for only two minutes." He prodded them constantly to check if they were done. "A little more salt. A little apple vinegar on top. Try this." He stabbed a liver strip with a cocktail stick and passed it to me.

"Mmm. That's very delicate. Very tender. Very moreish. That vinegar cuts the richness perfectly."

"Yes. It is more delicate than ordinary vinegar. What about the heart?" He passed over another cocktail stick.

"Nice and fresh. It has a sort of blue steak texture: that slight resistance, that fleshiness. It's cooked really well—delicious to eat."

Karl-Josef, however, preferred action to praise. "Well, since the head is in the oven for some hours, I think it is time for you and I to taste the produce I make."

We spent a while eating some of Karl-Josef's delicious meats and cheeses, but as soon as the time was up he was down in the kitchen again, eager to see how our boar's head had turned out. He opened the door of the oven, waved away the steam cloud and lifted out the trussed parcel on its tray. "We must unroll it carefully so it does not break." He cut the string and removed the wrapping. The head still looked blackish on the outside, but it had kept its shape perfectly. "Okay, we need to let it cool a little so we can cut it successfully."

"I'm excited to taste it, but its appearance is quite startling."

"I agree," said Karl-Josef. "It is one thing to read about boar's head on a menu, but seeing it in this form is something else. Once sliced, it will look different of course." And it did. Once the head had cooled we lifted it onto a meat slicer and cut thin shavings from the thicker end, behind the ears. The meat had the appearance of a coarse French pâté flecked with fat and little green roundels of pistachio. It was extremely tasty. "That will go very well at the hunters' feast," Karl-Josef said, "dressed with lamb's leaf, a few truffle shavings and hot stock."

I was pleased for him but couldn't help thinking that, while hunters wouldn't baulk at a boar's head, my guests might. Besides, my stay in the Black Forest had resolved into a group of images—huntsmen in the dark forest; smears of blood on white snow; a boar's heart on a chopping block—that pointed me back towards *Grimm's Fairy Tales*. I was considering taking my main course in a very different direction.

THE MAGIC PUMPKIN

For the first course of my Fairy Tale Feast, I wanted to start with something dramatic—a bit of magic worthy of the Fairy Godmother herself. But I couldn't look to the Grimms' *Cinderella* for inspiration, because the Fairy Godmother doesn't appear in their version. Perhaps this was fortunate, because the Grimms' account is, even by their standards, a sombre and savage one. At first it follows a familiar storyline: a stepmother and her daughters tease Cinderella and treat her as a skivvy. They go to a grand ball leaving Cinderella at home, but she attends in a gold and silver dress and captures the heart of the king's son, who then searches the kingdom for her, with an abandoned slipper as the only means of identification. It's at this point that the tale turns nasty: the stepsisters cut off their toe or heel to try to fit into the slipper (cynically urged on by their mother: "When thou art Queen thou wilt have no more need to go on foot") and eventually have their eyes pecked out by pigeons while attending Cinderella's wedding.

Fortunately, the version of the story that most of us know comes from the French author Charles Perrault's collection *Tales and Stories of the Past: Tales of Mother Goose* (1697). He introduced to the tale several of its most memorable, magical details, including the glass slipper and the Fairy Godmother who transforms a pumpkin into a beautiful golden coach to convey Cinders to the ball. It was this piece of vegetable alchemy that I hoped to play around with.

Such is the power of the fairy tale that the Rouge Vif d'Etampes pumpkin, with its doughnut shape, distinctive ridging and deep red-orange colouring, is also known as the Cinderella pumpkin. The Fairy Godmother hollowed it out "until there was nothing left but a shell, struck it with her ring and turned the pumpkin into a beautiful golden coach." I, too, would hollow it out, in order to roast half the flesh and cook the other half with onions, cream and stock before blending the two together to produce a velvety smooth purée—my first transformation of the pumpkin. Two spoonfuls of this went into a glass hemisphere, along with some toasted pumpkin seeds and tiny pickled cubes of cucumber, pumpkin and melon to cut the richness of the purée.

Of course, it needed something else to turn it into a tale—or tail. I blanched a langoustine tail for ten seconds: enough to help remove the shell without cooking the flesh. I then skewered it on a toothpick to prevent it curling up and fried it in a pan for a few seconds more to develop a nutty flavour that would complement the purée. Once it was drained (the stick removed), seasoned and cut into segments along the bodylines, the langoustine could be placed on top of the purée.

On the langoustine's back I perched a blob of caviar and then finished the dish with two crucial touches. A dish based on *Cinderella*

Service at speed—garnishing Cinderella's Pumpkins.

needed cinders. Luckily I'd found a Japanese technique that involved steeping baby leeks in salt water overnight, then drying them in the oven for twenty-four hours. The leeks carbonised, but in a way that avoided bitterness and retained an enjoyable leek flavour. When ground in a mortar, they produced a grey ash that looked exactly like cinders which could be sprinkled over the dish, like a seasoning.

Equally obviously, a *Cinderella* dish calls for a touch of fairy dust. I ground up pumpkin and sesame seeds and gold powder, sprinkled a shimmer of it on top of the purée, langoustine and caviar, and laid another glass hemisphere on top of the first to make a globe, which I then covered with orange-coloured flashpaper and placed in a small

Cinderella's carriage goes up in flames.

silver-wire model of a carriage. This was my second transformation of the pumpkin—back into a recognisable element of the fairy tale. For the final bit of magic, all it would take was a guest putting a match to their carriage to make the paper pumpkin vanish in a flash, leaving no trace and revealing the dish inside.

EYES WITHOUT A FACE

Plunking a whole boar's head in the middle of the table was undeniably dramatic but it wasn't particularly gastronomic. The blackened face looked a bit grotesque and, while the *farce* was classical *charcuterie*, cooking all the meat at the same temperature meant none of the cuts really achieved their full potential. I was still determined to serve up some form of boar's head to my guests, but I decided to explore cooking parts of the head separately—tongue, snout, cheeks, ears, eyes—using whichever methods seemed likely to bring the best out of each cut.

Cooking the tongue and cheeks would be easy: both had established culinary methods that I could adapt. But cooking the ears was going to be tough—literally. They were criss-crossed with thick strands of tensile cartilage which, if handled badly, would make them horribly chewy. I decided to try long, slow, gentle cooking, which breaks down the cartilage in a way that adds a lovely gelatinous quality to a dish.

In the Fat Duck lab, Stefan prepared aromatic vegetables for a simple braising liquid. A roughly chopped turnip, carrot and chunk of swede went into the pressure-cooker pot along with a leek that had been halved and quartered lengthways, some water and a couple of pinkish ears. I sealed the lid and left it to cook for a couple of hours.

"Did you eat ears, eyes, stuff like that when you were growing up?" I asked Stefan. He was born in Iceland where the harsh environment demanded that cooks be inventive with limited ingredients. The results were often surprising and occasionally—to the outsider at least—unpleasant. When Stefan offered me something new to taste, I approached it with trepidation because, although it was likely to be delicious, he had fed me a couple of real shockers in the past.

The eyes have it—a taste test for my boar's head main course.

"No, but one of our traditional dishes is a whole sheep's head. I've eaten that. The eyes taste quite creamy. Some people consider them the best bit. We should try cooking and eating the boar's eyes."

I searched Stefan's face for signs that he was winding me up. He looked back at me, poker-faced. Time to call his bluff.

"Okay. I will if you will." I could see the grins on the faces of the TV crew as they savoured the prospect of filming a controversial ingredient and a showdown at the same time. "Grab that severed head and scoop out the eyeballs for me, please, Stefan."

He took a sharp knife and ran it round the socket, grimacing. "It looks too human," he said in a voice even gruffer than usual. "A sheep's

eye has a rectangular pupil that makes it look alien-like. But this…"
He trailed off as the blade severed the last of the connective material
and the eye popped onto the board and rolled to a halt, staring up at
us. He savaged the second socket then picked up both eyes between
finger and thumb and carried them at arm's length to a pan containing
a little water. "What shall we simmer them for? Ten minutes?"

"To be honest, I've got no idea what the right time or temperature
is for cooking eyeballs. But I'd prefer them to be creamy rather than
crunchy when I eat them. I hope we see eye to eye on this."

"That's one of your cornea jokes," said Stefan, who seemed to have
recovered disturbingly quickly from his ophthalmic surgery.

"Just a bit of aqueous humour," I replied. For the next ten minutes
we waited, occasionally reluctantly checking the contents of the pan,
which, if anything, looked worse than before. The water had turned
cloudy with scum. The eyes sat on the base of the pan, grey and forlorn.
At some point the pupils fell out. When the time was up, I spooned out
two ragged grey globes and two smaller black-and-white spheres.

I sliced the ball in two—it looked like a cross between a whelk and
a stuffed olive—and handed one half to Stefan. "And you reckon these
are creamy?"

"Well… sheep's are. I've no idea about boar." He put it in his
mouth and chewed. And chewed. "Needs more cooking," he announced
finally, still chewing, his face blank. Stefan was determined to give me
no clue as to what I might expect from what I was about to eat.

The globe was squidgy to the touch and made a squelching sound
as I picked it up. "Here goes," I said, biting down. "Um… what can
I say? Crunchy and rubbery. It's how I imagine a salted rubber band
would taste that's spent time on a farm."

"Yes," Stefan agreed. "It needs cooking for a couple more hours."

"I don't care how long you cook it for, this isn't a good idea. But
I'm going to see it through—no pun intended, for once—so pass me
that pupil." I bit down once more, gagged, then broke into a series of
uncontrolled and uncontrollable kung-fu moves round the room.
"Aaaargh. That's *horrible!*" I said, perhaps unnecessarily, once the

spasms of disgust had subsided. "It reminds me of an old, chalky, unbelievably hard-boiled egg." Just describing the thing sent another tremor of revulsion through me. I knew I was going to need some form of eyes in my boar's head—it wouldn't look realistic without them—but there was no way I was going to serve up the real thing.

The eyes, then, didn't work. The ears, however, turned out much better than expected, and larking around with the film crew gave me a great idea for the presentation of the whole dish.

I had put the cooked ears in a container in the fridge overnight with a weight on the lid to compress the contents. Now I placed a green and white striped chunk on the chopping board and explained to the camera that the gelatine in the ears had created the jelly that had helped to make this into a kind of terrine. I cut off a slice and pointed out the wiggly white stripes of cartilage that doodled through it, then spooned English mustard onto it, dipped it in egg, flour, then egg again, then breadcrumbs and put it into a pan of hot oil. It fizzed angrily. A couple more minutes, a little seasoning, and it was ready. I lay it on kitchen paper to drain, cut it into pieces and handed one to Stefan.

"Mmm. That's nice. The jelly has the right amount of softness."

"Yes," I agreed. "Great texture. You don't notice the cartilage—it's broken down well. And I like the contrasts. The crispiness of the breadcrumbs. The rich, gelatinous centre. That prick of mustard. So there you have it," I declared. "My Crispy Boars' Ears." And, as if to illustrate the point, I held a piece to either side of my head.

"Like the ears of the Seven Dwarves," said Russell, our sound man. "You should use that in the dish, Heston. Another echo of Snow White." Characteristically, he then offered a volley of ear-based puns, but my mind was elsewhere. He was right. I could cut the terrine into pointy ears. And I could do the same with the other cuts: fashion the cooked snout into a nose, the tongue into a tongue. Create something that looked like an eye. And I could present them in a way that emphasised they were all parts of the head. Positioned, perhaps, over a diagram like those in meat cookery books that give the black-and-white outline of a cow with dotted lines inside to show where the cuts come from.

Enacting the little-known fairy tale The Chef with the Tongue of a Pig.

An idea was really taking shape here. Maybe I could somehow print the diagram inside what looked like an old-fashioned storybook (but in fact had a hollowed-out middle, as though to conceal a pistol). Waiters could solemnly present to each guest a book, *Snow White* in Gothic lettering on its red leather cover. They'd open it and find the boar's head from the fairy tale. And I could introduce other elements of the story to the dining room. The little plates, knives and mugs of the dwarves, perhaps, or the poisoned apple or the glass coffin. It'd be easy enough to put a mirror on the dining room wall and have it spring a surprise on my guests—a more welcome one than the Wicked Queen's news that her beauty had been surpassed by her stepdaughter's.

A POISONED APPLE

My development chef Ida offered me an apple. It was tiny and fragile with a lustrous red skin. She was justifiably proud of its beauty because it had taken her several weeks to perfect the technique for making it. Blowing sugar is a pretty rarefied culinary skill, one I'd never needed at the Fat Duck before.

Once I began thinking about which elements of the Snow White story should feature in my Feast, I realised that an apple had to be one of them as it's such a dramatic and memorable detail in the tale. When the magic mirror declares that Snow White is the most beautiful in the land, the Wicked Queen orders a huntsman thus: "Take the child away into the forest; I will no longer have her in my sight. Kill her, and bring me back her heart as a token." But the huntsman is unable to take the girl's life. He tells her to run away and returns to the palace with a freshly killed boar's heart, pretending that it is Snow White's.

When the Wicked Queen discovers the huntsman's deception, she decides to kill Snow White herself. Disguised as an old pedlar-woman, she visits the dwarves' cottage, but fails on her first two attempts because the dwarves manage to revive Snow White on their return home. So the Queen visits a third time to offer Snow White an apple that is "so cunningly made that only the red cheek is poisoned", while the other, non-red side is not. To prove it isn't poisoned, the old woman bites the non-red side of the apple, then passes it to Snow White, who takes a bite from the red side and falls down dead. Fortunately, however, when the Prince's servants stumble as they carry her off in her glass coffin, the piece of apple is dislodged from Snow White's throat and she lifts the lid, sits up and cries, "Oh, heavens, where am I?", which probably made the servants stumble even more, or even run away screaming.

Obviously I wouldn't be feeding my guests poison but I still wanted my apple to be not quite what it seemed. I wanted it to give them a shock, albeit a pleasant one. Mindful of Carême's *extraordinaires*, I wondered about the possibility of using sugar to make a very sculpted, decorative imitation apple which, when you bit into it, contained

The Wicked Queen's poisoned apples.

something unexpected. While I racked my brains for what this might be, I asked Ida to try her hand at sugar blowing.

It was incredibly delicate work. It takes a lot of time to develop a feel for the way the sugar mixture responds to heat and air, and a lot of patience to allow it to happen at its own slow pace. To make the apple, the sugar had to be softened under a heat lamp until it could be pushed onto a finger and massaged into a tube shape with only one opening. Then Ida inserted the nozzle of a little air puffer into this hole and gently huffed in air with one hand, while twisting the tube round and round with the other and blowing on its surface. Occasionally she would return the sugar to the glare of the heat lamp for a few seconds to make it more malleable. Eventually a bubble appeared at the other end of the tube and began slowly to grow, becoming increasingly translucent—and increasingly fragile—as it did so. Ida had learned fast and was now extremely skilful at sugar blowing, but even she would have to do it seven or eight times to produce a single apple. All too often the thinning skin would simply burst, like overblown bubblegum, and she would have to start again from scratch.

When it *did* work, the finishing touch was made by returning the bubble to the heat for a moment, then tentatively nudging a fingertip into it. Once a sugar stalk and leaf were placed in the dip this created, the whole thing looked remarkably convincing.

While Ida had been honing her sugar-blowing skills, I had come up with what seemed to me the perfect filling. And so, when she offered me the apple, I piped a parfait of boar's heart into it. Ever since my visit to the Black Forest I had wanted to include the heart in my Feast in some form or other. What better way than inside the apple—bringing together two symbols of the Wicked Queen's murderous intent?

THE GOLDEN EGG

My *rognon blanc* jelly bean idea was developing well. I had created a black coating using a Madeira reduction and squid ink, which gave it a lovely shiny liquorice blackness, and a red one using concentrated

Training a tiny beanstalk round a golden egg.

red pepper juice. I'd even thought up a way of serving the beans to my guests: each would receive a flattish rectangular box inside which was a piece of moulded plastic with little depressions that each housed a jelly bean, much like the classic Jelly Belly forty-bean gift box. *Heston's Magic Beans*, the box proclaimed in a curly yellow font, and I had to admit they looked pretty good through the lid's cellophane window.

However, I was bothered that, while all the other courses in my Feast were structured round a particular fairy tale, this one wasn't. To me it stuck out like a sore thumb. And my unease was compounded by the fact that I'd finally tumbled to something I should have thought of much earlier—there was a bean-based fairy tale that offered fantastic possibilities for a dish: *Jack and the Beanstalk*. An English tale, *Jack and the Beanstalk* first appeared in print a few years before the start of the Regency era, in a highly moralistic interpretation by the publisher Benjamin Tabart, but the most popular version comes from Joseph Jacobs' *English Fairy Tales* (1890). Jack's mother sends him to market to sell their cow, but on the way he meets a stranger and swaps the animal for five supposedly magic beans. When Jack returns home and proudly explains what he has done, his mother throws the beans out of the window in disgust. Overnight the beans grow into an enormous beanstalk that Jack, naturally, climbs to find a giant's castle from which he steals, over a period of time, a sack of golden coins, a goose (or hen) that lays golden eggs, and a golden harp that sings. The instrument almost proves Jack's downfall as it calls out to the giant for help, but he shins quickly down the beanstalk and chops it down, bringing the giant crashing to the ground.

I renamed my jelly beans "magic beans", and began thinking how other details from the story might complement them. Goose was the most obvious one, and I decided to make a confit: cooking the meat for a long time in fat with salt and spices, then shredding it. I put two of the beans on a plate and surrounded them with a delicate little salad of goose meat, fine slices of pickled lemon to cut the richness, and fine slices of radish for crunch and pepperiness. I added a little mustard vinaigrette, a couple of types of cress, some seasoning. It was delicious and the daintiness gave it the right air of fantasy, but there was something missing. If I had a goose, I had to have a golden egg, too.

At the Fat Duck I serve a Mandarin Aerated Chocolate that is made in half-egg-shaped moulds. I realised I could adapt both the recipe and its equipment for my beanfeast. I had larger moulds made and followed my usual technique for chocolate shells: pour chocolate into two moulds, swirl, then pour the excess back out and set the moulds upside down on a rack to dry, leaving a very fine coating of chocolate on the mould. However, this time I added some chicken fat that had been fried in cocoa butter to the melted chocolate, to give it a meaty characteristic and a lovely nutty note.

The golden eggs are served.

Once they had chilled to solidity, I had two egg halves that, with the application of a little heat, could be fused together to make a whole; and then, with the application of a little heat to the base of the egg, could be melted sufficiently to make a hole. I carefully brushed the egg with powdered gold leaf mixed with edible shimmer and set it on top of my magic beans, hiding them from sight, then draped a couple of peashoots around the golden egg, as though they were growing from the salad undergrowth banked around it. This was what I would serve up to my guests, along with a jug of white bean velouté. When they poured this over the golden egg, it would magically dissolve to reveal the two beans nestling beneath. ❋

MENU

❈

Cinderella's Pumpkin

*Pumpkin Purée, Langoustine Tail and Osetra Caviar
sprinkled with Golden Fairy Dust*

❈

The Goose That Laid
The Golden Egg

*Chicken Testicle Jelly Beans, White Bean Velouté,
Peashoot Beanstalk, Golden Egg and Shredded Goose Leg*

❈

❋

Snow White's Heart &
The Wicked Queen's Apple

*Deep-fried Boar's Ears, Braised Cheek and Tongue,
Snout Sausage, Gribiche and Radish Eye
Apples with Boar's Heart Parfait*

Wicked Quink

❋

Hansel & Gretel's Edible House

*Shortbread Roof Tiles, Marshmallow Bricks,
Sugar Stained-glass Windows, Aerated Chocolate Door,
Green Moss, Welcome Mat*

❋

CINDERELLA'S PUMPKIN

FOR THE PUMPKIN PURÉE

1 Cinderella pumpkin
12g butter
20g white soy sauce (shiro shoyu)
6g milk

Preheat the oven to 160°C.

Cut the pumpkin in half, remove the seeds and roast one half for 30 minutes or until soft (reserve the other half for the fairy dust).

Cut the roasted pumpkin flesh from the skin and blitz to a purée using a blender. Strain the purée through muslin to remove excess water. Weigh out 150g of the purée.

When ready to serve, heat the pumpkin purée and butter in a pan and stir in the white soy sauce and milk.

FOR THE PICKLES

1 cucumber (skin on), cut into 5mm thick
    strips
1 cantaloupe melon, peeled and cut into
    5mm pieces
1 butternut squash (neck only), peeled and
    cut into 5mm pieces
100g water
45g Chardonnay vinegar
33g unrefined caster sugar
7g salt

Put the cucumber strips, cantaloupe melon and butternut squash pieces into 3 different sous-vide bags and seal under full pressure.

Place the sealed bags back into the vacuum machine and run the cycle two more times to compress.

Remove the pieces from the bags and cut into cubes.

Combine the water, vinegar, sugar and salt in a bowl and whisk to dissolve.

Pickle each type of vegetable/fruit separately by covering the cubes with pickling liquid for 20 seconds. Drain well, pat dry and reserve for serving.

FOR THE GOLDEN FAIRY DUST

reserved Cinderella pumpkin half
    (see above), skin removed
2g toasted white sesame seeds
0.1g gold dust

Cut the pumpkin into thin slices and dry in the dehydrator for 12 hours.

Crush the dried pumpkin slices into fine flakes and weigh out 4.5g.

Thoroughly mix the pumpkin powder with the sesame seeds and gold dust. Reserve in an airtight container.

FOR THE PUMPKIN SEEDS

50g isomalt
50g water
50g white soy sauce (shiro shoyu)
30g pumpkin seeds with skin removed

Make a syrup by boiling together the isomalt, water and white soy. Remove from the heat.

Coat the pumpkin seeds in the syrup, then drain and dry them in the dehydrator. Reserve in an airtight container.

FOR THE LANGOUSTINE TAILS

6 langoustines
grapeseed oil, for frying
salt and freshly cracked black pepper

Remove the tails from the langoustines and insert a bamboo skewer through each one to hold the tail straight and prevent it from curling during the cooking process.

Blanch the langoustine tails in boiling water for 10 seconds, then immediately cool in an ice bath. Drain and remove the shells, leaving the skewers in place.

When ready to serve, pan-fry the blanched langoustine tails in a little grapeseed oil in a sauté pan.

Season with salt and pepper, drain on kitchen paper and carefully remove the skewers. Cut each of the cooked langoustines into 3 pieces.

TO SERVE
    pumpkin purée (see above)
    pickled cucumber, melon and squash
      (see above)
    pumpkin seeds (see above)
    sautéed langoustine tails (see above)
    sustainable Osetra caviar
    a pinch of golden fairy dust (see above)

Spoon the warm pumpkin purée into 6 bowls. Place alternate cubes of cucumber, melon and squash around the edge of each bowl. Arrange pumpkin seeds in between the pickle cubes.

Place the langoustine pieces in the centre of the dish and spoon a generous amount of caviar over the top.

Garnish with a sprinkling of the fairy dust.

THE GOOSE THAT LAID THE GOLDEN EGG

FOR THE CHICKEN TESTICLES

180g salt
3kg water
1kg cock's testicles, washed and
    trimmed

Dissolve the salt in the water to make a brine. Chill.

Add the cleaned testicles to the brine and return to the fridge for 2 hours.

Rinse the testicles in several changes of cold water over 30 minutes and dry.

Preheat a water bath to 68°C.

Place the testicles in a sous-vide bag, arranging them in a single layer, and seal under full pressure.

Put the bag in the water bath and cook for 2 hours.

Remove the bag from the water and chill in the fridge until cold.

Take the cooked testicles out of the bag and peel the membrane away with a small knife, keeping the shape of a bean.

The testicles are now ready for the gelling process.

FOR THE MADEIRA REDUCTION

200g Madeira
1g thyme
70g shallots, finely diced
1g coriander seeds
1g black peppercorns
5g tarragon leaves

Combine all of the ingredients except the tarragon in a saucepan and reduce the mixture to 100g.

Put the tarragon leaves into a bowl. Strain the reduced mixture onto the tarragon and allow to infuse for 10 minutes.

Strain and reserve.

FOR THE SQUID INK STOCK

25g grapeseed or groundnut oil
50g shallots, finely diced
1g thyme
1g black peppercorns
1g coriander seeds
200g water
30g squid ink
30g Madeira reduction (see above)

In a pan, heat the oil and sauté the shallots with the thyme, peppercorns and coriander seeds until the shallots are softened.

Add the water, then the squid ink and Madeira reduction. Bring to a simmer, then remove from the heat and strain.

Chill the stock thoroughly before proceeding to the gelling stage.

FOR THE BLACK JELLY BEANS

⅛ of the cooked cock's testicles (see above)
190g squid ink stock (see above)
1.4g Gellan F
0.4g Gellan LT 100

Place each cleaned, dry testicle on a toothpick to hold firmly for dipping.

Pour the cold stock into a pan, add the two gellans and bring to the boil, whisking gently, trying not to incorporate too much air.

Take off the heat and dip each testicle in the liquid for 2 seconds. Lift out and wait a few seconds until fully set before putting down.

Place the cold chicken testicles in a sous-vide bag and seal it under medium pressure. Preheat a water bath to 68°C. To serve, reheat the testicles in the water bath for 25 minutes.

FOR THE YELLOW PEPPER STOCK

4kg yellow peppers
10g grapeseed or groundnut oil
30g shallots
1g thyme
1g black peppercorns
20g Chardonnay vinegar
200g water

Wash and clean the peppers, then remove the stem and seeds. Place the flesh in a blender and blitz to a liquid. Transfer the liquid to a saucepan and reduce by half.

Pass through a fine sieve, return to a clean pan and reduce to a thick syrup that coats the back of a spoon. Cool the syrup and then weigh out 50g for the next step.

In a pan, heat the oil and sauté the shallots with the thyme and peppercorns until they are softened but without colouring them.

Add the vinegar and reduce to a syrup. Pour in the water and yellow pepper syrup. Bring just to the boil, then remove from the heat, pass through a fine sieve and cool.

Weigh out 200g and proceed to the next step.

FOR THE YELLOW JELLY BEANS
⅓ of the cooked cock's testicles (see above)
200g yellow pepper stock (see above)
1.4g Gellan F
0.4g Gellan LT 100

Follow the instructions for the black beans (see above).

FOR THE RED PEPPER STOCK
4kg red peppers
10g grapeseed or groundnut oil
30g shallots
1g thyme
1g black peppercorns
20g Chardonnay vinegar
200g water

Follow the instructions for the yellow pepper stock (see above).

FOR THE RED JELLY BEANS
⅓ of the cooked cock's testicles (see above)
200g red pepper stock (see above)
1.4g Gellan F
0.4g Gellan LT 100

Follow the instructions for the black beans (see above).

FOR THE GOLDEN EGG
500g chicken skins
120g cocoa butter
240g white chocolate
2g gold lustre powder
2g gold shimmer colour

In a large pan, slowly fry the chicken skins in 100g of the cocoa butter until browned. Strain the butter and leave to cool. Discard the skins.

In a tempering machine, temper the white chocolate and remaining 20g of cocoa butter. Add in the cooled chicken cocoa butter and mix for a further for 5 minutes.

Using a ladle, line egg-shaped moulds with the white chocolate mix and pour out the excess. Turn the moulds upside down so that any excess chocolate can drain off. Leave to set at room temperature for 10 minutes.

Place the moulds in the freezer for 1 minute, then un-mould the chocolate (if necessary return to the freezer for a minute and repeat).

Heat up a flat tray and carefully touch 2 half-shells on the tray for 1 second, just to melt the outer rim. Then hold them together to form an egg shape. Place in the fridge to firm up again. Repeat with the other egg shells.

Using a cloth or glove, hold an egg on its side on another cloth. Using a heated large knife, cut off the bottom so the egg can stand upright.

Brush the egg with gold lustre powder, then gold shimmer colour. Repeat with the remaining eggs. Store in a cool, dry place until needed.

TO ASSEMBLE
black, yellow and red jelly beans (see above)
peashoot, cress and herb salad
confit goose leg, shredded
pickled lemon, shredded
a little vinaigrette
golden eggs (see above)

Place a bean of each colour on a serving plate. Surround with the salad, confit goose and pickled lemon. Drizzle with a little vinaigrette and cover with the golden egg.

SNOUT "SAUSAGE"

FOR THE LAMB'S SWEETBREADS
200g salt
2kg water
1kg lamb's sweetbreads

Dissolve the salt in the water to create a brine; chill. Rinse and separate the sweetbreads and place in the brine in the fridge for 2 hours.

Rinse the sweetbreads in several changes of cold water over 2 hours and pat dry.

Put the sweetbreads in a medium sous-vide bag in a single layer. Seal under full vacuum.

Preheat a water bath to 65°C, put the bag into the water and cook for 1 hour.

Take the bag out of the water bath and cool quickly to 5°C in an ice bath. Remove the sweetbreads from the bag. Clean of all fat and membrane, then cut into small pieces.

FOR THE SNOUT "SAUSAGE"
2 boar's snouts, cleaned and boned
50g honey
50g sugar
2g allspice
3 cloves
1 star anise
2g pink peppercorns
5g coriander seeds, ground
¼ garlic bulb
25g carrot, roughly chopped
25g onion, roughly chopped
10g celery, roughly chopped
15g leek (white and pale green only), sliced

Preheat the oven to 160°C. Rinse the snouts under cold water for 5 minutes, drain and pat dry. Remove any excess meat from them.

Burn off any hair from the skin of the snouts with a blowtorch, without burning the skin.

Place a large (ovenproof) pan on the stove over a medium-high heat. Add the honey and once melted, add the sugar, stirring well. Cook to a deep golden brown caramel (155°C). Lower the temperature to prevent further colouring. Lay the snouts in the caramel skin-side down and colour them to a deep golden brown.

Slowly add enough water to cover the snouts, stirring to dissolve the caramel. Add the spices (tied in a muslin bag), garlic and vegetables. Bring to a simmer, lower the heat and lay a parchment cartouche over the surface of the liquid. Cover the pan with aluminium foil.

Place the pan in the preheated oven and cook for about 4–5 hours until the skin of the snout can be easily broken. Remove the snouts from the liquid and place on a tray; allow to cool before cutting into small cubes.

FOR THE PANADA
20g butter
15g olive oil
335g onion, diced
50g garlic, thinly sliced
900g whipping cream
2g black peppercorns
3g bay leaves
270g white bread, crusts removed

Heat the butter and olive oil in a saucepan. Add the onion and cook until lightly caramelised. Add the garlic and continue to cook for a further 5 minutes over a medium heat.

Add the cream, peppercorns and bay leaves. Bring to a simmer, then remove from the heat, cover the pan and leave to stand for 15 minutes.

Put the bread into a food processor and pass the infused cream through a fine sieve onto it. Blitz until smooth, being careful not to overmix.

Pass through a medium drum sieve and refrigerate until required.

FOR THE TURKEY BASE
500g turkey breast, minced
60g beaten egg (whites and yolks)
60g egg whites
14g salt

Combine all of the ingredients in a PacoJet canister and freeze.

Blitz the mixture twice through the PacoJet. Re-chill, then pass through a medium drum sieve. Refrigerate until required.

TO ASSEMBLE

240g turkey base (see above)

72g panada (see above)

44g whipping cream

0.1g ground ginger

0.2g ground nutmeg

60g bone marrow, cleaned and diced small

30g sweetbreads (see above)

60g cubed boar snout (see above)

25g black truffle, diced small

100g whipping cream, lightly whipped

finely chopped chervil, tarragon, parsley
   and chives, to garnish

whole white truffle, to finish

Mix the turkey base, panada and un-whipped cream together in a bowl. Fold in all of the other ingredients except the whipped cream. Slowly and gently fold in the whipped cream.

Divide the mixture into 6 portions and roll in clingfilm to make "sausages", roughly the size of the boar's snouts.

Preheat a water bath to 67°C and poach the "sausages" at this temperature for 25 minutes.

To serve, cut open the clingfilm and sear the "sausages" evenly in a little oil in a pan. Lift out and drain, then cut into slices. Sprinkle on chopped chervil, tarragon, parsley and chives.

Slice white truffle over just before serving.

ROOF TILES FOR HANSEL & GRETEL'S EDIBLE HOUSE

FOR THE OLIVE OIL BISCUIT BASE

- 400g unrefined caster sugar
- 700g plain flour
- 12g salt
- 6g baking powder
- 2.5g vanilla seeds
- 450g butter
- 150g extra virgin olive oil
- 180g egg yolks

Place the sugar, flour, salt, baking powder and vanilla seeds in a mixer fitted with a paddle attachment. Add the butter while on low speed and mix until it is fully incorporated and the mixture resembles breadcrumbs.

Add the olive oil on a low speed until just incorporated, then gradually add the egg yolks. When the ingredients come together to form a dough (be careful not to overmix), remove from the mixer. Wrap in clingfilm and rest in the fridge for 24 hours.

Place the dough between 2 pieces of baking parchment and roll out to a thickness of 2mm. Slide onto a baking tray and place in the fridge to rest for 1 hour.

Preheat the oven to 150°C. Remove the top sheet of parchment, then place the tray in the oven and bake for 15–20 minutes, until lightly browned. Remove and immediately cut into rectangles measuring 15x17cm. Leave to cool, then store in an airtight container.

FOR THE SALTED CARAMEL

- 800g double cream
- 750g glucose
- 750g caster sugar
- 600g butter
- 25g salt
- 750g whole milk

Pour the cream into a pan, bring just to the boil, then cover and set aside.

Combine the remaining ingredients in another pan and bring to the boil, whisking continuously. Continue boiling until the liquid has reached 151°C.

Reduce the heat and slowly whisk in the cream in 3 stages until the mixture is smooth and homogeneous. Pour onto a tray lined with baking parchment and leave to set at room temperature for 2 hours, then cover with parchment and refrigerate until needed.

Cut into rectangles measuring 15x17cm and store in the fridge.

FOR THE CHOCOLATE SHEETS

- 250g Amedei Chuao chocolate
  (70% cocoa solids)

Preheat a water bath to 53°C. Put 225g of the chocolate in a sous-vide bag, seal under full pressure and immerse in the water bath for 12 hours. Finely chop the remaining chocolate.

Temper the melted chocolate using the 25g chopped chocolate to seed it. Once the seed has been added, bring the chocolate down to 28°C, then take it back up to 32°C.

Ladle the chocolate onto 4 acetate sheets (A4 size) and spread to a thickness of 2–3mm. Cut into rectangles measuring 15x17cm, cover and store in a cool, dry place.

TO ASSEMBLE AND FINISH

- 15x17cm sheets olive oil biscuit (see above)
- 15x17cm sheets salted caramel (see above)
- 15x17cm sheets tempered chocolate
  (see above)
- 500g dark chocolate (70% cocoa solids)
- 200g cocoa butter

Lay the olive oil biscuit sheets on a flat work surface. Place the sheets of salted caramel on top evenly and peel back the parchment.

Place a sheet of tempered chocolate on top of the caramel.

Chop the dark chocolate and cocoa butter and melt gently in a bain-marie or microwave. Pour the melted chocolate into a paint spray gun and, working quickly, spray the entire surface and sides of the tiles evenly.

Return each assembled piece to the fridge to chill completely.

A Gothic Horror Feast

REVIVAL of the Gothic sentiment, particularly in architecture and literature, began in the 1760s. (The catalyst is usually considered to be Horace Walpole, who not only wrote *The Castle of Otranto* but also built Strawberry Hill, a fanciful villa with towers and battlements and churchy arched windows that still stands in Twickenham.) The Gothic novel took the spirit of Romanticism and added a few more astringent ingredients—a spot of violence, a dash of the supernatural, a smattering of paranoia. The Romantics prized "picturesque" scenes, such as a landscape dominated by a crumbling, ivy-clad tower. Devotees of the Gothic liked much the same thing, but with a leering face at the window or a shadowy figure at the door.

Many of the genre's seminal texts, such as *Melmoth the Wanderer*, *The Monk* and *The Mysteries of Udolpho*, are now largely the province of English Literature students. Some, however, remain mainstream classics because, like *Grimm's Fairy Tales*, they speak to something deep inside us. They articulate our most fundamental fears. The monstrous, destructive scientific ambition of Victor Frankenstein; Dr Jekyll's warring capacities for good and evil; the sinister and relentless menace of Count Dracula—these continue to trigger strong emotions, and so these would be my main sources of inspiration.

I just hoped that I would be able to find six guests who didn't scare too easily.

HYDE AND SEEK

When my guests stepped into the studio for my Gothic Horror Feast, they would leave behind the wide, treeless streets of Kentish Town and enter a room with skulls on the walls, cobwebbed body cages hanging from the ceiling and tables strewn with stoppered bottles and the instruments of dissection. I wanted to capitalise on this abrupt shift by serving an appetiser based on the most dramatic transformation in Gothic literature—Dr Jekyll's into Mr Hyde.

In Robert Louis Stevenson's story, the doctor becomes obsessed with the fact that he has within him two very different characters—one upstanding and altruistic, the other brutish and immoral—and looks for a way of separating one from the other. He manages to manufacture a compound that, when drunk, represses any trace of the Jekyll side of his personality, leaving only Mr Hyde, a creature who follows his own appetites and desires, no matter what damage they may cause to those around him. The compound, the author tells us, consists of a white powder which, when added to a red tincture, causes it to "brighten in colour, to effervesce audibly, and to throw off small fumes of vapour. Suddenly, and at the same moment, the ebullition ceased, and the compound changed to a dark purple, which faded again more slowly to a watery green." So I needed to create a green drink that fizzed and smoked when a white powder was added to it.

What kind of drink had an aura of Gothic Horror? I first thought of absinthe, which not only had a reputation for inducing madness and stupefaction but was also exactly the right colour. But the spirit's strong anise flavour is very much an acquired taste, and even though this Feast was intended to be scary, I didn't want my guests to be repulsed by what I served. I decided on gin instead. In the eighteenth century the widespread consumption of gin in Britain became a real problem, and William Hogarth's depiction of this in *Gin Lane* has many of the classic elements of the horror genre: a corpse loaded into a coffin; a child falling from its mother's arms to its death; sprawled, skeletal figures; men gnawing on bones like dogs. Gothic literature grew out of images like this, and the real-life scenes that inspired it.

Creating flavoured spheres by pipetting drops of G & T and gellan into oil.

Dr Jekyll's potion bubbling in true Gothic Horror style.

Gin, then, would form the base of my Jekyll-and-Hyde drink, but I needed to add flavours and textures that would give it a fantastic mouthfeel. I decided to introduce a little finely diced cucumber for crunch, but the green colour would come mainly from a technique using the heat-resistant setting agent gellan. If I added this, plus some green food colouring, to a warmed mixture of gin, tonic water and sugar, I could create tiny vibrant green spheres (not unlike frogs' eggs) by sucking up the liquid in a pipette and expelling it drop by drop into a beaker full of oil. These would burst in the mouth to give lovely sudden hits of flavour, intensifying the whole sensory experience.

I imagined these spheres sitting in a martini glass, perhaps on top of a scoop of gin granita. I wanted to make some link to the notion of split personality that underpins *Dr Jekyll and Mr Hyde*, and wondered if I could introduce both hot and cold elements to the drink. I'd have to look into the possibility of creating a warm foam to top the glass.

The other key element—effervescence—was easy to achieve. I had been using dry ice at the Fat Duck for years to produce just that kind of effect and, if I ground up the pellets in a pestle and mortar, they'd look like a white powder. It would be fun to get the guests involved in making their own potion and adding a white powder to it, just like Dr Jekyll. Dry ice is a superb carrier of flavour: pour any kind of fragrant liquid onto it and, as the vapour spreads out, wraith-like, it takes all the aroma with it. I could present to each of my guests not only a cocktail but also a set of test tubes containing flavourings and a flask with a tube attached to it. I'd encourage them to empty the test tubes into the flask along with a quantity of "white powder" and a hot liquid (cucumber juice, maybe), then stopper the flask and feed the tube into the liquid in the glass. Gradually the dry ice vapour would bubble into the cocktail, infusing it with all kinds of secret ingredients.

Now all I had to do was find those ingredients. In *Dr Jekyll and Mr Hyde*, the doctor discovers that he is doomed to remain Hyde for ever: he is no longer able to make the potion that would reverse this because he can't obtain the right ingredients in the right proportions. I hoped I would be more fortunate.

IN TRANSYLVANIA

> We are in Transylvania; and Transylvania is not England. Our
> ways are not your ways, and there shall be to you many strange
> things.
>
> BRAM STOKER, Dracula

In Stoker's novel, Jonathan Harker takes several days to reach Dracula's
castle, travelling first by train to Bistritz, then taking a carriage to the
Borgo Pass, where he transfers to Dracula's own coach, drawn by four
coal-black horses through a landscape of jagged, pine-clad rocks and
fine, powdery snow. Fortunately, my own journey involved only a plane
to the capital of Romania, Bucharest, followed by a short flight to Sibiu,
once the capital of the Principality of Transylvania. Here I was to meet
Alexandru Sonoc, curator of art at the Brukenthal Palace and an expert
on local history. I was hoping he could flesh out my ideas for a dish
inspired by Dracula.

The dusting of powdery snow on the pantiles of the buildings
surrounding Sibiu's main square reminded me of Harker's journey.
Across the cobbles I could see what looked like a giant birdcage: it was
the Fool's Cage, which once held thieves and adulterers for public
humiliation. I could imagine the Count flitting across this space at
night, skirting the Catholic church on its northern side. I made my way
through the heavy carved wooden doors of the palace and on through
the courtyards, until I reached the doorway that led to the Reading
Room and climbed the wooden stairs to the first floor, where Alexandru
awaited me.

In his black cords, black workboots and a black collarless shirt,
Alexandru might have had a vampiric air, had it not been for his
studious-looking, gold-rimmed glasses and the white rubber surgeon's
gloves that he wore to protect the old manuscripts he was about to
show me. He motioned me into a long, narrow, high-ceilinged room
with desks running along one side and banks of battered wooden card-
index drawers along the other.

Searching for inspiration in wintry Transylvania.

"Alexandru, I'm hoping to find some old dishes that Count Dracula would have approved of. Probably something involving blood. Do you know of anything along these lines?"

"Well, Heston, I've been searching through these recipe books from the seventeenth and eighteenth centuries." He lifted the leather-bound cover of a slim volume to reveal brittle pages covered in dense, slanting handwriting, and peered myopically as he leafed through them. "They're written in Gothic script and it's hard to read, even for me. There are recipes for, let's see, making steak from a stag... sour cherry jam... milk with pistachios. But there are no recipes for blood. One thing you have to realise is that Sibiu used to be mainly inhabited

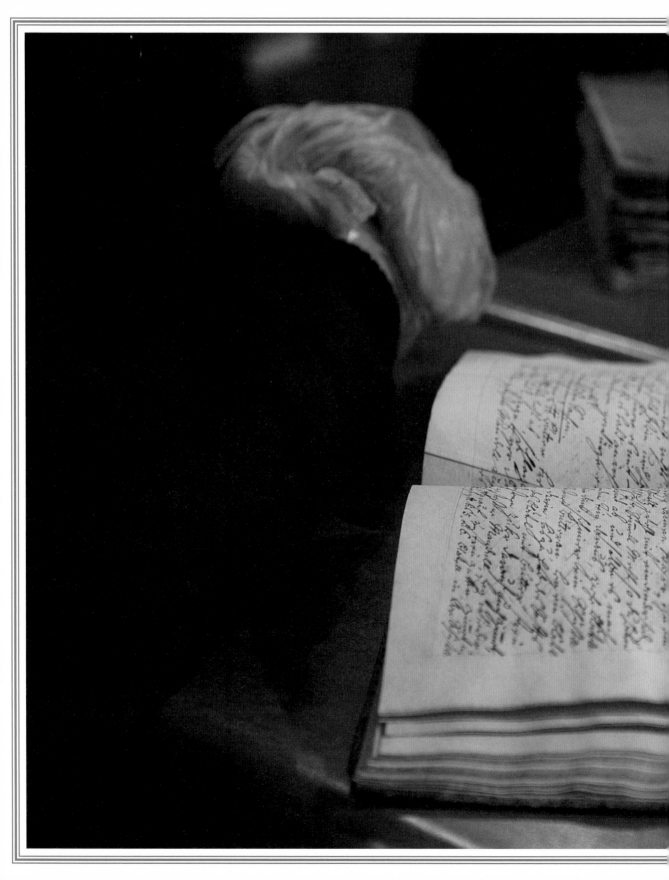

An encounter with the Count.

by Saxons—Protestant, god-fearing, orthodox people who didn't eat foods involving blood because it is forbidden by the Bible. There's a recipe for Baked Lungs, but it doesn't get more extreme than that."

"What about recipes linked in some way to Dracula himself?"

"No, this is not possible because there is no literary tradition of Dracula in Romania. This is something invented by you British."

"You're kidding me! This is like finding out that Father Christmas doesn't exist."

"Well, I'm sorry, but it's true nevertheless. Until recently we didn't really have movies in Romania and had no idea about Dracula at all. Most Romanians find the idea very funny. They know the word *Dracul*,

74

of course, which means 'the Devil'. But that's about it. For them Dracula just means 'son of the Devil'."

"So how has Transylvania come to be identified with the Count?"

"In the Middle Ages Transylvania was very much seen as at the end of Europe, bordered as it is on two sides by the Carpathian mountains. So it was quite a mythical place. I think Bram Stoker drew on stories of Vladimir III, the Prince of Wallachia, who was extremely cruel. He used impaling, which he probably saw the Turks doing—this country has a history of conflict with the Turks—for his own punitive ends."

"So Count Dracula isn't even a myth here?"

"No," said Alexandru, looking at me apologetically over the top of his glasses. "But we do have legends of The Undead."

"Ah ha!" This was more like it.

"But they don't suck blood. They take the milk of cows. Give people illnesses or scare them. They're more like ghosts than vampires."

"Oh." I don't know who was more disappointed—me, or Alexandru because he hadn't come up with anything gory enough.

"There's one other recipe," he offered. "But although I've searched the state archives, I've yet to find it written down anywhere…"

"Oh yes?"

"A story about a goose with leeches. Nobody cooks this, but every Romanian knows about it. Leeches are put on a slaughtered, spiced goose, which is then roasted in the oven; once cooked the goose is discarded and the leeches are eaten. Or leeches are attached to a live goose to feed, then made into a stew with vegetables; there's no mention of what happens to the goose in this version."

"Now that sounds *very* Dracula-like."

Alexandru shook his head and raised his hands, as though to defend himself. "I don't think I'd want to try something like that!"

Well, that showed that it had at least the requisite shock value. For now, however, it was time to move on before I put Alexandru off completely. "You say nobody now cooks this, but there is a tradition of cooking with blood in Romania, isn't there?"

"Certainly. Every region has recipes for this. People here are mainly poor farmers and they can't afford to waste any part of the animal. With the pig, we even use the trotters for glue and the hair for stuffing cushions. Pig's stomach with blood is a popular recipe."

"Is there any way I can see this being made?"

"Sure. Now is a very good time, in fact. It's not very economical to feed pigs through the winter so farmers tend to kill and cook their animals instead. They make it a kind of celebration—the Winter Feast—and the whole family gets involved."

Alexandru put on a tall, black astrakhan hat and we set off in the car for Gura Raului. A few kilometres outside Sibiu, the landscape resolved into a wide, flat, snowy plain with raptors flying overhead and a view of the gentle slopes of the Fagaras mountains in the distance. We drove through a series of villages that huddled close to the road, eventually swinging through an open set of barn-like double doors into a large cobbled courtyard. At its centre was a large trestle table stacked with enough cuts of meat to stock a small butcher's shop, and a tray full of shot glasses of fiery plum brandy that were pressed upon us as soon as we got out of the car. *"Noroc,"* said a man in a blue workman's jacket, pausing in his butchery long enough to clink glasses with mine. I'd learned my first word of Romanian. *"Noroc,"* I replied. "Cheers."

Two sides of the courtyard were bordered by terracotta-coloured houses. At one end stood an open-fronted ramshackle garage-cum-workshop, across which hung a line strung with a pig's lungs and liver. In the corner I could see a stockpot bubbling away on an outdoor range, cooking the pig's head and other organs. As young kids chased after skinny feral cats, Gheorghe got on with trimming and salting pieces of pork, adding them to the growing pile in the plastic tub at his feet.

"What happens to all this meat?" I asked.

"The slaughtering must take place in one day, in the open air. Some of the meat is eaten straight away. The rest is preserved. It's left in salt for three days and then smoked over oak. Sometimes we put spices on before the smoking. We eat some of it raw, with onions or chillies, some of it in stews and some of it cold. And some is cut into small pieces and minced to make sausages. That's what's in the tub here."

Gheorghe and son prepare for the Winter Feast.

"What you do with the blood is the key thing for me, as I'm here because of Dracula. Do you know Dracula?"

"I don't believe in this foolishness. If you keep God in your soul, no one can have victory over you."

"Yes, I see," I replied, not seeing at all. I tried a different tack. "What about garlic rather than God?"

"Garlic, like onions, is good for the heart. It purifies. Keeps you healthy and free of evil influences."

"Er... I meant more in terms of warding off Dracula. Sorry, I'm trying to get used to the fact that he's not really part of the mythology here," I explained. "Back home the story's so familiar that even little

The blood for blood sausage, and the end product neatly sewn into an intestine.

kids know about using the cross and garlic to protect themselves from him. They know it from films and books."

"You let your children read about Dracula?" Gheorghe's eyes narrowed. "How young did this happen?"

"Oh, when they were seven or eight. It's all around them. They can't fail to know about him."

"And you. How often do you go to church?"

This question was so unexpected that it jolted me into remembering something Alexandru had told me. *Dracul* means "the Devil". Thinking back over the conversation, I realised I had basically asked Gheorghe whether he consorted with the Devil, and then confessed to educating my kids in the ways of the black arts. I began to backpedal furiously.

It took half an hour to convince Gheorghe that I wasn't a rabid Satanist, but once fresh glasses of plum brandy were poured, I figured I'd established a fragile respectability and decided that the best way to keep out of trouble was to keep my trap shut for a while and watch the blood sausages being prepared. Gheorghe ground the chopped pork using a small hand-cranked mincer that was clamped to the table, a laborious process. Once this was done, Gheorghe left and two women in floral-print aprons and floppy Gatsby caps appeared, each carrying a blue enamel bowl. Butchery, it appeared, was man's work. Mixing and cooking the ingredients was women's.

One of the bowls contained cooked pork, the other a pool of bright red blood. They began cutting the meat and transferring most of it to the blood bowl, along with cubes of fat and some of the pig's skin, liver, spleen and lungs, as well as cooked meat from the head (taken from the pot on the range I'd spotted earlier). They worked fast and it proved impossible to slow them down. As Gheorghe had suggested, they were making sure that the preparation all took place in one day. Soon both bowls were filled with a sausage-stuffing mixture: the blood-rich one had the intense colour of stewed red fruits, while the other, which consisted of the braising juices in which the head had been cooked, plus a cupful of blood, looked like corned beef. The women waved their hands at me. "They want you to taste," Alexandru explained.

I dipped in a finger and put it in my mouth. The lumpy red mulch might have looked like a prop from a Hammer Horror movie but it had a very pleasant flavour—porky and salty with just a hint of raw garlic. As I was saying this to the camera, the women swooped, grabbing the bowls and scuttling inside. We hurried after them, hoping we hadn't already missed a vital stage in the sausage-making procedure.

Sure enough, they had already begun to spoon the meat mixture into the casing, which, my nose told me, was intestine: it gave off that characteristic faint faecal note. In France intestines are used to make *andouillettes*. I like them but they're undoubtedly gutsy stuff. It was going to be interesting to taste the Romanian version.

Four women were at work now, chatting sociably as they pushed in the mixture, making sure there were no air pockets to cause the meat to go off. The end product, lumpy and as thick as my forearm, was secured with twine and they moved onto the next, continuing until all of the casings had been filled, including the bladder, which required a lot of serious needlework to create a bulbous, haggis-like affair.

We filmed in the village, then returned to find the table in the dining room set for sixteen. At each place setting was a bowl of steaming soup. "You must eat it now," we were told, "it's no good once it's cold." We were about to dig in when Gheorghe asked permission to say grace first. I assumed this was the traditional way to start a meal rather than evidence of a lingering suspicion about my interest in the Devil, but I gave an enthusiastic response, none the less.

Once Gheorghe had finished saying grace, we turned from the spiritual to the physical. Following Alexandru's lead, I sprinkled grated horseradish onto the soup and took a mouthful. It was rich, fatty and perfect for a winter's day. The horseradish gave it a zing and the broth had a nice pickled aspect.

"This is Sour Soup," Alexandru told me. "An economical recipe that makes something very good to eat out of almost nothing. Just cuts and trimmings of meat—both fat and lean—plus water and cabbage brine. Bring it to the boil, add lard and an onion and simmer for a couple of hours. Dress it with egg, sour cream and buffalo milk."

Next, lidded earthenware pots were brought to the table. They looked like bulbous versions of the French *marmite* pot. It seems that every culture has its own version of the one-pot meal: something that can be assembled, then left to cook on its own for a while.

"This is one of our national dishes," said Alexandru, as he spooned sauerkraut, smoked pork and some little leaf parcels onto my plate. "*Sarmale*. It comes from the Arabic. Basically, stuffed cabbage rolls." The English translation didn't do the dish justice. The parcels contained cooked rice and incredibly tasty coarse-ground pork meat. The cabbage itself was firm and flavourful. "It's a dish of layers," he continued. "In the pot goes some lard, then shredded pickled cabbage. Sprinkle in some pieces of meat—smoked bacon, sausage and other, fatty cuts—then pack in the cabbage rolls. Top all this with more shredded cabbage, another centimetre or so of lard and a few allspice corns. Here we make them and then put on the lid and store them outside—in January, it's better than a fridge! When it comes to cooking, the pot must be put in a cold oven. Then it's cooked for two hours, turning regularly. This is the winter version, with sauerkraut. In the spring we use vine leaves, horseradish and greens."

The food kept coming. We ate thick slabs of yellow polenta with mouthwateringly gelatinous slow-cooked pork. At one point Alexandru disappeared into the kitchen and returned half an hour later with a thick brown stew. "This is a quick blood meal from my region. Pimentos, onions, fat, raw liver, a cup of blood, a glass of wine and some spices— pepper, marjoram, paprika. It tastes very good—better than it looks."

"Well, it looks okay to me, Alexandru. And you're right, it tastes great. I like the chilli heat in there."

"It's a very simple dish." He smiled shyly. "We eat this after church or during the Winter Feast, with some form of grain, like polenta."

Eventually I got to try the sausages. First up was the one with blood as its major ingredient. Not surprisingly, it looked much like a black pudding, and, when I took a bite, it tasted pretty much like one, too. Full-flavoured and well-balanced, it was very enjoyable but I realised this was way too familiar to give my guests a Transylvanian thrill.

Jonathan Harker crossed Transylvania in a carriage. My vehicle was less glamorous.

The other sausage looked more like a salami and turned out to have an extremely interesting texture. The stock had gelatinised to produce something softer, more akin to an aspic or a blood-flavoured jelly. I'd not had anything like it before, and it had a lovely delicate flavour, but again very little about it was Gothic, except its country of origin.

As far as Drac snacks went, I had drawn a blank. On the way back to Sibiu, I racked my brains for something that might take my Feast forward. Something grotesque, gory and repulsive. "Alexandru?"

"Yes, Heston."

"What was it you told me about a stew made from leeches fed on goose blood…?"

THEATRE OF BLOOD

The floor was laid with glistening black rubber mats. The silence was broken only by the thrum of the strip lighting, which cast a pallor over the room, and by the constant gurgle of water running through white pipes that labyrinthed down from the ceiling. Double-tiered, bolted metal shelving lined two of the walls; a third set ran down the middle of the room, bisecting it. Each shelf held five large rectangular plastic tanks covered with mesh. It looked like the incubation room from some Hollywood sci-fi dystopia. Gingerly I peeled back the Velcro.

In the liquid confines of the tank dozens of leeches rippled snake-like through the water or wormed their way up the sides. I pressed the mesh firmly back down and found myself nervously checking my forearm for bloodsucking stowaways.

"You know, leeches use their extraordinary sense of smell to detect prey. If you were to stand there for a while, Heston, the leeches would all congregate by that part of the tank," said a grinning, shaven-headed man in white gumboots and a blue sweatshirt with the logo BIOPHARM LEECHES *The biting edge of science*. It was my guide, Carl Peters.

Although most of us recoil in horror at even the thought of leeches, they play an important part in medical therapy, and have done so since ancient times. The European medicinal leech, *Hirudo medicinalis*, contains a valuable anti-coagulant called hirudin, which is used in preparations to treat ailments like rheumatism and thrombosis. And this is just one of several medically useful substances found in their salivary excretions. However, I wasn't here for their medical benefits but to try to recreate the recipe that Alexandru had told me about.

"They're funny things, leeches," Carl said. "The full-grown ones can go a couple of years without feeding."

"How do they survive?"

"They gorge themselves, then in winter or drought they hibernate." He pulled back the mesh again and gazed affectionately at the weird, writhing creatures. Extended, they were about six inches long and had a dark stripe down the centre of their speckled back. "These are adults. I should introduce you to the babies. They're the ones we'll

use for the dish. They haven't eaten for a year, so they'll be hungry."
We walked into the next room. Either the temperature had dropped
or I'd broken out in a cold sweat. "The cold slows their metabolism.
It helps them to go for a long period without eating," Carl explained
as he lifted the mesh on a tank. The leeches wriggled in the water like
tadpoles. They were as thick as a shoelace and about an inch long.

"So if I put my hand in the tank now, would they bite it?"

"Oh yes," said Carl happily. "They're attracted to sugars and salts
in the body, and they can detect the carbon dioxide in your breath.
You'll see—stick your hand in."

"What? Now?" I put my hand bang in the middle of the tank—as
far away from the leeches as possible—and flapped it nervously.

"That splashing won't attract them, Heston. Quite the reverse, in
fact. Don't worry—a leech takes about fifteen seconds to bite you, so
there's loads of time. I'll pull it off before then."

I held my hand still. Several leeches were now edging their way up
the sides of the tank. Others swam around with an eel's fluidity of
motion. Suddenly one of the swimmers made straight for me. It took
all my determination to keep my hand in place. When I lifted it out of
the water, the leech dangled from it. Almost at once the creature
compressed into a blob and began probing its way round my hand.

"It's sniffing for the best place to feed."

It felt creepy and sacrificial. I was beginning to wonder how long
Carl would wait before removing the leech, when it dropped to the
floor. "I guess it didn't like me. Must be last night's garlic," I joked.

"Actually, they *are* repelled by garlic. And beer."

"Interesting. Maybe there's something to the Dracula myth."

"Well, the use of leeches is widespread in Eastern Europe, where
they're considered a cure for depression, headaches, gout, all sorts."

"If that one had fed on me, how much blood would it have taken?"

"Generally, leeches will eat five times their own bodyweight. These
tiddlers weigh about a gram, so normally I'd say five grams of blood.
But as they haven't fed for a year, they'll probably manage fifteen."

"That should be enough to cook with. Let's do it."

Frying tonight—a blood-fattened leech ready for the pan.

I was glad to see that I didn't have to collect the leeches using my hand as bait. Carl showed me how to catch them by holding two fingers like a pair of chopsticks, pinching them round the creatures as they swam past and then flicking them into a small plastic tub. Then we poured goose blood into a sausage casing and lowered it into a beaker filled with water.

"Okay, Heston, tip in the leeches."

A couple thrashed round the beaker but the rest attached almost instantly to our tube of blood and began to probe, hauling themselves up out of the water as they did so. Eventually they stopped, ready to bite in with their three sets of jaws, each with a hundred teeth.

"The blood will be less diluted out of the water," explained Carl. "Look! One's started feeding."

Already the leech's body had grown fatter and flatter, and it began to look less like a shoelace and more like a slug. Soon the sausage casing was looped with leech bodies, attached and feeding voraciously. It was both horrible and fascinating to watch—a brutal, primordial experience. "Once they're full they'll start to drop off," said Carl. As the first one did so, blood leaked into the water from its puncture marks, clouding it red and making the whole thing look even more Frankenstein-like. Eventually all the leeches lay at the bottom of the beaker, fat, sated, inert. It was hard to believe they were the same creatures as the inch-long shoelaces I'd collected minutes before.

"Have you ever eaten leeches, Carl?"

"No. Never. It'll be interesting to see whether the blood coagulates when they're cooked. I've often wondered that."

Blimey! And I'd thought I puzzled over obscure culinary questions... "Now's your chance to find out. You fish out the leeches—I've guddled enough today—and kill them while I get the stove going."

We moved into the kitchen. I wasn't sure how best to cook leeches. After all, there wasn't much guidance in *Larousse*. Since a fed leech was, in effect, a blood pudding, it seemed wise to try frying it, like a sausage. I softened some butter in the pan, added chopped garlic and sautéed briefly, hoping that would impart some flavour to what I doubted would turn out to be a delicacy. In went three of the leeches. They didn't look at all appetising, and a few minutes in the pan didn't change that. I lifted them onto a plate and prodded one with a fork.

"I tell you what, Carl, these are still rock hard."

He stabbed at one. "Yes, the skin is taut. But maybe they're still liquid inside..." He was keen to persuade me they still had potential, but it was no-go. "Or maybe not..." He looked a little crestfallen.

"The heat's made the skin contract. Perhaps leeches would be best stewed like snails—poached for a long time in a gentle heat," I offered, letting him down gently. "I'm not sure about eating these. I hope the blood's congealed. I don't want a burst of goose blood in my mouth."

"The Count would approve, though," Carl said, eagerly. "Maybe we should cut one in half and see...?"

I sliced a leech in two. It was firm inside. The blood *had* congealed. I put a piece in my mouth. "Hmmm," I said. "My first taste of goose-blood-stuffed fried leech. All I can taste is congealed blood, which, frankly, isn't that nice. A bit like overcooked liver pâté. I guess it could be improved if you added spicings to the blood the leeches feed on. But as it is, it's not that appetising. And the skin is thicker and chewier than a sausage casing. What do you think, Carl?"

"I've had worse."

"Really?"

"Yes. My mum's cooking's not that great. Of course, you could try pickling the skin before cooking. Maybe that would improve it."

I was beginning to think that this Transylvanian recipe was a myth. I doubted that anyone could find pleasure in such a dish. It might be macabre enough for Count Dracula but, as far as I was concerned, it was a "lost" recipe that should stay lost. I would have to go back to the beginning and rethink the recipe entirely. Something involving blood pudding and liver and garlic and a good, meaty stock, perhaps with a little kick of horseradish as a nod to Transylvanian culinary custom. It still had to have lashings of blood, of course, but that could probably come from forms of beetroot: juiced, puréed, diced, pickled. And I'd need a stunt double for the leeches. Maybe snails would fit the bill.

THE ANATOMY LESSON

In *Frankenstein*, Mary Shelley is famously vague about how the monster is created. Most of Frankenstein's scientific investigation takes place in dissecting rooms, charnel houses and graveyards. "To examine the causes of life, we must first have recourse to death," he explains. "So I became acquainted with the science of anatomy."

Bones, therefore, were an appropriate centrepiece for my Feast. I would wheel out a gurney upon which lay a life-size model skeleton. Somehow, all the elements of my main course would involve this skeletal serving dish. My first idea was to create edible bones to replace their plastic counterparts. Guests would be able to pick out and munch on a metatarsal, snack on a scapula. I tested various techniques for making bone casts, and decided to try out the one I liked on John Morris, a professor of anatomy at Oxford University. If he found the results convincing, then I could be pretty sure my guests would too.

The department's lecture hall was built in 1893, around the time the Gothic classics *The Picture of Dorian Gray*, *Dr Jekyll and Mr Hyde* and *Dracula* were published. The moodily lit room was shaped like an amphitheatre, with tiers of curved wooden benches and desktops banking steeply away and up towards the ceiling. In the small semicircle in front of these—the lecturer's arena—was an octagonal table with a solid stone worktop bordered by a deep groove: the original Victorian dissecting table. I hefted a sack of alginate, a plastic tub and a couple of bone-models onto it, and got to work.

Alginate is extracted from seaweed. It absorbs water quickly and in quantity (up to three hundred times its own weight) and sets to a thick gum. It is used in a variety of ways, from slimming aid and food thickener to mould-maker. It was this last property that I needed to make use of. I poured the bluish powder into the tub, added the same amount of water and stirred. The mixture turned almost instantly to a slurry and with each whisk became thicker and more porridge-like. I grabbed a couple of models of a shoulderblade and half-submerged them in the mixture, then reached for an arm bone. I had to work fast if I was going to get all four models in place before it set too hard.

In a little over five minutes, the alginate had firmed up and I prised out the bones, which gave a satisfying squelch as they came out, leaving behind neat bone-shaped hollows. I wasn't sure what flavour I'd like my bones to have, but for the moment I had opted to line the moulds with marzipan, as it had a bone-like ivory colour. After I'd baked them, the marzipan had a bone-like brittleness, too. They were very fragile. Many broke as I tried to glue two halves together with white chocolate, but eventually I managed to construct one example of a shoulderblade and one arm bone. I invited the professor in to check them out.

A femur comes in handy to roll out marzipan for the bone-mould.

My audience in the anatomy department's lecture theatre seems unimpressed.

John looked bemused at the carnage I'd caused in the lecture hall. Broken bone shards littered the dissecting table and spatters of alginate freckled the floor. I tried to distract him from the mess. "How much anatomical knowledge did they have in Mary Shelley's time?"

His brow furrowed with concentration. "Actually, it was pretty good. Since the bones are what remain after death, scientists had been able to investigate them much more fully than other parts of the body. This is why the grave-robbing industry came into being."

"So science was basically dependent on bodysnatching?"

"In a way, yes. Medical schools used to pay for this."

"And what about re-animating bodies? In films of *Frankenstein* they make a big play of using electricity to achieve this, even though there's only a glancing reference to it in the book."

"Now, of course, electricity is routinely used to restart the heart. But in the 1800s people were already beginning to research and understand how electrical impulses go through the nerves to the muscles to stimulate reactions. It's not impossible that Mary Shelley has this in mind when talking about the creation of the monster."

"I don't want to make a monster—just an edible skeleton," I said, realising that John might consider this to be frivolous lunacy. "I was wondering which bones might best serve my purpose."

"Some bones are much more complex shapes than others. Some of the long bones should be relatively easy to make in a recess mould. The more intricate shapes will be far more difficult. Particularly in an edible form, I would think, though that's more your end of things."

"Well, I've got a couple I'd like your opinion on." I held out my two bones. John took the one that looked like a dog's bone. "A humerus. Not bad. You've got all the lumps and bumps. Quite convincing. And what's this?" He examined the other bone. "A scapula. You've got the flat part but not the large projection that attaches to the muscles. So, pretty good. Eight out of ten," he declared with a grin.

"Must try harder. I used to get that a lot at school too."

"The acid test for you, I imagine, is what it tastes like."

"Please, go ahead."

"It seems almost a shame to break it after all this work." He bit in nevertheless. "That's a nice mix of textures, and a very nice flavour."

"Excellent. So I just need to work on my anatomy studies."

BLYTHE SPIRIT

The Betty Blythe tearoom in Kensington seems like a portal to a more innocent age. Parked in the window is a heavy black tandem. Pink gingham bunting crisscrosses the ceiling, shelves are stacked high with brightly coloured boxes of Tunnock's Teacakes and tins of Glenryck Pilchards, a blues number by Bessie Smith warbles weakly from a wireless somewhere. Demure girls in black uniforms with a white bow at the neck serve tea in floral-patterned china.

The shop's basement, however, was a different proposition. At a long table sat thirteen women who wouldn't have looked out of place in a risqué Hollywood period piece. Style seemed to be divided between Moulin Rouge Showgirl (black lace, fishnets), French Revolution Courtesan (corset, extravagant wig, even a bustle) and 1930s Madam (silk dressing gown, pearls and little else). This was Zoe Fletcher and the Time for Tease girls, who put on "events that combine a delightful afternoon tea with a burlesque cabaret in a scrumptious package", and their conversation, like their dress, seemed a world away from the innocent atmosphere upstairs. "Has anyone else done a ladies' buffet where you lie on the table? I smelled like a cow's udder afterwards."

I had come here to try to gauge how far I would have to go to create a provocative dessert for my Feast, but it seemed unlikely that I'd be able to produce much that would shock this lot. Zoe (white corset, severe dark bob, pillbox hat) beckoned me over. "Hello, Heston. Before you show us what you can do, let us show you what we do."

Two women took the stage behind a table set for a cooking session, each with a cookbook to show their allegiance to a particular TV chef and dressed in the spirit of their idol: one in tight, flirty black skirt and shirt with bright red heels and red and white polka-dot pinny; the other in fawn rollneck and pale lemon skirt. The voice of Gracie Fields burst onto the stereo, "If I knew you were coming I'd have baked a cake…", as they began to act out a choreographed scene in which each tried to outdo the other in the kitchen until the spoon-licking vamp played her trump card and stripped down to pearly grey satin underwear. The staid woman failed to top this (her undergarment was a sensible nightie) and chose instead to drive a custard pie into the face of the other. Funny, teasing and over the top, it was classic burlesque and the audience loved it. I hoped my efforts would get a similar reception.

I had read that, among his many ungovernable appetites, the Marquis de Sade had an incredibly sweet tooth. I had also read about a recipe for Minni di Virgini, little ricotta-filled cakes shaped like breasts and topped with a cherry nipple, and wondered whether my Feast should end with a dessert that de Sade might have enjoyed. So I had made up a batch of Minni that I was now going to feed to a troupe of hungry dancers who were busy baying, "Bring on the breasts." I hurried upstairs and brought down the tray of cakes, which got a cheer and a clap. "They really *are* boobs," somebody declared.

"Those don't look anything like mine," said another, and then began licking one suggestively. Soon everybody was grabbing a bun and pantomiming erotic pleasure as they ate them. To calm things down, I explained that the cakes were traditionally made by the nuns of the Monastery of the Virgins in Palermo. They didn't seem impressed. "All those women. There were breasts everywhere already. You'd have thought they'd have made a cock instead."

"I know someone who made a banana fritter penis," one girl said wistfully. "I don't think I ate it. I just giggled a lot."

"So you don't find this shocking in any way?"

This caused incredulous laughter. "I think you're probably asking the wrong group, darling," advised deep-voiced Monique. But in fact more than one of the others admitted that it felt a bit weird to eat a nipple, and then I told them that the ricotta was supposed to represent breast milk. "*Ugh*. That just makes me feel *bleugh*!" It seemed that even in a worldly age, among very worldly people, these cakes could provoke a reaction, so they must have caused a real stir in the eighteenth century. Even so, I wasn't convinced this was the right direction for my dessert to take. It wasn't really dark and Gothic enough. "What about the flavour and texture—does it work for you?" I asked.

"I thought it'd be like a fondant fancy," one girl told me. "But they're nicer than that. They'd be good for Christmas. As gifts."

"Yeah. Those cakes aren't really shocking. They're fun. And delicious," said Zoe. "But you know what, Heston? That shaved head of yours is shaped a bit like a Minni di Virgini. Have you ever tried putting a nipple on top?"

"Oh no. I think that's a terrible idea," I said, as she tweaked the pink bit off the top of a cake and advanced towards me…

THE BONE COLLECTOR

My skeleton service was coming together. I had been thinking about getting my guests to pick up and eat edible versions of real bones, and realised I could extend this idea: they could literally eat ribs—short ribs, a well-marbled, tasty cut of beef. I could brine and slow-cook these, then sear and cut them into strips before placing them back where they belonged, in between the bones of the ribcage. And I could cook brains and serve them in the brainpan. I deep-fried a mixture of sheep's brains and savoury choux to make little fritters. Guests could pick these out of the skull, perhaps to immerse in a dipping sauce. And there was a Fat Duck recipe that would fit perfectly into this anatomical gastronomy. I've always found vegetarian dishes that resemble their meaty counterparts comical. Why would you want to eat food that looks like the things you've given up (particularly if you've done so on moral grounds)? With this in mind, for the tasting menu I had developed a Vegetarian Pot au Feu, a rich, meaty-seeming broth surrounding what looked like a marrowbone but was in fact a hollowed-out heart of palm.

For the Feast I could follow pretty much the same process—boil the trimmed hearts of palm for half an hour with rosemary, thyme, salt and black peppercorns, then fill them with a savoury custard made from milk, cream, salt, grated horseradish root, mushroom-and-red-wine broth and the setting agent gellan—and then slice the hearts of palm into vertebra-sized pieces and lay them on top of the spinal column of the model skeleton, as though they were part of it.

I began to wonder whether I could add one more play on words to the dish, using half a calf's bone as a sort of serving vessel, and placing upon it a filling made from the bone marrow that had once been inside. Bone-in-a-bone. It had an appealing symmetry and wouldn't be hard to do. Bone marrow is utterly delicious and would need very little in the way of garnish and seasoning—some parsley, chervil, tarragon and lemon zest perhaps, breadcrumbs for texture, and maybe a few smoked anchovies, a surf 'n' turf thing that alluded to the patchwork mix 'n' match of Frankenstein's creation.

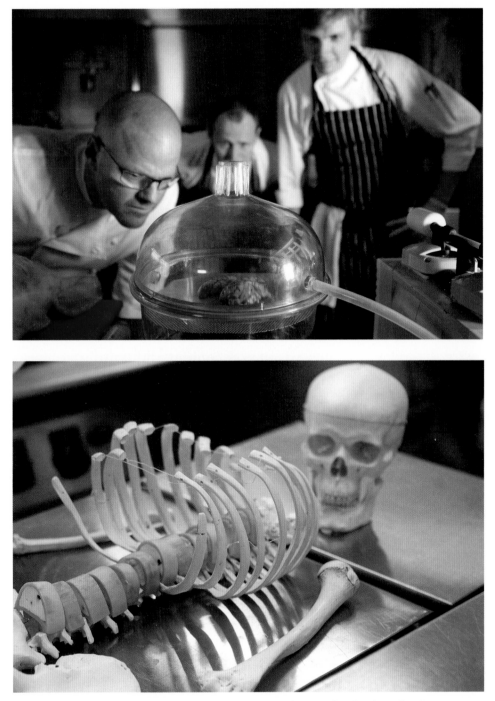

Inflating a sheep's brain and constructing a heart-of-palm spinal column.

THE EDIBLE GRAVEYARD

The set designers had done a fantastic job. In front of me on the table was a perfect model graveyard. A 4ft x 2ft oval of grass was fenced in by straggly, spiky, wrought-iron railings. At one end two miniature stone pillars flanked a pair of forbidding-looking gates. In the middle of the cemetery was a stone plinth surrounded by six deep cavities—plots ready to be filled with the coffins for which I was busy preparing a recipe, because I'd decided to make the graveyard edible.

Some of the elements were already in place. I knew what was going in the coffins: soil. One dish at the Fat Duck calls for edible sand, and it had proved easy to adapt this. The key ingredient was a form of light tapioca with the ability to absorb oil without becoming fatty. To this I added ingredients that would provide a range of flavours and textures: ground Rice Krispies; caramelised chocolate (for crunch) and ground, caramelised grapenuts; rich, bitter, crunchy cocoa nibs; cocoa powder and drinking chocolate; small ganache balls for smoothness; silver lustre to lend a shimmering mineral content and powdered black-coloured chocolate to give it the right appearance. Once some hazelnut oil was poured in—to add more flavour and an earthy dampness—it looked almost offputtingly convincing, but tasted lovely. I'd also come up with something that allowed me to hold onto the idea of de Sade and the Minni di Virgini—carving up a Barbie doll and pressing her bust in some alginate to produce a breast-mould so that each coffin could contain an unexpected, raunchy body part amid the soil.

The gravestone was solved, too. I'd fashioned a mixture of nuts and marzipan to a brittle, stony-looking texture and turned it into a classic gravestone shape: a flattish cuboid rounded at one end. Mine, though, was not solid but hollow, and I piped into it blobs of gore-red raspberry compote and slime-green pistachio paste, sprinkled on freeze-dried raspberries and pressed into place a gravestone-shaped sheet of dark chocolate—for a touch of bitterness and a fine crunch—and then began the process all over again. Once I'd got three such layers I laid the other face of the gravestone on top, sealed it in place and began to think about what I should write on it to unsettle my guests… just a little. ▨

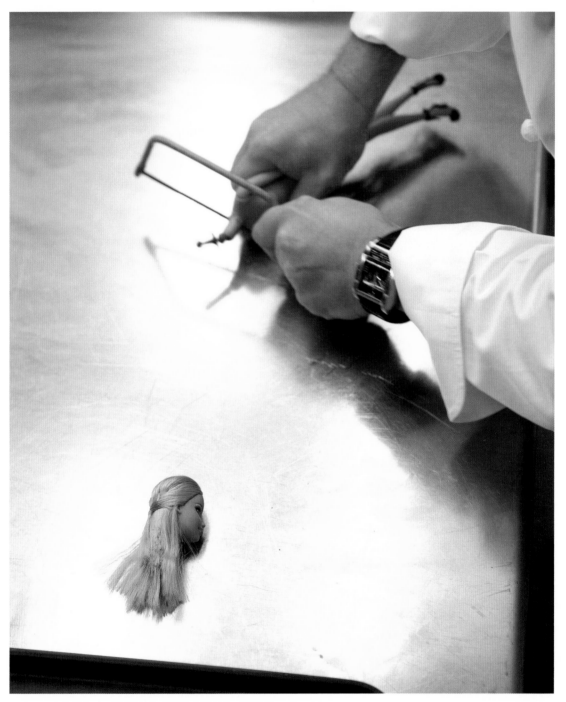

The Texas Hacksaw Massacre—cutting up Barbie to make a mould of her breasts.

MENU

Jekyll & Hyde's Bubbling Potion of Transformation

*Gin & Tonic with Granita, Green Gin Spheres
and Effervescing Gin Aroma*

Dracula's Little Bites

*Beetroot and Blood Civet of Spelt with Nitro-frozen
Horseradish Cream, Charred Pickled Beetroots,
Fennel Salad and Deep-fried, Impaled,
Garlic Butter Snails*

Hestonstein's Monster

*Seventy-two-hour Ribs, Heart-of-palm Spinal Column,
Deep-fried Brains-within-a-brain, Bone Marrow
served-in-the-Bone, Deep-fried Crispy Eel Bones*

The Gourmand's Graveyard

Edible Gravestones, Soil, Coffin and Breasts

DEEP-FRIED, IMPALED, GARLIC BUTTER SNAILS

FOR THE BRAISED SNAILS

100g Roman snails
1kg water
120g onions, halved
40g split carrots
½ garlic bulb (split vertically)
90g trimmed leeks, halved
2 celery sticks
2 bay leaves
50g rosemary
50g parsley
50g thyme

Rinse the snails in several changes of fresh water until all the grit has been removed.

Preheat the oven to 120°C.

Place all the remaining ingredients in a flameproof casserole dish and bring to a simmer on the stove.

Place the snails in the simmering liquid, cover and cook in the oven for 3–4 hours or until the snails are soft and tender.

Remove from the oven and let the snails cool in the liquid in the casserole dish.

Remove the snails and trim away the intestine and white sac. Refrigerate the snails until needed.

FOR THE GARLIC BUTTER

100g shallots, finely sliced
20g garlic, very finely chopped
230g butter (at room temperature)
15g flat-leaf parsley, chopped
salt and freshly ground black pepper

In a sauté pan, sweat the shallots and garlic in 30g of the butter. Once softened, leave to cool.

Once cool, mix in the chopped parsley and remaining butter.

Transfer the garlic butter to a container and refrigerate until needed.

TO PREPARE THE SNAILS

garlic butter (see above)
snails (see above)
thinly sliced lardo

Wearing gloves, rub the garlic butter into the snails so that they are well covered. Allow to set in the fridge.

Wrap the buttered snails in the slices of lardo. Keep chilled until needed.

FOR THE TEMPURA BATTER

50g cornflour
50g plain flour
2g bicarbonate of soda
5g salt
120g iced water

Combine the dry ingredients in a bowl.

Add the iced water and gently incorporate the dry ingredients using chopsticks or a fork, being very careful not to overmix as this will create lumps.

Place the bowl of batter over an ice bath to keep it cold.

TO SERVE

grapeseed or groundnut oil, for deep-frying
prepared snails (see above)
tempura batter (see above)

Heat the oil in a deep-fat fryer to 180°C.

Dip the prepared snails in the tempura batter and deep-fry until golden brown and crispy. Drain on kitchen paper and impale each snail with a toothpick to serve.

BEETROOT CIVET OF SPELT WITH HORSERADISH CREAM

FOR THE BEETROOT SOUBISE

30g butter
250g onions, thinly sliced
200g chicken bouillon
2.5g salt
225g beetroot juice, strained through
    a fine sieve
2.7g Gellan F

In a sauté pan, melt the butter and sweat the onions for 5 minutes until just soft but not coloured. Add the bouillon and salt.

Bring to the boil, then add the beetroot juice. Return to a simmer and cook for 3 minutes.

Blitz the mixture in a blender and pass through a fine sieve.

Weigh out 400g of the mixture and place in a Thermomix. Begin blending on medium speed and set the temperature to 100°C. When the liquid comes up to temperature sprinkle in the gellan and heat at 100°C for another 2 minutes.

Pour the mixture into a bowl surrounded by iced water and leave to set. When cold, blitz using a hand blender until smooth. (If necessary, heat the mixture a little whilst blitzing to melt the solidified butter.)

Pass the mixture through a drum sieve and reserve in the fridge until needed.

FOR THE PICKLED BEETROOT DICE

200g Chardonnay vinegar
4g sugar
2g salt
100g beetroot, diced into 4mm cubes

Combine the vinegar, sugar and salt and whisk until dissolved. Add the beetroot dice and leave to marinate for 20 minutes.

Strain and reserve the beetroot cubes.

FOR THE PICKLED BABY BEETROOTS

1kg baby beetroots
600g water
45g sugar
6g salt
180g Chardonnay vinegar

Wash the baby beetroots and top and tail them. Combine the water, sugar, salt and vinegar in a bowl and add the baby beetroots. Put into a sous-vide bag and seal at full pressure.

Bring a pan of water to 95°C. Immerse the bag of beetroots in the water and cook for 45 minutes to 1 hour until just softened.

Remove and cool to room temperature. Peel the beetroots, halve lengthwise and reserve.

FOR THE SPELT

300g spelt
10g grapeseed oil
40g shallots, finely diced
1g garlic, finely diced
150g Madeira
500g chicken bouillon, warmed

Toast the spelt in the grapeseed oil in a wide-bottomed pan, then add the shallots and cook for 1–2 minutes. Add the garlic and cook for an additional 2 minutes.

Pour in the Madeira and reduce the liquid by three-quarters. Add half of the bouillon and cook gently, stirring gently and adding more stock as required, until the spelt is cooked.

Pour the spelt onto a tray, cool and reserve.

FOR THE VINEGAR REDUCTION

100g Cabernet Sauvignon vinegar
100g sherry vinegar

Combine the vinegars in a pan and reduce by half. Allow the mixture to cool and reserve.

FOR THE GARLIC PURÉE

4 garlic bulbs
150g grapeseed oil

Break the garlic into cloves. Blanch in boiling water for 10 seconds, then refresh in iced water.

Place the garlic cloves in a pan, cover them with grapeseed oil, bring to 100°C and cook until tender. Leave to cool, then drain the garlic, peel and blend the flesh until smooth. Pass through a drum sieve and reserve.

FOR THE FOIE GRAS PARFAIT

This recipe makes one terrine (26x10x9 cm) and the best results are achieved using the quantities specified below, rather than scaling them down.

  100g shallots, finely sliced
  3g garlic, minced
  15g thyme sprigs, tied with string
  150g dry Madeira
  150g ruby port
  75g white port
  50g brandy
  250g foie gras (trimmed weight)
  150g chicken livers (trimmed weight)
  18g table salt
  2g nitrite salt
  240g eggs
  300g unsalted butter, melted

Place the shallots, garlic and thyme in a pan with the Madeira, both ports and brandy. Set aside to marinate for 24 hours.

Heat the marinated mixture until nearly all of the liquid has evaporated, stirring regularly to prevent the shallots and garlic from burning. Remove from the heat and discard the thyme.

Preheat a water bath to 50°C and the oven to 100°C. Fill a bain-marie with 5cm water and place in the oven.

Cut the foie gras into pieces roughly the same size as the chicken livers. Sprinkle the table salt and nitrite salt over the livers and mix well.

Put the livers and foie gras in a sous-vide bag. Put the eggs and the alcohol reduction in a second sous-vide bag and the butter in a third. Seal all the bags under full pressure, then place them all in the water bath for 20 minutes.

After 20 minutes, remove the bags from the water bath.

Combine the eggs, alcohol reduction and livers in the Thermomix and blend at 50°C until smooth. Slowly blitz in the butter.

Pass the mixture through a fine sieve, using the back of a small ladle to push it through.

Pour the mixture into a 26x10x9 cm terrine dish and place in the bain-marie. Cover the bain-marie with aluminium foil and cook the parfait until the temperature in the centre reaches 64°C.

Remove from the oven and allow to cool. Refrigerate for 24 hours before serving.

FOR THE WALNUT VINAIGRETTE

  20g Dijon mustard
  300g walnut vinegar
  645g walnut oil
  275g grapeseed oil

Combine the mustard and walnut vinegar in a bowl, then whisk in the oils until emulsified. Set aside until needed.

FOR THE FENNEL SALAD

  1 bulb fennel, white part only, cored
  walnut vinaigrette (see above)

Using a fine slicer, shave the fennel very thinly and place directly into iced water.

Just before serving, drain the fennel and dress with the walnut vinaigrette.

FOR THE ICED HORSERADISH CRÈME FRAÎCHE

  100g crème fraîche
  25g horseradish sauce
  5g lemon juice
  10g sugar
  salt and freshly ground black pepper

Mix all of the ingredients together in a bowl. Taste and add more horseradish and/or seasoning if necessary.

Pass the mixture through a drum sieve and, using a pipette, drop small balls of it into liquid nitrogen.

Remove the frozen crème fraîche balls from the nitrogen using a tea strainer and keep in the freezer until needed.

TO SERVE

prepared spelt (see above)
200g chicken bouillon
150g braised oxtail, diced
beetroot soubise (see above)
foie gras parfait (see above)
garlic purée (see above)
pickled beetroot dice (see above)
vinegar reduction (see above)
pickled baby beetroots (see above)
fennel salad, dressed at the last minute
  (see above)
iced horseradish crème fraîche (see above)
cress

In a pan, combine the spelt and bouillon and bring to a simmer. Add the oxtail and beetroot soubise and cook to a risotto consistency.

Remove from the heat and add enough foie gras parfait to achieve a creamy consistency, then add garlic purée to taste. Fold in the diced beetroot and add vinegar reduction to taste, seasoning with salt and pepper.

Sear the pickled baby beetroots in a dry pan.

Spoon the spelt into 6 bowls and place the charred baby beetroots and fennel on top.

At the last possible moment, spoon the iced horseradish crème fraîche onto the dish and garnish with cress.

SEVENTY-TWO-HOUR RIBS AND BRAINS-WITHIN-A-BRAIN

FOR THE SHORT RIBS

    5kg beef short ribs, bones removed
    sea salt

Cover the meat liberally with salt and leave for 1½ hours.

Preheat one water bath to 56°C and another to 85°C. Soak the meat for 30 minutes in several changes of cold water.

Divide the meat between 2 sous-vide bags and seal under full pressure.

Place both sous-vide bags of meat into the 85°C water bath and cook for 7 minutes. Transfer directly to the 56°C water bath and cook for 72 hours.

Remove the bags from the water bath and cool completely in a bowl of iced water. Reserve in the fridge.

When ready to serve, reheat the bags of meat in a 56°C water bath for 45 minutes.

Remove the meat from the bags and trim away any remaining heavy connective tissue. Set aside.

FOR THE RED WINE SAUCE

    7.5kg beef bones
    2kg oxtail, chopped into sections
    grapeseed or groundnut oil, for frying
    7.5kg boneless shin of beef, in pieces
    3kg carrots, thinly sliced
    3kg onions, thinly sliced
    30g star anise
    2.25kg red wine
    12kg water
    salt
    red wine vinegar
    40g flat-leaf parsley
    25g chervil

Preheat the oven to 190°C.

Combine the beef bones and the oxtail pieces in a roasting pan and place in the hot oven. Roast them until golden brown on all sides, turning regularly.

Heat a thin film of oil in a pressure cooker over a high heat. Brown the pieces of beef in batches, colouring them deeply without burning. Take out the meat and set aside.

Add the carrots and onions to the pan. Sauté the vegetables until soft and then add the star anise. Continue to sauté the vegetables until evenly coloured, but not caramelised.

Add the red wine and, when hot, flame off the alcohol. When the flames have died out and the wine has reduced by half, add the beef bones and the meat and cover with water.

Put the lid on and bring to full pressure. Cook at full pressure for 2 hours.

De-pressurise and remove the lid. Strain the liquid through a muslin-lined sieve. Return to a clean pan and reduce to a sauce consistency.

To serve, season the sauce with salt and red wine vinegar to taste, then add the chopped parsley and chervil.

TO PREPARE THE BRAINS

    1kg calf's brains

Rinse the brains and soak in several changes of water in the fridge for 2 days.

Trim away any red pieces from the brains and then cut into pieces. Dry well on kitchen paper and set aside.

FOR THE CHOUX PASTRY

    250g water
    100g butter, cubed
    150g plain flour
    3 eggs
    prepared calf's brains (see above)
    salt

In a pan, bring the water and butter to the boil.

Whisk in the flour, then use a spatula to mix together until no longer sticky. Add the eggs one at a time and mix well to fully incorporate. Continue to heat for 5 minutes.

Cool the mixture to room temperature and transfer to a piping bag.

Weigh out the choux pastry and for every 600g of choux add 400g of the brains (60% choux, 40% brains).

Place the choux and brains in a food processor and blitz until smooth.

Pass through a fine drum sieve, season and transfer the mixture to a piping bag.

TO SERVE
grapeseed or groundnut oil, for deep-frying
choux pastry mixture (see above)
short rib meat (see above)
red wine sauce (see above)
tartare sauce, for dipping

Heat the oil in a deep-fat fryer to 180°C. Pipe out the choux into small profiteroles and drop into the hot oil, using scissors if necessary to trim the batter off evenly.

Deep-fry the choux balls until they are evenly golden brown, then remove and drain on kitchen paper.

Meanwhile, heat a sauté pan and sear the short rib meat in a little oil to colour on both sides. Slice thinly lengthwise.

Place 3 slices of short rib in between the ribs each side of the ribcage. Serve with the red wine sauce.

Season the choux fritters with a little salt and serve in a skull accompanied by tartare sauce for dipping.

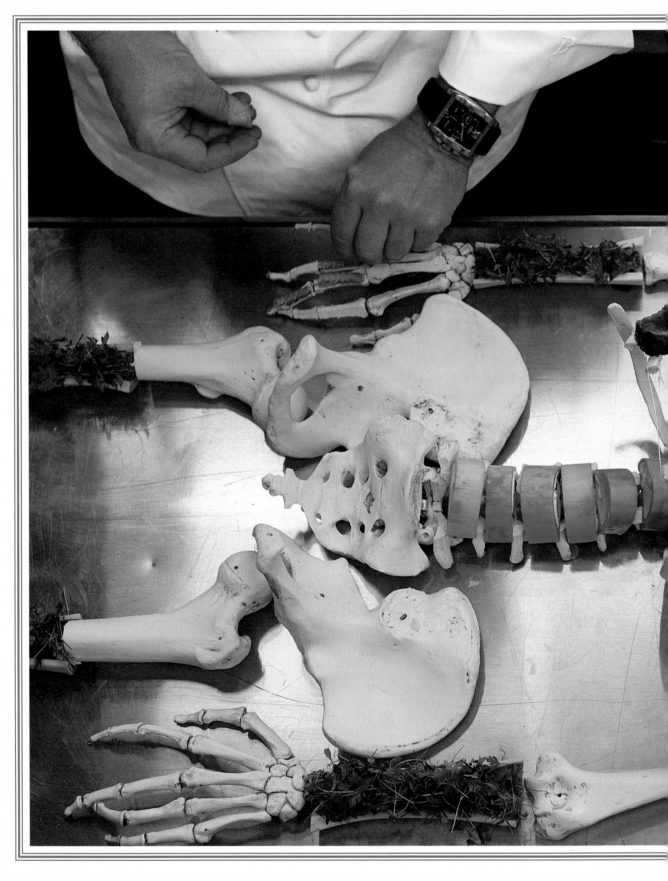

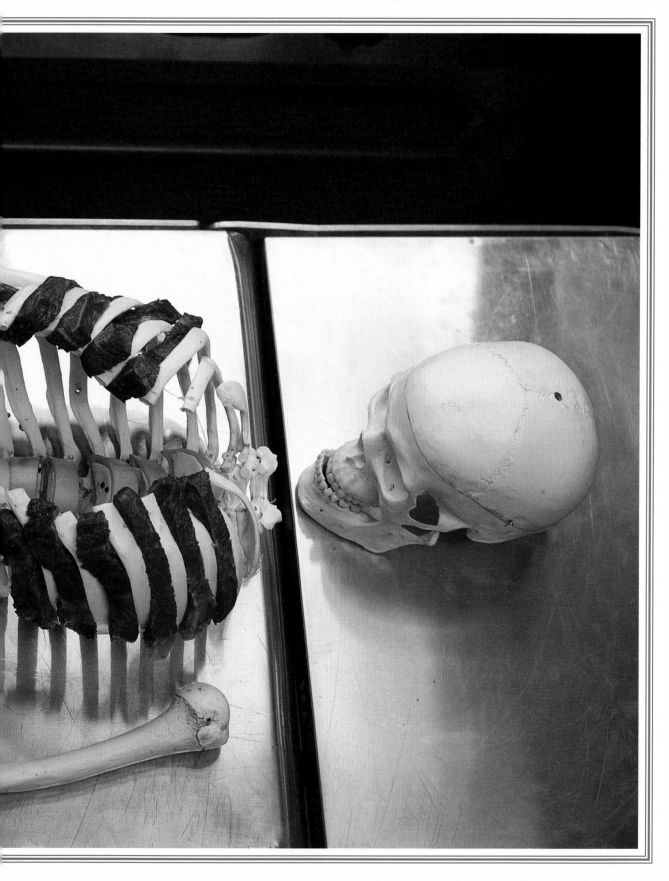

EDIBLE GRAVESTONES

FOR THE MARZIPAN SHELLS

15g chopped hazelnuts
100g white marzipan

Fold the chopped hazelnuts into the marzipan and then roll it out on a piece of parchment to a 2mm thickness.

Carefully line the inside of gravestone-shaped moulds with the thinly rolled marzipan. (The moulds measure 10cm from the top of the semicircle to the base, 5cm wide and 1cm deep.)

Leave the marzipan shells to dry at room temperature for 24 hours.

FOR THE PISTACHIO ICE CREAM

140g egg yolks
250g unrefined caster sugar
1kg whole milk
500g soured cream
140g natural yoghurt
40g brandy
400g pistachio paste
200g salted shelled pistachio nuts, quartered

Whisk the egg yolks and sugar together in a bowl until the mixture is light and creamy.

In a saucepan, heat the milk to 52°C and then, using a whisk, gradually add it into the egg mixture to temper.

Return to the pan and place over a low heat. Bring to 70°C, stirring constantly, and hold the custard at this temperature for 10 minutes. Strain through a fine sieve into a container set in a bowl of iced water and allow to cool.

Before churning, add the soured cream, yoghurt, brandy and pistachio paste to the custard base, mixing well to incorporate fully.

Churn in an ice-cream machine until -5°C, then fold in the pistachio nuts. Transfer to a suitable container, seal and store in the freezer until needed.

FOR THE OLIVE OIL BISCUIT

450g butter
400g unrefined caster sugar
700g plain flour
12g salt
6g baking powder
2.5g vanilla seeds
180g egg yolks
150g extra virgin olive oil

In a mixer fitted with the paddle attachment, cream the butter and sugar together until smooth, taking care not to overmix.

Combine all the dry ingredients and add them to the creamed mixture. Continue to mix for 2 minutes.

Add the egg yolks and olive oil to the bowl and mix briefly, just enough to bring the dough together. Cover with clingfilm and leave to rest in the fridge overnight.

Remove the clingfilm and roll the dough between 2 pieces of parchment to a thickness of 2mm. Place in the freezer for 15 minutes to rest.

Preheat the oven to 150°C.

Peel off the top layer of parchment and place the dough on a baking sheet. Bake in the preheated oven for 14 minutes.

Remove from the oven and allow to cool.

FOR THE RASPBERRY PÂTE DE FRUIT

550g raspberry purée
100g glucose
350g caster sugar
13g pectin jaune
9g tartaric acid
9g water
120g olive oil biscuit (see above)

Place the raspberry purée and glucose in a saucepan. Mix the sugar and pectin together in a bowl, add to the pan and bring to a simmer. Stirring constantly, bring the temperature up to 69° Brix.

In the meantime, dissolve the tartaric acid in the water.

Remove the pan of raspberry purée and glucose from the heat. Add the tartaric acid solution and pour into a PacoJet container. Allow the mixture to cool and set completely.

Break the biscuit into pieces and add to the pâte de fruit. Run through the PacoJet machine and reserve for serving.

TO ASSEMBLE
   marzipan shells (see above)
   pistachio ice cream (see above)
   raspberry pâte de fruit (see above)

Half-fill the marzipan shells with the ice cream. Pipe in the pâte de fruit to create a ripple effect, add more ice cream and flatten with a spatula.

Close with a marzipan shell and place in the freezer to set before serving.

A Titanic Feast

A NEW CENTURY, a new beginning. Edward VII came to the throne in 1901, and provided a sharp contrast to the staid and sober outlook of his mother, Queen Victoria. Edward was a big man with a fondness for gourmet food, pretty women, horses, hunting and huge cigars. The upper classes seemed to take their cue from this, indulging in luxury foreign travel, haute couture, garden parties and plenty of Champagne. For them it was a golden age, even if the growth of the newly formed Labour Party and the women's suffrage movement showed how big a gap was developing between the haves and have-nots.

Edward died in 1910 but it's difficult not to see 1914 as the real cut-off point for Edwardian confidence and innocence. When we read about that period, we're always aware that the First World War is just over the horizon, implacable and destructive, like an iceberg. This is probably why so many iconic figures and events of the period are at the same time gloriously heroic, and doomed. The "unsinkable" *Titanic* with its luxurious fittings and lack of lifeboats. Captain Robert Falcon Scott and his ill-thought-out expedition to the South Pole. Lawrence of Arabia swapping messing about in Mesopotamia for guerrilla warfare in the Arabian peninsula, before becoming a recluse and dying in a motorcycle crash. These were the things that held my imagination, and they would form the starting points for my *Titanic* Feast.

SCOTT OF THE ANTARCTIC

> The pulling this afternoon was fairly pleasant; at first over hard
> snow, then on pretty rough ice with surface snow-filled cracks,
> bad for sledges, but ours promised to come through well... The
> weather is beginning to look dirty again, snow clouds rolling in
> from the east as usual. I believe it will be overcast tomorrow.
>
> ROBERT SCOTT'S JOURNAL, *17 December 1911*

The ice sheet in front of me radiated a blinding whiteness. Rain stippled
its surface, creating shallow puddles in places. The weather had turned
and gusts of viciously cold wind buffeted the area, making me doubt
that we'd be able to keep the camping stove alight. I settled my ski hat
more firmly on my head.

Unfortunately, however, my research on Scott hadn't brought me
to the Antarctic but to Hyde Park, where a tourist attraction called
Winter Wonderland offered a sort of Yuletide Experience. I had walked
past cutesy wooden huts selling wooden toys or hearty German fare:
Steak mit Krautsalat, Bratwurst, Krakauer. The flapping mouth of a
mechanical reindeer head—attached to the eaves of one of the stores—
belted out Christmas tunes or, somewhat incongruously, the opening
of *Cabaret*. *"Willkommen, Bienvenue..."* had echoed round the park as
I made my way past mulled-wine kiosks and decorated-gingerbread
stalls to the point of my visit: the ice rink. Nearby I had set up a portable
marquee and gas stove so I could cook and offer to skaters and passers-
by one of the basic foodstuffs of Scott's expedition—pemmican.

Pemmican was originally made by Native American Indians who
needed a non-perishable foodstuff to sustain them as they travelled
the North, trapping animals and trading fur. It had to contain the
basics for survival: some form of protein to keep the body healthy and
operational, fat for insulation, carbohydrates for energy and fruit for
vitamins. So they melted whale or seal fat, added berries, grain and
meat that had been dried in the sun or over a fire, then let the mixture
cool and solidify into portable bricks.

Although Scott's journal records that their meals were "simple enough", to modern eyes they can seem surprisingly extravagant. Their Christmas dinner, while the *Terra Nova* was stuck in pack ice in 1910, consisted of tomato soup, stewed penguin breast, roast beef, plum pudding and mince pies, asparagus, Champagne, port and liqueurs. Six months later, their celebration of Midwinter Day (the turning point of the Antarctic winter) meant more Champagne and liqueurs, as well as roast beef with Yorkshire pudding, fried potatoes and Brussels sprouts. Of course these were special occasions, and it was important to counter the boredom and slog of the expedition with entertainment (they even brought a pianola with them to base camp). But their Norwegian rivals in the dash for the South Pole disapproved of the British habit of dragging "many of the luxuries of civilisation into the wilderness", and initiatives such as ferrying an ice-house full of mutton to the Antarctic (rather than relying on the plentiful local fresh seal meat) seem to confirm the doomed naivety of Scott's expedition.

By the time they reached the final leg to the Pole, their fare was very different, even on Christmas Day. "We had four courses. The first, pemmican, full of whack with slices of horse meat flavoured with onion and curry powder and thickened with biscuit; then an arrowroot, cocoa and biscuit hoosh [a sweetened hot soup usually made from melted snow and pemmican]; then a plum pudding; then cocoa with raisins, and finally a dessert of caramels and ginger." From then on, references to pemmican litter Scott's journal, and seem to act as a litmus test of his state of mind. "Tonight we had a sort of stew fry of pemmican and horse-flesh," he notes in his journal on 19 February 1912, "and voted it the best hoosh we had ever had on a sledge journey." This comes a couple of days after the death of Lieutenant Evans (and little more than a month before Scott's own death), and it feels as though the explorer is desperately trying to persuade himself into a positive frame of mind. Two weeks later, he no longer allows himself such comforting self-delusions. "We started march on tea and pemmican as last night—we pretend to prefer the pemmican this way." The last meal recorded in his journal, on 19 March, ten days before his death, is "cold pemmican and biscuit and half a pannikin of cocoa", which cruelly contrasts with an entry from a year earlier, at Hut Point, when the adventure was just beginning, and Scott still thought he could beat Roald Amundsen in the race to the Pole. "We gather around the fire seated on packing-cases, with a hunk of bread and butter and a steaming pannikin of tea, and life is well worth living."

Grain, fat, dried meat and fruit—I liked each of pemmican's ingredients on its own, particularly the dried meat because my father, who grew up in South Africa, used to give me biltong as a treat. But I wasn't at all sure about how well they'd go together. I unwrapped a pack of Britannia Dripping (a name that had a suitably Edwardian ring to it), carved off a big chunk, let it melt in the pan, then added shredded biltong to create a dark pulp that looked like stewed currants. The bratwurst-sellers had little to fear from my efforts, I reckoned. The few people who glanced in at my little tent as they passed seemed to quicken their step once they'd seen what was in the pan.

I added blueberries to the mix, along with enough ground oats to thicken it and absorb some of the fat. I had read that pemmican tasted better in extreme cold. I hoped so because it would look fairly awful whatever the weather—a grey-green sludge that, if I were being generous, looked a little like olive tapenade. Reluctantly, I tasted a spoonful. The biltong and blueberries were nice enough but the liquid beef fat was hard to stomach and left me feeling queasy. "I'd have to be near death to enjoy that," I told the camera. "And I'd feel like death after eating it." I shovelled the thick paste into a foil tray. Once it had cooled and hardened into a block, I'd have to see if I could find someone adventurous enough to try this adventure food.

It turned out that, despite its unappetising appearance, my chilled pemmican found a number of takers. A large family crowded round the marquee, bribing their little girl with promises of a trip on the helter-skelter later. I tried the granddad first, on the carefully thought-out premise that, since his baseball cap showed he supported the same football team as me, he might be suitably game. "Tastes a bit like corned beef. And Bovril. Not bad," he declared. His granddaughter looked unconvinced and clamped her mouth firmly shut, forcing her mum to pick up a piece out of politeness. She regarded it sceptically. "It looks like the stuff they hang from bird feeders," she said, but put it in her mouth anyway. Her face puckered. "Don't cry, Carol," chorused the rest of her family, cackling. Carol shook her head. "It's all right," she claimed, unconvincingly. "I'd eat it if I was literally starving to death, but otherwise…"

She echoed my own feelings, and I expected pemmican to get a pretty frosty reception from everyone, but for every person who found it revolting there was another who gave it an enthusiastic endorsement. It was impossible to predict who would like it and who wouldn't. The producer pounced on a passing policeman who diplomatically suggested it was: "Different. A strange taste—like cold bacon." I asked him if he thought it could fuel him on the beat and he said, "Yes, why not?" but didn't seem sure. A woman in a sharply tailored red leather jacket decided, "It could be nice as a starter—a kind of pâté," and her young daughter, who had also eaten a piece, nodded vigorously. "It's better than the sausage I had here earlier," commented one man. "Put it in a roll with some ketchup and it'd be okay."

Of course, pemmican was designed as a power food for people in demanding physical circumstances. Today the nearest I was going to get to replicating those conditions was at the rink, where a number of wannabe skaters were effortfully pushing round the perimeter. I took over my foil tray and set about drumming up some custom.

The two ice marshals on duty were pretty enthusiastic. "That's pure sustenance," said one. "Not bad," the other agreed. "The blueberries really give it something. Maybe it'd be a good idea to add a bit of spice. The fat's strong but I guess if you're out in the Antarctic it'd be okay."

The fact that many of the less-skilled skaters spent most of their time anxiously gripping the guardrails meant I had a captive audience and I doled out cubes of pemmican to anyone who looked as though they might be able to stay upright while eating it. The majority liked some combination of the ingredients involved, but most agreed that the high fat content got in the way of enjoyment. A couple of people who'd eaten the stuff earlier called out to me as they glided past, claiming that the pemmican had given them extra energy.

"You know what'd improve the taste of that pelican or whatever it's called?" One of the marshals skidded to a halt right in front of me. Clearly he'd been considering spice rather than watching the ice. "At first I was thinking cinnamon. But what'd work is nutmeg."

It was a good idea that helped confirm what I was already thinking. I didn't want to serve pemmican to my Feast guests, but ditching the format didn't mean I had to ditch the ingredients too. Seasoned correctly, they could all contribute to the deliciousness of a dish, and provide a kind of homage to Scott at the same time.

FIRESTARTER

With its grand restaurants and lavish menus, the Edwardian era is often seen as a golden age for British food. It was a time of celebrity chefs—none more celebrated than Auguste Escoffier (1846—1935), a favourite of Edward VII who achieved a reputation for unrivalled culinary excellence at the Savoy and Carlton hotels in London, wrote the classical chef's bible, *Le Guide Culinaire* (1903), and created many famous dishes, including *homard à l'américaine* and Peach Melba. He also invented a number of recipes that satisfied the Edwardians' enthusiasm for the drama of the flambé, a technique in which a spirit or fortified wine is warmed until the alcohol begins to vaporise, then set alight, poured over the food and allowed to burn.

Thinking that it would be appropriate to introduce an Escoffier flourish to my dessert, I began by cooking his Bombe Nero—a flaming moulded ice cream—on the Dover-Calais ferry and serving it to passengers to see whether it ignited the same kind of excitement now as it did then. Everybody enjoyed the flavours but the flambé effect was too familiar to impress. Clearly, if I wanted my Feast guests to be blown away, I'd have to get a lot more pyrotechnical.

Preparing to turn a chocolate cake into a raging fireball.

Which is why I found myself in a freezing-cold breeze-block warehouse that the TV company used for set design, standing behind a workbench upon which were a couple of chocolate cakes, a bottle of washing-up liquid, a candle on a long pole and a canister of highly flammable methane gas connected to a nozzle by a piece of plastic tubing. Surrounded by these odd bits of kit and clad in fireproof overalls, I looked like a *Blue Peter* presenter—though I couldn't imagine Valerie Singleton introducing the craft section of the programme with the words: "Today children, we're going to make a cake explode into a twelve-foot fireball."

I placed one chocolate cake on top of the other, then hollowed out the centres sufficiently so that they could house a small plastic tub. Into the tub I poured some water and most of the bottle of washing-up liquid, then stirred them to create the sort of mixture used for blowing bubbles. It was the next bit that turned this from a child's plaything into something more dangerous. I turned the tap on the gas canister and pushed the nozzle into the tub. Because methane is lighter than air, it bubbled quickly and impressively into a tall narrow column. Was it big enough to produce something spectacular? I had no idea.

"Okay, boys. Get your safety goggles on," I directed, snapping my own into place and picking up and lighting the taper. Set-designers Matt and David edged back a respectful distance. I backed away too and moved the long pole towards the column of bubbles, holding my breath. The little flame on the candle danced towards the mixture. Suddenly a four-foot tongue of flame erupted from the cake and, just as abruptly, was swallowed up again. For several long seconds nobody spoke. We all looked over at the director.

Jay is like an overgrown kid. He has the sweetest tooth of anyone I know, and an innocent, boundless enthusiasm for anything new or dramatic. Now, his eyes were as big as mill-wheels. "Let's go bigger!"

We put water in the tub, mixed in washing-up liquid, turned on the gas canister, bubbled the mixture, retreated and extended the taper. Flames leaped twelve feet in the air. "That's more like it. *Now* we're in FX territory," yelled Matt. Again we looked at Jay.

It's not every day I have to extinguish one of my dishes.

"Let's go BIGGER!"

I reckoned we had one more go at it before the cake disintegrated. The little canister of methane had already run out, so we dragged over a huge orange tank of propane, rigged it up to the nozzle and fed gas through the liquid until the tower of bubbles could barely support its own weight. As it began to tilt precariously I hurriedly lit the candle, shoved the taper towards the mass and WHOOOOOOOOOOOOMPH!

The mushroom cloud of flame thrust up to the ceiling, licking the metal girders. David jumped forward and hit it with a long powerful blast of foam from the extinguisher. Jay didn't say anything but his face was split by the biggest grin I had ever seen.

"I think I've cracked the art of the flambé..." I said as I gazed at the table, where a pool of lumpy white foam dotted with ragged lumps of soggy brown chocolate cake spread across the surface and dripped onto the floor. It looked as though some prehistoric animal had just thrown up. "But I may need to work on the presentation..."

SCOTT OF THE ANTARCTIC ROLL

Originally, taking my cue from Scott's extravagant Christmas and Midwinter celebrations, I had thought of creating a kind of deluxe pemmican, with the meat and fat content provided by foie gras. This wasn't inappropriate: exploration in the early part of the twentieth century had a distinct whiff of privilege about it. The most famous example is the provisions list for Mallory and Irvine's 1924 attempt on Everest, which included sixty tins of quails in foie gras, but even the Antarctic base camps were stocked with Fortnum & Mason goods.

Over time, however, as is often the way with recipe development, this idea evolved into something different, influenced by my memories of the 1970s dessert Arctic Roll and the terrible play on words that it prompted. The Arctic Roll was sweet—a rectangle of sponge smeared with jam and rolled around a cylinder of vanilla ice cream—but I could see a way of creating a savoury version by fashioning cooked foie gras into a sausage shape and then wrapping it in something with the springiness of sponge but not so sweet. I wouldn't put cream in—the foie gras would be rich enough on its own—but the fruit layer gave me the chance to introduce another essential pemmican component: a dried fruit, something suitably sharp to cut the foie-gras richness.

I could imagine this cut into thickish roundels and served rather like a slice of terrine. It would need a garnish, of course. For the Fat Duck dish Sound of the Sea I'd developed an edible sand, and I began to wonder if this could be played around with to create edible snow. A little snowdrift of this could lie beside the foie gras, perhaps with a Union Flag on a cocktail stick poking out of it, as though Scott really had made it to the Pole first.

Wrapping brioche around a foie-gras ballotine.

ROAD TO MOROCCO

Lawrence met a camel for the first time... He was new to the game, could not get the most out of the splendid animal he rode. He realised there was a knack in it, and silently determined to acquire it if he ever got the chance.

HARRY IRVING SHUMWAY, War in the Desert

One of the things we associate with Lawrence of Arabia is the camel. It was his transport as he harried trains and blew up bridges along the Arabian Peninsula during the First World War. His epic trek to Akaba to take the port from the Turkish forces was only possible because of the camel's perfect adaptation to its desert environment. And, once the animals collapsed and could go no further, they became the food that sustained Lawrence and his forces during their 600-mile journey. It seemed appropriate that my guests should eat camel too, so I visited a butcher in Fes to find out about cooking "the ship of the desert".

Founded in the ninth century, Fes el bali is the biggest medina (walled city) in the world, as well as one of the oldest. As I walked through its passageways, avoiding donkeys and trolleys amid cries of *"Balak! Balak!"* (Move on!), that long-establishedness appeared to be reflected in the layout of the place. It was less ramshackle than markets I had been to in India and Egypt: the alleys were wide enough to make donkey-dodging easy, and the shops were often beautifully tiled, with ornate wrought-iron grilles and old, heavy wooden shutters for doors. Over our heads, though, protection from the elements consisted of a patchwork of pieces of trellis. It had been raining heavily since daybreak, and every so often the trellis would let through an avalanche of water. As we arrived at Omar's stall, a sudden gush nearly caught the director as he wrestled with the camera's rain-cover.

Behind the counter of the tiny white-tiled stall, there was just enough room for Omar and his dad, Abd-el Aziz. It was pretty obvious what kind of business they were in: hanging from the meat-rack at the front of the store was the fresh, unskinned head of camel. Impaled

The camel's head in front of Omar's stall.

on a butcher's hook, it seemed to float, grinning, in mid-air, like the Cheshire Cat. I shook the surreal image from my mind and examined the cuts of meat that lay before me on stubbly green plastic matting—a ragged cone-shaped piece that I took to be the tail, some XL-sized ribs and thighs, and a sort of white, knobbly pyramid that looked like bone marrow and smelled like it too. "Is this from the hump?"

"Yes. The fat of the camel. Very important for the cooking."

"Yes, I can imagine it'd be delicious once melted. A bit like beef dripping. What other pieces of the camel do you use in dishes and what's your favourite way of cooking the meat, Omar?"

"Roasted maybe. Or a shish kebab. In a brazier. Whatever way, it needs time because the meat is tough. That's why it's often minced. Another good method of cooking is the tanjia. You know it?"

"No. I know the tajine—stew cooked in an earthenware pot with a lid—but I've not heard of the tanjia."

"It's another sort of pot. More like a water carrier, with handles. We put ingredients in the pot. Tie a paper lid on top. Take it to the hammam."

"The Turkish bath?"

"We give it to the man who looks after the oven that heats the water. He puts it in the oven. We come back the next day and it's had a nice, slow cook."

This was such a beautifully economical process that I felt I had to try it. Besides, how often would I get the opportunity to do a hammam-cooked dish? While our resourceful researcher, Charlotte, hurried off in search of a tanjia, I asked Omar's advice on what to put in it.

"You need some of the fat from the hump," he told me as he took the pyramid from the matting to the chopping board and began cutting. "It gives richness and flavour." He passed over a large handful of soft squashy cubes, which I popped in the pot that had just been handed to me. "And shin for flavour." More chopped chunks went in the pot.

"Shin is a cut that needs a long cooking time. It'll have plenty of connective tissue and it'll be tough from all that walking around."

Omar nodded. "The final thing is the tail." He sawed it into half-inch sections and added these to my tanjia. "This is a man's way of cooking," he added. "Lazy. Just throw it all in together. Okay, Heston. You are ready. Now you walk through the souk. Choose whatever you like. Add it to the pot. Add some water. Take it to the hammam and it's ready in time for dinner."

It was already mid-morning and the tanjia needed a good ten hours in the oven. If I was going to eat it for dinner I had to get a move on. I bagged a few chopped onions and some garlic from Omar, and set off in search of other flavourings. Soon I came across a store virtually barricaded in with pale blue plastic buckets containing neat powdery cones of vibrant colour—intense yellow turmeric, pillar-box red sweet

In Fes it was inevitable that I would be filmed wearing a fez.

paprika—and bought little scoops of each, plus some of the classic North African spice ras el hanout, a mix of as many as twenty ingredients, including cardamom, ginger, cinnamon, cloves, coriander and chilli.

"Here we say ras el hanout is for the lazy housewife," the trader told me. "Because you can put it in any kind of dish. This is a hot blend, with rose petals. You want to try it?"

It did have a distinct and very pleasant floral character. There was an earthiness to it, too, and touches of wood and citrus. Exactly the sort of thing that would make the tanjia sing. I added it to the pot. Then my eye was caught by a tub containing a hummock of what looked like cream cheese. "What's this?"

An entrance to Fes's walled city.

"Rancid butter. Preserved in salt. Two years old. This with eggs and honey is a Moroccan aphrodisiac. Very good. Also for the tanjia."

The trader had a moustache like Richard Pryor's and a similar ready grin. Was he having me on? I took the piece he offered and chewed. It tasted like pig's cheeks and had a definite sour cream characteristic. In the pot it went.

There was one other ingredient that was essential to my tanjia: preserved lemons. Packed in jars with salt (and, occasionally, spices), then covered with brine or lemon juice and allowed to cure, the flavour of the lemon settles to something sour, sweet, salty, fragrant and utterly distinctive. It's a characteristic ingredient of North African dishes.

132

I was just handing over a few dirhams for a jar of them when I noticed an old woman in a long brown robe, black shawl and pale blue and white headscarf paring cardoons on a tiny portable trestle table to one side of the alleyway. She plucked the long green stems that resembled celery and swiftly trimmed them of their leaves, thorns and stringy bits, then cut them into bite-sized pieces. A relative of the globe artichoke, cardoons benefit from a long, slow cook. Just right for the tanjia, and they would bring a lovely vegetal, nutty, faintly bitter flavour to the dish. In the pot they went, too. Now all I needed was a hammam.

Fes el bali is not only the biggest medina in the world, it's also the world's largest car-free zone, so we left the walled city, drove as far as the Blue Gate—the imposing blue-tiled, triple-arched main entrance to the medina—and set off on foot once more. We were guided along narrow streets selling musical instruments and curl-toed slippers to an opening in the wall with just enough space for one person to haul themselves up and onto the mound of sawdust-filled nylon sacks stacked inside. I pulled myself in and sat for a moment, waiting for my eyes to adjust to the darkness. The room was tall and narrow. The only light came from two small holes in the side of the oven, which was a six-foot-high stone dome that took up most of the available space.

A skinny, hollow-eyed man in a ragged T-shirt and wool cap was hunkered on a split sack, alternately flinging handfuls of sawdust towards one of the holes, as though it were confetti, and stoking the other with a long metal pole. I held up the tanjia and mimed putting it in the oven. He nodded curtly and handed the pot to a man I hadn't spotted in the gloom, who nestled it into a hole at the base of the oven. "See you later," his hands told me, and I clambered back to the entrance and levered myself out.

In the souk I had been to a stall where they sold tubs of dried camel meat stored in fat or olive oil and flavoured with cumin, salt, coriander and thyme. They served it spread on the traditional thin pastry known as *warka,* which is cooked on something that looks like a metal egg. It was delicious: the pastry was light and tasty, with a nice kick from the spices, and the meat reminded me of beef jerky—full-flavoured

and salty. I wondered whether more modern camel-meat recipes could match up to this and decided that, while I was waiting for the tanjia to cook, I should visit the Café Clock.

The café is the brainchild of Mike Richardson, a thin, denim-clad bundle of energy who was previously maître d' at the Ivy and Wolseley restaurants in London and has now restored a 250-year-old house to create a place that really captures the magic and colour of Fes. After making my way along a pitch-black alleyway between two buildings I found myself in an open courtyard with an intricate blue, ochre, white and black mosaic floor and rackety octagonal tables set before leather-cushioned banquettes that lined the walls. I could see a mezzanine above with more mosaic-work, ornately carved wooden window frames and distempered walls covered with Arabic script. I climbed the thin, twisting staircase and found myself on a flat roof, looking out over the medina. The tops of other buildings spread out in a series of endless geometric planes. Roofs were cluttered with satellite dishes and washing lines, the clothes flapping like prayer flags. I settled onto a bench beneath a little pergola, enjoying the sun and breeze on my face, and awaited the speciality of the house: a camel burger.

Mike was keen to showcase the camel's versatility and brought me three dishes in succession. The first he called "hump bread", a flat loaf that looked almost like thick pizza dough, with the edges folded inwards and the whole thing nicely browned and speckled with herbs. It had been cooked with camel fat and stuffed with olives, onions and spinach or cardoons, plus something sharper that I couldn't identify. It had a lovely flavour—fresh, exotic, almost perfumed. I'd need to get some of this fragrance into whatever I finally served at my Feast.

Next up was scrambled eggs. Apart from a certain richness, it was hard to tell what camel fat contributed here. The most defining feature was the seasoning of ras el hanout. The aroma of cinnamon triggered memories of custard tarts, even though this was a savoury dish. Again it was the spicing, rather than the camel, that made the difference.

This turned out to be true of the burger, too. In fact, I'm not sure that I would have recognised it as camel meat, had I not been told. But it was undoubtedly moist and tasty. Here the ras el hanout relish was less welcome, giving the burger a perfumed aspect that took away from what I wanted in the dish, but overall it was an encouraging experience. Before coming to Fes I had worried that camel meat might be tough or flavourless and difficult to work with, but already I could see ways of making it delicious. I was looking forward to getting back to the lab and experimenting, but first I had to get a taste of my tanjia.

In the magnificent colonnaded and chandeliered atrium of the Riad Fes, where I was staying, the staff had set up a table with silver cutlery, thick white napkins and a candelabra, as though my translator, Youness, and I were on a date. The glazed earthenware pot looked a little incongruous amid such surroundings and tableware. Youness carefully prised off the paper lid, trying to keep flakes of ash from falling into the pot, and I began awkwardly ladling juice and chunks of meat and fat from the tanjia's narrow mouth. A delightful aroma caught my nostrils—spicy, a bit like lamb stew.

"Mmmm," said Youness, breathing in. "I'm sure you'll have lovely ras el hanout and rancid butter flavours."

"Considering that we pretty much just bunged everything in, it'll be interesting to taste it. I hope it's as good as it smells." I took a spoonful of the juice. Cooking had softened the butter's harshness nicely. Now it accentuated the meat flavour, giving it an aged character. I'd got the balance just right. Had I put any more in, I suspect I'd have ended up with braised camel in a sort of blue-cheese sauce.

The most unexpected thing was that the hump fat hadn't dissolved. I took a bite and the texture was slightly crunchy. It took some getting used to, and I wasn't sure that I could expect my Feast guests to eat it with enthusiasm. The shin, though, was nice and soft. "This is delicious, and the spice mix is wonderfully fragrant and really complements it. What d'you think, Youness? Does this taste of Morocco to you?"

"Oh yeah."

This was good to hear because that's what I had to get into my main course—the taste of Morocco. I only hoped that I'd be able somehow to reproduce it back home.

Aligning the strands of meat for camelburgers.

Back in Bray, however, I gradually became more taken with the idea of a camelburger than a tanjia, partly because the beginnings of a skit on fast food were forming in my mind (I could serve a Humpy Meal), and partly because I had already developed a great technique for making a lovely loose-textured burger. The key was to align all the strands of meat in one direction as they came out of the grinder. Then, once they had firmed up in the fridge, I could cut across the "sausage" so that all the strands in the burger ran vertically. This meant the teeth would be biting between the strands rather than across them, which offered much less resistance and made for a much more pleasurable eating experience.

Once I'd gone down this road, the dish took on a logic of its own. A burger had to be accompanied by the classic condiments—mayo, ketchup and mustard—but I decided I'd give them little Moroccan twists. Some chopped preserved lemon in the mayo, perhaps, and some ras el hanout in the ketchup. I began to wonder, too, whether I could make my own version of chicken nuggets, but using marrowbone because that's what the camel's hump had most forcibly reminded me of. It would be a nice hidden allusion to my visit to Omar's.

MRS MARSHALL'S LITTLE DEVILS

For my appetiser I had decided to make a form of curry ice cream. This might at first seem distinctly un-Edwardian, but in fact curry had by then become a popular and familiar dish, as had many Indian (or Anglo-Indian) recipes and condiments, such as pilau, khichari, mulligatawny, piccalilli, curry powder and mango chutney. The English had, by means of the East India Company, controlled large areas of Indian trade since the 1600s, and when the company was abolished in 1858, Britain took over the country. A large number of Britons spent much of their working life on the subcontinent and, when they retired, often returned home with their ayahs (nannies), manservants and a taste for Indian food. "Empress" Currie Powder and Selim's True Indian Curry Paste began to appear in the shops, and cookbooks began to feature recipes for spiced dishes.

The Edwardians were also keen on savoury ices, which gave me an opportunity to draw on the work of a culinary hero of mine—Agnes Bertha Marshall (1855–1905). In her book *Fancy Ices* (1894), she has a recipe for Little Devilled Ices in Cups, which involves pounding chicken and adding spices, cream and gelatine before piping the mixture into little glass cups and placing them in an ice cave for about an hour. She suggests serving these "for a ball supper" but instead I tried them out on passers-by in Brick Lane. People were polite about the flavour but it became clear that the modern-day association of ice cream with sweetness is so strong that people find it difficult to accept the idea

Poaching mint, coriander, cucumber and lime mousse in liquid nitrogen.

of a savoury ice. Serve up the same ingredients cold, in the form of Coronation Chicken, and they wouldn't bat an eyelid. Frozen, however, was a step too far.

So I had to find another way into my Indian appetiser, and I took my inspiration from another enthusiasm of Mrs Marshall's: liquefied gas. As early as 1901, a mere ten years after James Dewar had first liquefied oxygen on a large scale, she was advocating cooking with it. A century or so later, I began using liquid nitrogen at the Fat Duck to "poach" a green-tea-and-lime-flavoured meringue that I served as a palate cleanser. I reckoned I could adapt this recipe: flavour the meringue with Indian spices and perhaps even give it a liquid centre

A glass of nitro raita.

so that when my guests bit in, there would be a nice contrast of textures, and a second wave of flavours.

Even though the dish had shifted from the idea of ice cream, it was still essential to keep the sweetness in check. The ingredients of the meringue would have to emphasise freshness and acidity. I developed a stock syrup that used not sucrose (ordinary sugar) but fructose (the sugar found in fruits and honey) to introduce a chutney note, and then cut it with salt and malic acid, which has a Granny Smith sharpness. To build up the Asian character of this base I decided to raid elements of a classic raita: lime, chopped mint and coriander. Infused in the syrup for a couple of hours, these produced a lovely delicate spicing.

141

I was pretty sure that, once I added some yoghurt, bound the mix with egg white and then pressurised and chilled it in a whipping cream canister, it would produce a savoury herb crust that wasn't too dominant and so would gently complement whatever was put inside it.

Mrs Marshall's Devilled Ices reminded me of Coronation Chicken, so I wanted to keep faith with her original dish by using some of the classic ingredients of that recipe to create the filling. I blitzed cooked chicken with countless combinations of curry powder, mango chutney, Worcestershire sauce, anchovies and egg yolks until I had a smooth piccalilli-yellow purée that captured the Coronation character in a nicely balanced way. All I had to do now was develop a foolproof technique for poaching the meringue so that it was frozen to a crisp crunchiness on the outside while the filling remained liquid, and sort out the technical difficulties of injecting that filling and then sealing the hole so that it looked perfect!

"ICEBERG RIGHT AHEAD"

A flaming cake was all very well, but for my *Titanic* dessert what I really wanted was a burning berg. I had a picture in my mind of an iceberg in the centre of the dining table with flames angrily flickering round its perimeter before abruptly snuffing out. The iceberg itself would be easy—it could be commissioned from an ice sculptor—and methane would provide the conflagration. But I had to decide what food to put on such a spectacular centrepiece. Of course I could still introduce a version of the bombe to the dessert by using specially shaped moulds to produce mini bergs—jagged white chocolate outer shells filled with vanilla ice cream, alcohol and other flavourings—which could sit at the base of the big berg, as though they had sheared off it. But the dish still looked too bare and disparate. I needed to find a way to tie these elements together.

My inspiration came not from the 1900s but from the 1980s Ice Magic, marketed by Bird's. It came in a cool conical bottle that looked like a miniature mountaintop, and when you squirted the sauce onto

Making and decorating mini icebergs.

My iceberg waiting in the wings, ready to make an impact.

ice cream, it instantly hardened to a brittle chocolate topping. Why not make my own Ice Magic, I thought, but in white chocolate rather than dark? Then drip it over the iceberg to resemble melting snow. Jocky and I played around with ingredients until we had the texture and pourability we wanted. It was fun breaking off shards of snowcap and eating them, and I reckoned it would give my guests the kind of thrill that I remembered getting from the original Ice Magic.

On its own, though, the effect didn't offer enough complexity: I wanted my guests to be rewarded with a real range of flavours and textures when they began to demolish the iceberg. We developed a meringue mix that could be piped on and then palette-knifed into little snowdrifts, and a lemonade jelly that could be cut into rough chunks to look like ice blocks. To top this off, we began work on a slushy Champagne granita that could be spooned into the ice sculpture's ledges and fissures—a final touch of luxury to round off my *Titanic* Feast. 🏵

MENU

"We Are Not Amused"
Amuse-Bouche

Nitrogen-poached Raita Mousse, Coronation Chicken Curry,
Tandoori Chicken, Lentil Dal

Scott of the Antarctic Roll

Duck Liver Ballotine, Brioche, Rhubarb and
Freeze-dried Raspberry Jam, Edible Snow
and a Proud Union Flag

Heston's Humpy Meal

*Camel Burger, Triple-cooked Chips, Bone Marrow Nuggets,
Rose and Coriander Sandcastle, Harissa Ketchup,
Smoked Aubergine Mustard, Pickled Lemon Mayo*

Camel Consommé Drink

Titanic Dessert
"Iceberg Right Ahead"

*Iceberg covered with White Chocolate Snow,
Meringue Spindrift and Lemonade Jelly Ice Blocks,
Edible Mini-bergs floating in Flaming Sea-foam*

WE ARE NOT AMUSED "AMUSE-BOUCHE"

FOR THE CORONATION CHICKEN CURRY

80g table salt

1kg water

3 skinless, boneless chicken breasts, cleaned of any sinews

40g spiced mango chutney

20g Worcestershire sauce

8 smoked anchovy fillets

15g curry powder

250g whipping cream, plus extra to finish

180g brown chicken stock

5 hard-boiled eggs, peeled

In a large bowl, mix the table salt and water together, whisking until the salt has completely dissolved. Place the chicken breasts in the brine and refrigerate for 1 hour.

Remove the chicken breasts from the brine and rinse in several changes of cold water, then pat dry.

Preheat a water bath to 60°C.

Place the chicken breasts in a sous-vide bag and seal under full pressure. Place the bag in the water bath and cook for 45 minutes.

When cooked, take the bag out of the bath and place it in iced water to cool.

Remove the chicken breasts from the bag and cut into chunks. Place them in a food processor with all the remaining ingredients and blend until smooth; add a little more cream if necessary.

Pass the mixture through a fine drum sieve into a bowl. Cover and store in the fridge until needed.

FOR THE NITROGEN-POACHED RAITA MOUSSE

1kg water

175g unrefined caster sugar

16g high methoxyl pectin

1g malic acid

180g pasteurised lime juice

130g pasteurised egg whites

30g mint leaves, chopped

30g coriander leaves, chopped

180g fat-free yoghurt

120g fresh cucumber juice

Bring the water to the boil in a large pan. Meanwhile, combine the sugar and pectin in a jug, then whisk into the boiled water. Continue whisking over a high heat for 1 minute. Remove from the heat and allow to cool.

Weigh out 650g of the syrup and place it in a bowl. Add the remaining ingredients and whisk well. Allow to infuse for 2 hours, then pass through a Superbag, making sure to squeeze the bag to get all the liquid out.

Completely fill a cream whipper with the mixture and charge with 2 nitrogen dioxide charges. Shake well and leave in the fridge for 2 hours before using.

TO SERVE

coronation chicken curry (see above)

5g whipping cream

raita mousse mixture (see above)

crushed poppadoms, toasted

Heat up the chicken curry in a pan with the whipping cream, stirring to prevent the mixture from catching. Use a syringe to suck up a quantity of the hot mix.

Siphon a ball of the nitro raita mousse onto a warmed spoon and drop it into liquid nitrogen for 8 seconds on each side while basting with the nitrogen.

Remove the now firm ball and immediately inject it with the warm curry mixture.

Sprinkle the top with the crushed poppadoms and serve immediately.

SCOTT OF THE ANTARCTIC ROLL

FOR THE SPICE MIX
5g sugar
10g piece of nutmeg
20g cinnamon sticks
20g cloves
20g allspice

Combine the ingredients in a spice grinder and blitz to a powder. Pass through a tea strainer and reserve.

FOR THE ALCOHOL MIXTURE
150g Armagnac
375g Sauternes
375g Solero sherry

Heat the Armagnac in a small pan and when boiling, remove from the heat and flame off the alcohol.

Add the Sauternes and sherry and reserve.

FOR THE DUCK LIVER BALLOTINE
800g foie gras, cryogenically frozen
250g alcohol mixture (see above)
6g salt
0.3g finely ground black pepper
1g spice mix (see above)

Preheat a water bath to 60°C.

Combine the foie gras and the alcohol mixture in a sous-vide bag and seal under full pressure.

Immerse the bag in the water bath for 25 minutes. Remove the bag from the water bath and place in iced water for 10 minutes.

Take out the cooled foie gras and trim away any veins or mushy pieces.

Weigh out 450g of the foie gras, season it with the salt, black pepper and spice mix and allow to come up to room temperature.

Roll the seasoned foie gras into a tight tube, 6cm in diameter. Pierce the roll in a few places with a needle to let out any air that might have collected in pockets.

Tie a piece of string to one end and hang the tube in the fridge for 5 days.

FOR THE RHUBARB AND FREEZE-DRIED RASPBERRY JAM
500g rhubarb juice, plus extra for finishing
50g glucose
200g caster sugar
9.5g pectin jaune
150g maltodextrin IT-19
3.5g malic acid
30g water
freeze-dried raspberries

Mix the rhubarb juice and glucose in a pan.

Combine the sugar, pectin and maltodextrin thoroughly and whisk into the rhubarb juice. Place over a medium heat and bring to the boil.

Continue to heat, whisking constantly until the mixture reaches 69° Brix. Meanwhile, dissolve the malic acid in the water.

Remove the rhubarb juice from the heat and whisk in the malic acid and water. Pour into a bowl. Let cool and set at room temperature.

Transfer the mixture to a food processor and blitz until smooth, adding fresh rhubarb juice and freeze-dried raspberries to taste. Transfer to a piping bag and reserve.

TO ASSEMBLE
1 brioche
butter, for frying
duck liver ballotine (see above)
rhubarb and raspberry jam (see above)

Cut the brioche into thin slices, 2cm thick, trimming off the crusts. Heat some butter in a pan wide enough to fit the long brioche slices. Gently fry the brioche on each side until light golden brown. Remove to a board, placing the slices side by side and close together.

Spread the jam evenly across one side of the brioche. Unwrap the ballotine and place on one end of the brioche. Roll the brioche around the ballotine. Trim off the excess brioche from the sides and the end. Wrap in clingfilm and return briefly to the fridge to set.

Slice the roll into rounds using a warmed, long, thin knife and serve.

BONE MARROW "NUGGETS" WITH ROSE AND CORIANDER "SANDCASTLE"

FOR THE BONE MARROW

2kg marrowbones, cut into 5cm pieces
1kg water
50g salt

Rinse the marrowbones thoroughly.

Combine the water and salt, stirring to dissolve. Pour the salted water over the bones until they are well covered and refrigerate for 24 hours, changing the water every 4 hours (whenever possible).

Remove the bones and soak in several changes of unsalted, cold water for 30 minutes.

Push the marrow out of the bones and place on kitchen paper to dry. Cut into 7cm cubes and refrigerate until needed.

FOR THE ONION AND HERB COATING

100g butter
120g shallots, finely sliced
8 garlic cloves, finely chopped
6g thyme leaves, finely chopped
8g flat-leaf parsley, finely chopped
60g Savora mustard
finely grated zest of 2 lemons
salt and freshly ground black pepper
bone marrow pieces (see above)

In a sauté pan, heat the butter and sweat the shallots and garlic over a medium heat until they are soft but not coloured. Remove from the heat and add the herbs, mustard and lemon zest and season with salt and pepper.

Transfer the mixture to a food processor and blitz until smooth. Allow to cool until at room temperature.

Line a tray with parchment. Coat the bone marrow pieces completely with the onion and herb mixture, then place them on the lined tray, cover and freeze.

FOR THE ROSE CORIANDER SALT

3g coriander seeds, lightly roasted
0.3g ground ginger
1.5g dried rose buds
4g sea salt
1g maltodextrin IT-19
0.05g rose essential oil
50g vodka
1 rose tea bag

Grind the coriander seeds, ginger and rose buds together, using a pestle and mortar. Add the salt and the maltodextrin and continue to grind to a powder.

Combine the rose essential oil and the vodka in an atomiser and spray a single spray onto the rose tea bag.

Place the tea bag in a sous-vide bag and add the spice mixture. Seal the bag under full pressure and allow to infuse for 12 hours.

Open the sous-vide bag. Carefully scrape the powder off the tea bag and reserve; discard the tea bag.

FOR THE MISO-INFUSED OIL

500g red miso paste
200g white miso paste
10g cod liver oil
500g grapeseed oil

In a bowl, fold all the ingredients together very carefully, then cover and refrigerate for 48 hours.

Gently strain through damp muslin to separate the top layer of oil from the miso below. Reserve the oil.

FOR THE SAND COLOURING

25g dried kombu, blitzed to a fine powder
10g blue shimmer powder
17g brown carbonised vegetable powder

Combine the powders thoroughly and weigh out 40g for the next stage.

FOR THE "SAND"

240g tapioca maltodextrin
40g sand colouring (see above)
2.5g sea salt
335g miso-infused oil (see above)

Combine the tapioca maltodextrin, sand colouring and salt in a mixing bowl.

Slowly add the miso-infused oil while whisking gently to form a wet "sand".

FOR THE "SANDCASTLE"

180g "sand" (see above)
1g turmeric powder
0.75g yellow cocoa powder
0.4g orange cocoa powder
rose coriander salt (see above)

Fold together all the ingredients thoroughly and pack into 6 small sandcastle moulds.

Turn the "sandcastles" out onto plates.

TO SERVE

grapeseed or groundnut oil, for deep-frying
2 eggs
100g water
1g salt
200g plain flour
200g panko flakes (Japanese breadcrumbs), crushed lightly
frozen bone marrow pieces (see above)

Heat the oil in a deep-fat fryer to 180°C.

Crack the eggs into a bowl and whisk in the water and salt.

Place the flour in a second container and the panko in a third.

When nearly ready to serve, roll the bone marrow pieces first in the flour and then in the egg mixture. Drain off excess egg and roll in the panko to completely cover each piece.

Deep-fry the pieces until golden brown and drain on kitchen paper. Serve immediately with the "sandcastles" as a dipping salt.

EDIBLE MINI-BERGS

FOR THE VANILLA AND DARK RUM ICE CREAM

500g whole milk

3 vanilla pods, split lengthways

120g egg yolks

200g unrefined caster sugar

50g dark rum

350g soured cream

Pour the milk into a pan, add the vanilla pods, bring up to 90°C and remove from the heat.

Place the egg yolks and sugar in the bowl of a food mixer and beat for 5 minutes until light in colour.

Return the milk to the heat and allow it to reach 50°C. Whisk in the egg yolk and sugar mixture and bring the temperature up to 70°C. Hold at this temperature for 10 minutes.

Remove from the heat and allow to cool in a bowl over an ice bath. Cover and allow to infuse in the fridge for 8 hours.

Strain the custard through a fine sieve, then stir in the rum and soured cream. Churn in an ice-cream machine to -5°C. Place the ice cream in a chilled container. Cover and store in the freezer until needed.

FOR THE CHOCOLATE CARAMEL SAUCE

120g caster sugar

300g water

90g cocoa powder

20 coffee beans

2g table salt

30g chocolate (70% cocoa solids)

Place the sugar in a pan and bring to 150°C over a high heat. Once melted and caramelised, reduce the heat and whisk in the water, cocoa powder, coffee beans and salt. Bring the mixture to the boil and simmer for 5 minutes, stirring frequently. Remove from the heat.

Finely chop the chocolate and add to the pan, whisking until the chocolate has melted.

Cool over an ice bath to 5°C and refrigerate until needed.

FOR THE CARAMEL YOGHURT SAUCE

500g whipping cream

1kg caster sugar

240g unsalted butter

100g yoghurt

Pour the cream into a pan and bring to a simmer. Remove from the heat and keep warm.

Place the sugar in a large pan and bring to 150°C over a high heat, melting the sugar and caramelising to a golden brown.

Gradually whisk in the butter and the warm cream. Strain through a fine sieve and cool over an ice bath. As the mixture begins to cool, whisk in the yoghurt. Refrigerate until needed.

FOR THE PASSION FRUIT PÂTE DE FRUIT

500g passion fruit purée

100g glucose

350g unrefined caster sugar

13g yellow pectin

In a pan, heat the fruit purée and glucose.

In a bowl, mix the sugar and pectin together and add to the fruit purée mixture. Stirring regularly, bring the mixture to 69° Brix.

Pour the mixture into a PacoJet container and allow to set at room temperature and cool completely before placing in the fridge.

Run the mixture through the PacoJet machine and transfer to a piping bag.

FOR THE ROASTED ALMOND PASTE

200g whole blanched almonds

5g egg white

5g table salt

Preheat the oven to 180°C and line an oven tray with a silicone mat. Mix the ingredients evenly in a bowl and spread over the prepared tray. Bake for 10–15 minutes or until golden brown. Remove from the oven and leave to cool.

Roughly chop 15g of the almonds; set aside.

Place the remaining almonds in a food processor and blitz until smooth.

FOR THE FEUILLETINE AND ALMOND BASE

40g Amedei Toscano chocolate
    (32% cocoa solids), chopped
100g roasted almond paste (see above)
15g toasted chopped almonds (see above)
50g feuilletine (caramelised puff pastry)

Melt the chocolate in a microwave or over a bain-marie. Stir in the almond paste, almonds and feuilletine until it comes together, being careful not to overmix.

Line a baking tray with parchment. Spread the mixture on to a 5mm thickness. Place in the fridge to set. Cut to the dimensions of the iceberg bases. Keep in an airtight container.

FOR THE CHOCOLATE PIECES

250g Amedei Chuao chocolate
    (70% cocoa solids)

Preheat a water bath to 53°C.

Put all but 25g of the chocolate in a sous-vide bag, seal under full pressure and place in the water bath for 12 hours.

Finely chop the reserved 25g chocolate. Temper the melted chocolate using the chopped chocolate to seed it. Once the seed has been added, bring the chocolate down to 28°C, then take it back up to 32°C.

Ladle the chocolate onto 4 acetate sheets (A4 size) and spread to a thickness of 2–3mm. Cut into pieces to fit inside the iceberg, then cover and store in a cool, dry place.

FOR THE CARAMELISED BANANA AND RUM PURÉE

6 bananas, peeled
70g rum
grated zest of 2 limes

Place the bananas and rum in a pan and cook until soft. Transfer to a bowl, add the lime zest and allow to cool.

Use a whisk to purée the mixture until smooth. Store in the fridge until needed.

FOR THE WHITE CHOCOLATE ICEBERGS

1kg white chocolate

Preheat a water bath to 53°C.

Put all but 100g of the chocolate in a sous-vide bag, seal under full pressure and place in the water bath for 12 hours.

Finely chop the reserved 100g chocolate. Temper the melted chocolate using the chopped chocolate to seed it. Once the seed has been added, bring the chocolate down to 28°C, then take it back up to 32°C.

Use the chocolate to line an iceberg-shaped mould. Knock out the air bubbles by tapping the sides of the mould. Pour out the excess chocolate by turning the mould over and scraping the bottom. Place the mould on a wire rack to allow the chocolate to cool and harden.

Once fully set, remove the iceberg and store in an airtight container in a cool, dry place.

TO ASSEMBLE

vanilla and dark rum ice cream (see above)
white chocolate icebergs (see above)
chocolate caramel sauce (see above)
caramel yoghurt sauce (see above)
passion fruit pâte de fruit (see above)
caramelised banana and rum purée
    (see above)
chocolate pieces (see above)
feuilletine and almond base (see above)

Temper the ice cream enough to make it spreadable and spoon into the icebergs until they are one-third full.

Make several holes in the ice cream and fill with the sauces, pâte de fruit and fruit purée. Place a sheet of chocolate over the top.

Cover with more ice cream so that the icebergs are two-thirds full. Make several more holes and fill with the sauces. Place another chocolate piece on top.

Repeat the steps again up to the top of the iceberg and place the feuilletine and almond base on top, fitting securely to seal.

A Chocolate Factory Feast

WHICH is the quintessential book of the 1960s? Joseph Heller's *Catch-22*, with its surreal, anti-authoritarian comedy? John Fowles's blend of esoteric philosophy and psychology in *The Magus*? The feminist concerns of Doris Lessing's *The Golden Notebook*? The Cold-War tensions of John le Carré's *The Spy Who Came in from the Cold*? Tom Wolfe's account of Ken Kesey's magical mystery tour across America in a multicoloured school bus, *The Electric Kool-aid Acid Test*?

For me, one of the front-runners has to be *Charlie and the Chocolate Factory* by Roald Dahl. First published in the US in 1964, it was to be another three years before it found a publisher in the UK, probably because the tone of the book was so subversive. Establishment Britain simply wasn't ready for its deliberate bad taste, raucous humour and sneaked-in jokes for adults—things that are now staples of children's literature but were radically unconventional back then.

Of course, Willy Wonka's dress sense is suitably groovy. With his bottle-green trousers, plum-coloured velvet tailcoat, gold-topped cane and neat goatee, he wouldn't have looked out of place on the cover of *Sgt Pepper*. And his feverishly inventive, original, psychedelic, experimental, flamboyant imagination ties him to the spirit of that era. So my Wonka-inspired Chocolate Factory Feast would have to draw on elements of the 1960s as well.

One of the reasons I was so keen to do a Feast centred on Willy Wonka is because I have a personal connection to the Dahls. A few years ago I was called out of the Fat Duck kitchen by a waiter who told me one of the diners had enjoyed the tasting menu and wanted to see me. As I walked over to the table an elegant woman greeted me with, "If only my husband were alive to see this. You are the real Willy Wonka." It was Felicity Dahl, who has since become a good friend. At her house in Great Missenden, I've seen the little shed in which Roald used to write, wrapped up in a sleeping bag in an old armchair, and I've had the chance to look at the handwritten manuscript of *Charlie and the Chocolate Factory*—an unforgettable moment for me. Liccy's a terrific person and I wanted to repay her generosity by creating a Feast that properly reflected her husband's extraordinary imagination.

MR WONKA'S WACKY WALLPAPER

When I first read *Charlie and the Chocolate Factory* I loved the way that, as Willy Wonka takes his guests on a tour of the factory, he is forever reeling off ideas—*everlasting gobstoppers... hair toffee... fizzy lifting drinks... has beans... eatable marshmallow pillows... cows that give chocolate milk...* Out they'd tumble, unstoppable, as though his mind was in permanent overdrive. The one I liked best was lickable wallpaper, printed with pictures of fruit—bananas, apples, grapes, pineapples, snozzberries—that actually tasted of the fruit when you licked them. "Lovely stuff," Willy Wonka declared. I couldn't think of a better opener for my Feast than to have my guests licking the walls, as though they were on a psychedelic trip. Very off-the-wall—but on the wall!

At first glance, lickable wallpaper might seem a tall order, but in fact the decorator's trade and the chef's have more in common than you might think. Lots of the equipment is similar—scrapers, knives, spraygun, blowtorch—and even some of the terminology. Both talk about emulsions and about lining things (walls, baking trays), both brush on shimmer effects, and at the Fat Duck when we spray chocolate onto the Black Forest Gâteau we call it "flocking".

All the equipment you need for lickable wallpaper.

It was this last practice that formed my starting point for this dish. I developed a chocolate recipe that could be sprayed onto paper to give it a flocked effect. I had considered using a template to introduce some sort of swirly patterning to it—a nice little Berni Inn touch—but realised that a simple chocolate coating really wasn't ambitious enough. No matter what pattern I used it was, in the end, a single hit of chocolate. Wonka had managed to include a whole fruit bowl's worth of flavours. I had to try to match that.

I took the flock idea in a different direction, freeze-drying all kinds of fruit to turn them into little granules. To stick them in place I created a gel of the same fruit. I fixed a fruit template to the wallpaper with

Wonka meets Warhol in the designs for the wallpaper.

masking tape, painted on a smear of gel, brushed on the powdered fruit, let it all set and got a nicely flocked image of, say, an apple. Repeated, these looked convincingly like a pattern. Some fruits proved better than others, and we had to experiment with different setting agents, but the idea worked so well that I moved beyond fruit to things that had more of a sixties feel to them. What about prawn cocktail, I wondered? Or sausage on a stick? Or cheese and pineapple chunks? Or—for a neat bit of Warholian pop-art—tinned tomato soup?

I had to give up on cheese. Freeze-dried cheese had a vomit-like aroma that reminded me of the cardboard tubs of pre-grated Parmesan we'd had when I was a kid. However, some of the others turned out to be delicious, and eventually I had a wallpaper that might even live up to Mr Wonka's exacting standards, though I wasn't sure about the commercial appeal of a paper with a repeat pattern of apples, pineapples, tomato soup cans and sausages.

FERGUS THE FORAGER

Alice remained looking thoughtfully at the mushroom for a minute... at last she stretched her arms around it as far as they would go, and broke off a bit of the edge with each hand.

LEWIS CARROLL, *Alice's Adventures in Wonderland*

It had rained heavily overnight. I squelched along the track through Blean Woods, skirting sumps of muddy water, making for the dark-haired man standing on the verge, staring at the ground. He wore dusty grey cords tucked into green gumboots and a thick, rufous sweater— the colours of the forest. This was my guide for the day, forager Fergus Drennan, who views the natural world quite differently. Where most of us see merely a mass of trees and plants, he sees foodstuffs and other basic essentials. Foraging is a way of life that was once common, but is now much less so. In the foragers' bible, *Food for Free*, Richard Mabey observes that in times of serious scarcity we turn to wild foods, "yet each time with less ingenuity and confidence, less native knowledge about what they are and how they can be used." Apart from people like Fergus, we no longer know the land.

"Fergus, I want to find out about the 'toadstool' of fairy tales—the fly agaric mushroom. D'you think we can find some?" I asked.

"Well, autumn's a good time of year for *Amanita muscaria*—damp but not too cold. Frost stimulates some mushrooms but it kills off this one. And it likes to grow with birch and pine trees, both of which are plentiful here, so there's a good chance." He handed me a small wicker basket and a hunting knife and began threading his way between thin silvery trunks. "Fortunately," he said over his shoulder, "the fly agaric's bright red cap makes it pretty easy to spot."

I struggled to keep up with his more practised footsteps. "What is it you like about foraging?" I called to him.

"Some people dismiss it as a kind of gastronomic thrill-seeking. I guess that's understandable when things like the fly agaric—which is both poisonous and a hallucinogen—are involved. But for me it's about fully engaging with nature and making full use of what it has to offer. It's absolutely amazing what's out there and what can be done with it. Take this, for example." He pulled a kidney-shaped, brown mushroom cap from a shattered trunk. "Birch polypore—that'll make a couple of sheets of A4. And you could make mushroom ink to write on it, too. People have been doing this stuff for centuries. I've tried a couple of times to live on nothing but wild and foraged food for a whole year. The first time I did my back in and had to stop. This time I've run out of money so I need to get some work, which makes foraging almost impossible as it's a full-time job."

"How did you get into it in the first place?"

"Actually, the fly agaric played a part in that. When I went, briefly, to catering college I got into gourmet mushrooms in a big way but ended up very frustrated at how difficult it was to obtain delicacies like *Amanita caesarea*—Caesar's mushroom—so I decided to start foraging for native varieties, such as *Amanita muscaria*, which, as the name suggests, is a very close relative."

The classic toadstool—a fly agaric mushroom.

As we talked, part of Fergus's attention was elsewhere, his eyes restlessly hunting back and forth. He soon found what we were looking for. "This one's a bit ragged, but the good thing with fly agarics is that if you find one you're almost certain to find more."

Sure enough, a minute later he did. It was a classic: the stem snowy white, the cap deep orange-red sprinkled with little white speckles. Fergus pulled it out of the ground, snicked off the splayed base of the stem and handed it over. A childlike excitement welled up in me. "So this is it! The fly agaric! It's so pretty!" I sounded like Willy Wonka, which was appropriate since it was one of his confection inventions that had got me interested in the fly agaric in the first place.

One of my favourite moments in the film *Willy Wonka and the Chocolate Factory* is in the Chocolate Room, when guests are encouraged to find out whether everything in it really is edible. Mike Teavee's mum tentatively dips a finger in the white spot of a toadstool, discovers it's not only edible but delicious, and scoops out a whole handful. It's a things-are-not-what-they-seem moment that brought to mind the hippies' enthusiasm for the mushroom's mind-bending properties. The fly agaric meshed perfectly the themes of my Feast and so I really wanted to use it in my starter. However, I wanted the experience to be pleasurable and entirely safe. Willy Wonka might have let his guests shrink or turn blue, but I'd no intention of making a similar mistake. "Is this mushroom really dangerous?" I wanted to know.

"There are toxins in the fly agaric with hallucinogenic properties but they're soluble in water and in alcohol so they can be leached out of the mushrooms, which are then safe to eat as far as I'm concerned. I've been cooking and eating them for fifteen years without any side effects, though I guess you have to take into account that each person's body reacts differently. I'd suggest trying a small amount to see how you react to it." Fergus's knowledgeable tone inspired confidence.

"Is the 'high' worth it? I've read that the hallucinogens can affect your sense of perspective. Everything seems either exaggeratedly big or incredibly tiny. Some people have suggested the effects of fly agaric inspired Alice's changes of size in *Alice's Adventures in Wonderland*."

"I don't know about changes in size. It's very energising. Everything seems great and completely understandable. Which is delusional, but enjoyable at the time. It's like having ten espressos but without the caffeine jitters … or so I've been told," he added hurriedly.

Fergus took off to scout out enough fungi for us to cook something. Occasionally I caught glimpses of his distant, hunched figure passing between trees. Apart from the odd cry of a rooster, the place was silent. I could feel the cold creeping into my fingers. I felt a bit like I was in the *Blair Witch Project*. Was I even sure of the way back to the path?

"I once saw a forager nearly stabbed to death," declared Fergus, emerging from the undergrowth. "He'd picked some fly agaric, tried them out straight away, and then collapsed, almost skewering himself on his own knife. It just goes to show how careful you have to be. Treat things like these," he gestured towards his basket, "with respect."

Without me to distract him, Fergus had collected several varieties, including ceps (or porcini) with their fat brown caps and small orange-yellow, trumpet-shaped chanterelles, both great cooking mushrooms and full of flavour. There were plenty more fly agarics too.

"I've picked up loads, so let's go back to my place and get cooking." We tramped back along the forest path and clambered into Fergus's decrepit van. Anyone could have guessed Fergus's occupation from the state of his Peugeot. Scaly grey-brown parasol mushrooms littered the dashboard. Walnuts wobbled in the recess by the speedometer. A fat marrow sat beneath the gearstick. "Sorry about the mess," he apologised. He floored the pedal and we were off.

Fergus drove at breakneck speed, as though the switch from the natural world to a mechanical one made him restless and uncomfortable. "Plants can make you ill if you don't do some research and follow the rules," he shouted over the roar of the engine. "But I'm not interested in playing mycological Russian roulette. I'm not aiming to dice with death every time I dice a mushroom. Foraging's not about the thrill of doing something perilous, though mushrooms have often been prized for the properties we now think of as dangerous. Ninth-century Viking warriors called 'berserkers' were noted for their inhuman rage during battle, supposedly encouraged by eating the fly agaric."

We barrelled down narrow roads, rarely stopping to let traffic pass. Whenever we did screech to a halt, I had to play goalie as mushrooms skittered off the dashboard. "Like the Vikings, Siberian tribes made use of the fly agaric's toxins, but for rituals rather than warfare," Fergus continued, as I tried to save the fungi. "They'd have a ceremony in which the shaman would ingest the mushroom—and get visions, presumably—then others would drink his urine because the toxins go through the body relatively untouched. They'd get the same hallucinogenic effects." He turned off the main road abruptly and drew to a halt. "Some say that's the origin of the term 'getting pissed'."

As we entered Fergus's house, I could see the rewards of his foraging spread over every surface. I'd have liked to spend the rest of the day exploring them but I had a mushroom mission to fulfil. "Okay, Fergus, how do we turn these fly agarics into a risk-free risotto?"

"Well, before we add the fly agaric to a risotto, we need to boil them to leach out the toxins. Mycologists William Rubel and David Arora advise using a litre of water for every 110 grams of mushrooms. So we're going to need a pretty big cookpot." He grabbed one from the draining board, measured the water into it and set it on the stove. "That'll take a while to come to the boil. Enough time for you to do some chopping. There's a knife in the drawer. It's none too sharp, I'm afraid."

According to Rubel and Arora, the mushroom slices had to be no more than 3—4mm thick to hasten the leaching. Fergus had given himself the easier task of gathering the more usual risotto ingredients: rice, garlic, wild mushroom stock, onions, wine, parsley, Parmesan.

"Sadly, when it's cooked, the fly agaric loses those lovely colours—the deep red of the cap and the creamy orange of the underside," said Fergus, taking some wild mushrooms from the fridge. "And since it's got a very subtle flavour we'll need other varieties in there as well." He peered into the cookpot. "It's boiling. Are you ready, Heston? Let's weigh those fly agarics and get them in. Then, when the water has come back to the boil we must cook the mushrooms for fifteen minutes."

We set the timer and Fergus began cooking the rest of the ingredients in the usual way, softening the onions and garlic in a little butter, adding the rice, the wine, the first ladleful of the wild mushroom stock. Alongside, he sautéed wild mushrooms in butter, adding some chopped parsley. Once the rice was ready, he combined the two and added the boiled and drained fly agarics. Finally, Fergus scattered some Parmesan and cubes of butter over the top, turned off the heat, put on the lid and let it stand for a few minutes to get that lovely risotto unctuousness.

"There you go, Heston. Fly agaric risotto. You can have the honour of the first taste. Dig in." He handed me a fork.

I hadn't been looking forward to this moment. "I can't."

"Why not? Surely my cooking's not that bad."

Cooking hallucinogenic mushrooms to remove the toxins.

"No, not at all. It's the insurers for the TV series. They won't let me. I can't believe it. I've travelled the world eating weird and wonderful things. Yet here I am, unable to try a mushroom in my own country!"

"I'm sorry to hear that, Heston, because this is very tasty. But I'm not surprised," said Fergus. He'd grabbed a radish and was gouging out bits with a knife. Perhaps people's ignorance about mushrooms was getting to him. "In Britain only twenty or so species of fungi are seriously poisonous, yet people still see wild mushrooms as dangerous. Anyway," he concluded, "here's a consolation prize—the only thing I learned how to do in catering college." He handed me the radish, now neatly carved into a miniature facsimile of the fly agaric.

173

THE GODDESSES OF CHOCOLATE

I woke up dry-mouthed, my head throbbing slightly. The previous night's filming in a private bar had got a little out of control, and I'd ended up drinking a bit more than I intended. I closed my eyes again and tried to piece together the events. At first, only fleeting impressions came back to me. My arms being massaged with a paste of cocoa butter, lime and bath salts... Eating chocolate flavoured with cardamom, pistachio, macadamia, geraniums... Had I made a cocktail big enough to serve everyone in the room, emptying bottles of liqueur into the ice bucket and using it as a cocktail shaker? And had I really drunk a shot glass of Choctini poured from the penis of a golden Greek statue?

———*———

It has been said that fiction writers must have a sadistic streak because of what they put their characters through. I think the same could be said for television companies. I've come to realise that the Feast film crew like nothing better than to put me in an explosive situation and wait for the fireworks to start. Now the producer had discovered a women-only event in Brighton called the Goddess of Chocolate, which he insisted would make great TV *and* give me ideas about the direction to take with the chocolate dessert that was to finish off my sixties Wonka Feast. I was doubtful—the event was billed as "a saucy, sassy way to nurture your inner goddess". But some of my best recipes have come from the most unlikely sources so I thought I'd give it a go.

Which is why I found myself in a private room at the Koba bar. The dark purple walls were decorated with impastoed geometric abstracts in burnt orange or lavender, which gave the place an appropriate 1960s vibe. Groups of women sat around amicably chatting and exchanging information. Other, louder groups were working their way through the cocktail list with hen-night dedication. Almost everyone wore killer heels. If a bunch of good-time girls launched a hostile takeover of a Tupperware party, I thought, it might look something like this.

"These girls really know how to have a good time," observed the dark-haired lady to my left. "I'm Fay MacDonald and it was me who thought up these 'Goddess of...' events. They're turning out to be really popular. We've already got a couple planned for next year—the Goddess of Wellbeing and the Goddess of Vintage Glamour."

"How did it all come about in the first place?" I asked.

"My company does PR and marketing. That's my day job. I'm pretty good at putting on events, and I suddenly thought, why not organise one for myself and my friends. It just grew from there."

"It's an opportunity for women to dress up and rock out on a Friday night," interrupted a woman wearing a pink satin corset, her blonde hair cut in a short, boyish style. "I'm Sam, and if you want to know what gets adults excited about chocolate, Heston, I have the answer."

Sam took me firmly by the arm and steered me towards a table on which chocolates were laid out beneath a placard that challenged: LOVE CHOCOLATE? MAKE CHOCOLATE! "Smell, smell, smell," she directed, nudging my head forwards. "That's raw chocolate. And this", she pointed to the Hispanic woman standing behind the table, "is Galia Orme—the ultimate Choc Chick, so that's what she called her company. Try one," she said, thrusting a chocolate towards my mouth.

"Mmm, that's lovely. Big flavour and I like the touch of cardamom. How do you make them, Galia?"

"At its simplest, you get a pan of water on the simmer, then set a bowl on top of it in which you whisk together 100 grams of raw cacao butter, a pinch of salt..."

"Which really lifts the flavour," I chipped in, for the camera's benefit. Many people still don't realise that salt can have just as dramatic effect on the flavour of desserts as it does in savoury dishes.

"... six tablespoons of cacao powder and two or three of agave syrup."

"The juice from the core of those plants that look like pineapple leaves? The ones used to make tequila?"

"Exactly. A lot of people think agave are cactuses because of the spikes, but they're not. They're actually related to the lily and the amaryllis. The syrup is a natural sweetener that's much better for you than processed sugar—lots of minerals and a low GI."

"Yes. The sugar in agave is fructose—fruit sugar. I use it a lot at the Fat Duck because it's sweeter than sucrose so you can use less, and it really enhances fruity flavours. It's great for macerating strawberries. It also dissolves more easily, which I can see would be a benefit when adding it to melted chocolate. What set you off on the raw idea?"

"When I was growing up in South America I used to make chocolate in this way. I guess the memories of it have never left me. I wanted to get back to that pure unadulterated flavour so I began making it myself and the business just grew around my enthusiasm. Raw chocolate has got loads of health benefits, especially if—as I do—you avoid adding 'bad' fats or dairy products or processed sugar to the mix. It's got more antioxidants than green tea or red wine or blueberries or goji berries or whatever. You can forget all those other so-called superfoods!"

I noticed that Galia had flavoured some of her chocolates with geranium, which is something that I also do at the Fat Duck. Clearly we thought along similar lines and she seemed just the sort of person who might trigger an idea for my dessert. I was about to explain my task when Sam decided it was time to move on. "Cocktails. Let's go."

"You're very bossy, Sam. Maybe you should work in my kitchen."

She grinned. I thought this was either because she liked the idea of working at the Fat Duck or because she liked to be seen as bossy. In retrospect I think it was because she knew what was coming next. "Almost no man is allowed to cross the 'Goddess of…' threshold," she announced. "You should feel honoured, Heston. Only one other male has ever been invited—the God of Chocolate. Are you ready for him?"

She stepped aside and I was confronted by a black plinth topped by a golden statue of a muscled and very obviously male torso. Sam held a shot glass between his legs and pressed a button at the back of the plinth. Onlookers whooped as a stream of liquid filled the glass.

"I think he needs to see a doctor if he's got brown pee," I said.

"It's a Choctini. Sip," said Sam. I did as I was told. "There. You have tasted the God of Chocolate."

The atmosphere was becoming more Carry-On by the minute. Even the slightest hint of an innuendo was greeted with loud cheers.

I decided the best tactic was to play it straight. "This Choctini's not at all bad. Using a chocolate base instead of a syrup means you can really taste the other ingredients…"

"CHOCOLATE MONKEY!" shouted the crowd. Were they registering their disapproval of my overly sensible comments, I wondered, or calling for me to be put through some kind of dubious ritual? Fortunately it turned out they'd decided it was time to make a type of cocktail and we shuffled en masse to the bar counter.

Even if I hadn't noticed that I was being plied with far more drinks than anyone else, the schadenfreude smiles on the faces of the TV crew would have alerted me to the fact. It was time to set up a little distraction. I picked up an ice bucket, flung its contents in the sink, grabbed a bottle of rum, upended it into the bucket, then reached for the crème de cacao and roared, "Okay. Let's make a cocktail for EVERYONE!"

It worked as well as I could have hoped. Scaling up the ingredients and deciphering the instructions in the dim light after a few drinks took some doing and slowed things down for a while. I escaped to the relative tranquillity of a chocolate body treatment and got my arms done, then returned to the raw chocolate-making table. So far I hadn't found much inspiration for my dish. I decided to have one last go.

"I'm developing a menu for a Chocolate Factory Feast. I'm hoping to create a dessert based on one of Willy Wonka's creations, perhaps his chocolate waterfall…" I tailed off, momentarily taken aback that I'd managed to say "willy" without triggering a reaction. "I'm keen to find out what you think should go into a chocolate dish for adults."

"It's the aroma that's important," one of the chocolate beauticians said. "It triggers memories. Everyone who comes in for a treatment— it's the smell that gets them." She lifted her hands and cupped them to her face. "It's sort of comforting and erotic at the same time."

"It's certainly comforting," I agreed. "Chocolate melts at mouth temperature. It's been suggested that there's something womb-like about that, and that's what makes it comforting for us."

"Chocolate's also very sensual," Galia pointed out. "You smell, taste, touch it."

"It needs something like vanilla," said one woman.

"Chilli," said Galia decisively. "Gets the endorphins going."

"Liqueur. For more depth," added a husky voice, and got an "oooh" from the people round the table. They were warming to the idea.

"What you need is dark chocolate," someone declared. "Chocolate so intense that even with the tiniest bit you can really taste it."

"So it's better to have something smaller but with a bigger impact?" I only realised the innuendo when the crowd started whooping again. I knew that was it for the evening—I'd get no sense out of anyone now.

THE ROCKET

"This is my private yacht!" cried Mr Wonka, beaming with pleasure. "I made her by hollowing out an enormous boiled sweet!"

ROALD DAHL, *Charlie and the Chocolate Factory*

The mini-skirt and the mini, the Beatles and the Stones, *The Avengers* and *Alfie*—swinging sixties Britain was successfully creative in almost every sphere except one: food. Package travel had opened up Europe and we flocked to Spain, Italy, Greece, Germany and France and came back with a taste for moussaka, spaghetti Bolognese, duck à l'orange and Black Forest gâteau. These began to appear on British menus but, cooked by chefs who had little access to the right ingredients and little idea of how the dishes were supposed to be put together, the results were often dire. As a kid, I was thrilled by the theatre of duck à l'orange, the bird reverentially borne to the table on its willow-pattern platter. But looking back, I know that what I ate was clumsily cooked: half a roasted cheap duck garnished with a chunk of raw orange and swimming in an insipid sauce that tasted mainly of boiled sweets. If possible, I wanted to get that aspect of the sixties into my Feast as well—the Brits' newfound excitement about food, and our quirky, faltering first steps towards a polished, more cosmopolitan cuisine.

Putting the smoke in Smoky Duck crisps.

Duck à l'orange crossed with Terry's Chocolate Orange.

I began by trying to create the kind of sauce, fragrant with bitter orange, which would temper the richness of the duck meat. Over a couple of months I developed a demi-glace made from roasted duck bones, Shiraz and various spices that had a wonderful intensity of flavour. To intensify it even further, I decided to put it in The Rocket.

With its strobe and purple flashing light, The Rocket mesmerised my development chefs and they welcomed any opportunity to use it. It's more properly known as a vacuum centrifuge and its main benefit for the chef is that it causes water to boil off at very low temperatures, leaving a highly concentrated liquid that retains all of the lovely, fragile fresh notes that are normally destroyed by heat. The Rocket created a

Stop me and buy one: duck crisps, duck pastilles and duck à l'orange.

flavourful demi-glace with a beautiful glossy sheen, but I kept thinking of the boiled-sweet flavour of my childhood duck à l'orange. Surely there was some way of getting that into the dish, too?

Somehow I made the leap to turning the sauce into actual sweets. I had two moulds made—one with depressions in the form of orange segments, the other in the form of thick discs—and filled them with a mix of gelatine and either rocket-concentrated orange juice or demi-glace. Wrapped in edible cellophane, they looked exactly like boiled sweets. I was looking forward to my guests' reactions as they watched the sweets magically turn into an accompaniment to roast duck. Except that now the duck was changing as well.

The sweetie theme, I realised, could be expanded to encompass the whole dish. It would provide the kind of theatrical excitement I was looking for, and was aptly Wonka-like too. The duck could take its cue from Terry's Chocolate Orange: instead of a ball of chocolate packaged to look like an orange, I'd have an orange with duck meat inside.

At first, I imagined this warm. I explored methods of binding the meat into a ball using either protein and salt or transglutaminase, an enzyme that acts as a kind of culinary superglue, sticking proteins together. But I had to use the heat-resistant setting agent gellan gum, which unbalanced the flavours of my sauce and didn't look particularly attractive. Instead I decided to serve the orange cold, which meant I could set the skin using gelatine, which melts in the mouth, avoiding the problem of a shapeless piece of orange skin cluttering the plate.

As if to confirm that I was on the right path, an unexpected touch of magic appeared as I was working on this new, cold version. I made a duck liver parfait, cooked it gently in a bain-marie, and then placed it in the freezer in hemispherical moulds. Once it was frozen, I took two halves, put them together to make a ball and dipped it in the gelatine. When I removed the ball, now covered in its orange "skin", I found it was dimpled with tiny pock-marks, just like a real orange!

A TASTE OF CAESAR'S MUSHROOM

I leaned against a tree, trying to appear shrewd and nonchalant. The ground was covered in spiky chestnut burrs that made it look as though a mass migration of tiny hedgehogs was under way. Teasing one with the end of my shoe, I sized up the opposition crowded around the small table on the village green, waiting for the auctioneer. The tall man with the frown seemed nervous—I hoped he'd be too jumpy to cause trouble. An older guy in flat cap and fleece appeared more confident. It was harder to read the man next to him in a checked shirt and workman's boots. Did a baseball cap turned the wrong way round suggest he knew nothing about mycology, or was it the fashion statement of the Italian mushroom hunter? And what to make of the man with pebble glasses

Serious scrutiny of the lots on offer in an Italian mushroom auction.

and swept-back silver hair, wearing a sky-blue sleeveless sweater? He looked like a professor but maybe he was a ringer.

As the Caesar's mushroom is scarce and doesn't travel well, I had come to the tiny hamlet of Bagnolo, on the slopes of Monte Amiata in Tuscany, to try to buy some at auction. I wanted to taste this close relative of the fly agaric, to get some idea of the flavour and texture.

The crowd's chatter suddenly stilled. A spruce man in jeans and a striped half-zip sweater appeared, carrying a large plastic crate of mushrooms and an ancient set of portable scales. He began apportioning fat, large-capped brown mushrooms to wicker baskets.

"That's Moreno," whispered my translator, Graziella.

We edged closer. I realised I wasn't even sure how to make a bid. Should I call out? Make a hand signal? Wave a mushroom in the air?

Thwack! Thwack! Thwack! The auctioneer's walking stick rapped against the table. He delivered a well-rehearsed eulogy on the basket of mushrooms before him, *"Eccezionale... belli... guarda, guarda,"* ("Exceptional... beautiful... look, look," Graziella repeated).

"Io—ventidue," broke in the man in the reversed baseball cap, as though he couldn't hold out any longer.

"Trenta," parried a voice from the back. As the auction of *ovoli* (Caesar's mushrooms) would come later, I was free to see my rivals in action and work out the rules. The bidding continued, with intermittent outbursts from Moreno, talking up his mushrooms as he marched up and down with the basket balanced on the stick over his shoulder. "He's saying, 'Forty-five euros? C'mon. The basket alone is worth fifteen'," Graziella explained. I'd heard much the same line in London markets. Traders' patter appeared to be the same the world over.

Eventually the bidding slowed and the increments became smaller. The final bid, *"Sessanta—tre..."* came from the tall man, who looked a little happier as Moreno handed the basket over to him.

The auctions were raucous affairs, punctuated by a lot of laughter—a travelling spectacle for little villages where little normally happened. Non-bidders heckled the proceedings in a light-hearted way. When the basket I was interested in was placed on the table, an "aaaah" rippled through the crowd. The mushroom caps didn't have the deep red of the fly agaric nor the white spots. The crowd was enthusiastic but, to me, *ovoli* lacked the fairy-tale magic of the fly agaric.

Moreno did the shroomspiel and Graziella translated. "Ovoli. An excellent product. Great in a salad with olive oil and Parmesan..." Scales were flourished, the weight announced. "Two and a half kilos. Worth at least thirty-five euros. Who'll bid thirty-five?"

"Trentasei," someone offered, cheekily one-upping the auctioneer's figure, but that was quickly superseded by more realistic offers—45... 46... 48... 49... In earlier auctions there'd been a kind of lull and I'd hoped to use such a moment to join the action, but this was different.

"Cinquanta," called out the professor in sky blue. *"Cinquantatre,"* countered a woman in glasses. Things were speeding up, I needed to get in there before it was all too late. There was no time to ask Graziella the Italian for fifty-four, I just had to jump in: *"Cinquanta quatre."* My Franco-Italian mishmash didn't matter because I was already being outbid—55... 56... 57. *"Cinquantotto,"* the Professor said. He seemed to be my main rival so I offered *"Cinquantanove"* and got an *"et uno"* ("going once") from Moreno. It looked like it was in the bag.

"Sessanta!" shouted the man with the baseball cap. *"Sessantadue,"* called the tall, frown-faced man who had bought the first basket of mushrooms. *"Sessantatre,"* I said, wondering how much longer my language skills could hold out. And then, as is often the way with auctions, it was suddenly over. No one opposed my "sixty-three".

Moreno hit the stick on the table for the final time and congratulated me on my purchase. "At sixty-three euros you've got a bargain, my friend," he told me. "Plus a fine wicker basket."

Most of the crowd were still hanging around in groups, joking and trading snatches of Italian folk song. I took my fine wicker basket off to the other end of the clearing where the crew were ready to film.

"So here it is," I announced, peeling off the outer skin of an *Amanita* cap, "the mushroom so valued by the Caesars," and I bit in. At first, the *Amanita*'s flavour seemed almost bland. But it built with each successive bite: there was an earthy richness to it, and a faint flavour of chestnut. There was an intriguing sharpness, too, reminiscent of unripe banana or cobnut. Italians had advised me not to cook Caesar's mushroom, and I could see why. Unless it was handled with extreme care, its lovely creamy texture and delicate flavours wouldn't survive the process.

I was worried that this meant I would be unable to use Caesar's mushroom in my Feast, but there was also a more pressing concern. I wasn't sure if I was being hoodwinked, but I had been told that local tradition required that the successful bidder in a mushroom auction prepared some of his winnings for the villagers. Before driving back to the airport, I had some cooking to do.

The tiny kitchen was already set for dinner. Bright yellow plates and white bowls were formally set out on a white lace tablecloth, with a large decanter of red in the middle of the table. As we took our seats, more and more people squeezed round the table, including several who'd been at the auction. The professor was introduced as Egino; the frown-faced man as Leonardo. Even Moreno was there. It appeared I was cooking for the man from whom I'd bought the mushrooms, and the people I had bid against for them! Figuring I had been gently gulled, I got on with cleaning the *ovoli* and finely slicing them.

The legendary status of foodstuffs like the Caesar's mushroom in Italy comes partly from fierce regional pride—this is, after all, a country that was unified a mere 150 years ago—and partly from a desire to protect the local economy by talking up local produce. Italians are unbelievably passionate about their food, and the crowd around the table was no exception. It wasn't long before they began to question the way I was preparing my mushroom salad.

"*Troppo*—it's too much. *Stop! Stop!*" they called out as I began crushing garlic and peperoncino seeds in a pestle. I wanted the flavours of garlic and chilli in my salad, but none of the harshness, so instead of adding them raw I had decided to make an infusion. I added extra virgin olive oil to the pestle and got a grudging: "*Olio. Va bene.*"

From then on, they watched keenly, pouncing on anything they considered a transgression. The chopped parsley that I scattered over the mushrooms was, like the garlic, thought to be *troppo forte*—too strong—for the mushrooms' delicate flavour. I decided that the way to get through this was to ask the table to vote on the addition of each item. By the time I'd got to grating over Parmesan, I had little control over the dish. Despite their collaboration, they were unimpressed with the result. "They think there's too much garlic," Graziella explained. "It cancels out the flavour of the mushrooms." I took a mouthful: it didn't seem at all strong to me and I asked Graziella to tell them that. "That's just because you're used to it like that," came the reply.

The diners were more impressed with what came next. "*Zuppa di funghi!*" they exclaimed as our host, Sabrina, lifted a big glazed

Preparing Caesar's mushroom salad for the sceptical villagers of Bagnolo.

earthenware pot onto the table. She put cubes of toasted bread in each bowl and began spooning over a thick, dark soup containing different mushrooms. It looked and tasted lovely, with a nice mix of textures. A real celebration of the mushroom.

"This is a four-hundred-year-old recipe," Sabrina told me.

"Well, it's delicious—"

"It's delicious because here we can actually *taste* the mushroom," cut in Egino, playfully putting me in my place.

"To be honest," I said, trying to keep a straight face, "I think there's possibly too much garlic…?"

The table erupted in mock-uproar, but they soon moved on to arguing over the characteristics of the local Montalcino wine instead. It's this passion that maintains Italy's food culture, and I'd have loved to stay and listen, but I had a plane to catch, so I left them to it…

A CHOCOLATE FOUNTAIN

Like a bank-holiday-weekend shopper, I strolled along the aisles of Waterlands garden centre, looking at the selection of water features, hoping one would catch my eye. There were stone hippos and cavorting otters, amorous rustic couples and plenty of pagodas and buddhas and Bacchuses. After my experiences with the goddesses of chocolate I was relieved to see there was no reproduction of the Belgian Manneken Pis, just a wistful Hebe unaware of the water spilling incessantly from the jug held at her side. The modern fountains usually took the form of an upright sculpted slab, like *2001: A Space Odyssey*'s monolith with a bad case of rising damp.

None of them was quite what I was looking for. In *Charlie and the Chocolate Factory*, Willy Wonka insists that the waterfall is what makes his chocolate special—"It mixes the chocolate! It churns it up! It pounds it and beats it! It makes it light and frothy! No other factory in the world mixes its chocolate by waterfall! But it's the *only* way to do it properly!" I thought it might make my chocolate dessert pretty special too, so I had come to find the right kind of fountain to try out the idea. I wanted something with a bit of theatre and a Wonka-like surreality. Eventually I found a tiered edifice with two pools supported by trios of entwined, big-lipped sea monsters. At the top an angry cherub yanked back the head of a baby monster below. The faint air of menace reminded me of Wonka, who, for all his apparent friendliness, has a sharp tongue for any child who asks an inconvenient question, and appears almost gleeful at the unpleasant plights of his guests. The staff told me the fountain would need at least forty litres of liquid in order to work properly, so I had a fair bit of work on my hands.

I had set up my portable gas stove in a trelliswork gazebo, hoping the flame would be sufficiently sheltered from the wind. The chocolate goddesses had suggested that alcohol was the key to creating an adult chocolate experience, but pairing chocolate and wine is a tricky thing to pull off: chocolate bombards the palate with sweetness, fruitiness, bitterness and acidity all at once, and any wine that doesn't have a similar intensity of flavour is simply going to get lost. The grenache-heavy fortified wines from Banyuls and Maury in the south of France have a concentration of black fruits, a tobacco-like aroma and a level of acidity robust enough to stand up to chocolate, so I began by upending a couple of bottles of Mas Amiel's Vintage 2007 into the stockpot, bringing it to the boil on a high heat and then flaming the alcohol to make sure the wine's acidity wasn't too dominant.

Once the flames had died down, I added chips of two types of Callebaut dark chocolate—Madagascar (66% cocoa solids), which has a pronounced red wine note to it, and their Dark Callets, which has flavours and aromas of exotic fruits. Here it was important to add enough chocolate to take down the temperature: put too little in a mass of hot liquid and the chocolate scorches, affecting the flavour. I definitely didn't want that to happen.

By now the gazebo was surrounded by an audience of Waterlands staff and customers, who looked distinctly dubious about my preparations. I hoped to dispel that look from their faces and give them the most fantastic chocolate experience, served straight from the fountain.

It wasn't long before the contents of the pot looked convincingly river-like—viscous and flowing, with a watery sheen. I added some whole milk to keep the chocolate from overheating and clumping together, and continued this balancing act for a while—a new slew of chocolate chips, a little more milk—stirring continuously as the small gas ring meant the base of the pot got hotter in the middle than at the edges, which could easily cause the ingredients to burn if left alone.

By now the ten-litre stockpot was three-quarters full. I dipped in a finger and tasted the liquid. The wine certainly gave the chocolate a more adult dimension: the flavour was deep, rich, fruity and only slightly sweet. But the mix was still quite volatile and the wine too dominant. I poured in a couple of tubs of passion fruit purée to pick up on the exotic fruit flavours of the chocolate and calm the red wine notes and got the balance I was looking for. It was delicious, exotic and had a kick to it.

Now all I had to do was cook up three more stockpots of the stuff and pour it into my fountain. Later there was a brief panic while we searched around for a receptacle large enough to transport forty litres of chocolate to the fountain itself, but eventually Mark and Steve, the two strongest of the Waterlands staff, were effortfully hefting a plastic storage box full of chocolate over the rim of the fountain and sloshing in the contents. The semi-circle of onlookers had shuffled over from the gazebo and stood, waiting.

I hit the switch and heard the pump grind into action. For a moment nothing happened. I was sure the amount of milk in the mix would keep the chocolate from solidifying, but there were a thousand other things that could go wrong. After all, the fountain was certainly not designed for this.

Then it spluttered to life and the surreal spectacle of chocolate cascading where water should be became wonderfully, tangibly real. It collected in the fountain's main pool where it bubbled, geyser-like, and the crowd clapped enthusiastically. "Quick! Dip in a cup!" I said, getting caught up in the excitement of it all. "Go on Mark, Steve. You deserve it! What d'you think?"

"Mmm. That's really nice. And it looks great. We really should do this as a customer attraction—perhaps as a Christmas special or something like that."

Now that somebody had tried it and liked it, everybody was happy to grab a cup and scoop up some chocolate. I was thrilled that it had worked, and Steve was right—it did look great. But to me it was more surreal than spectacular.

If possible, I wanted the guests at my Feast to be as awestruck by my chocolate waterfall as they would be by Willy Wonka's. This was quite a challenge: in the book they end up "too flabbergasted to speak. They were staggered. They were dumbfounded. They were bewildered and dazzled... They simply stood and stared." I didn't think my chocolate fountain was going to provoke that kind of response. I needed to go further.

THE MAGICALLY MINUSCULE ENOKI MUSHROOM

Although the insurers had swatted any chance of using the fly agaric in my starter, I was still determined that my guests would have a psychedelic experience, one way or another. I looked into all sorts of natural highs, but their effects wouldn't manifest until long after the course had been served. I considered using light and sound to create a trippy experience but couldn't find a convincing combination. In the end it was *Alice's Adventures in Wonderland*, with its hallucinatory switches in size, that pointed the way forward.

There's a mushroom called the enoki (or enokitake) that is popular in Japanese cuisine, particularly in soups, where it gives a lovely crunch. It's tiny, not much bigger than a matchstick, and it looks like one too: a pale off-white stem topped by a small reddish-brown ball. Adding a few white spots would turn the enoki into a miniature fly agaric. As soon as I thought of it I knew I'd found the detail around which I could structure this course. It had exactly the touch of fantasy I had been searching for, and was bound to induce an enjoyable disorientation in my guests.

Enoki mushrooms disguised to look like miniature fly agarics.

In some recipes, the discovery of the central ingredient or technique or idea brings with it a compelling logic: all the chef has to do is hang on and follow it through. This was one of those. At the Fat Duck I serve Jelly of Quail on a bed of moss (beneath which is hidden some dry ice), accompanied by *pain de seigle* toast and truffle and oak butter. When the diners are ready, the waiter pours a mixture of oak moss essential oil, alcohol and hot water over the moss-bed to produce a vapour that wafts the scents of the forest across the table.

Damp greenery, the smells of earth and bark, autumn mist—these were the sensory hits I'd had while foraging with Fergus, and they would be the perfect set-up for my magical minuscule *Amanitas*. (The

The mushroom starter ready for service in toadstool bowls on a bed of moss.

moss was particularly appropriate for a mushroom dish because the word "mushroom" actually comes from the Old French *mousseron*, which derives from *mousse*, meaning "moss".) I could see a way of using the truffle butter, too. If I got the set designers to construct a giant toadstool with depressions where the white spots would be, I could replicate the edible toadstool that Mrs Teavee greedily gobbled. Each depression would be filled with delicious white truffle butter.

Each idea chain-reactioned another. Butter had to be spread on something—what about toast? Or mushroom-flavoured bread? Or mushroom-*shaped* bread? It had to be something that looked right nestled in moss. And what about adding edible twigs or leaves…? And

I knew of a great bit of science that'd bring a little Wonka-like lunacy to the service of the dish. Inhaling sulphur hexafluoride makes the voice go disconcertingly deep. What if I could get my guests to take a hit of that from a toadstool balloon?

THE CHOCOLATE WATERFALL

"Check this out, Heston." Jocky, my pastry chef, scattered cocoa powder onto a baking tray, lifted a large polystyrene box full of liquid nitrogen high above it and began to pour. For a moment the work surface was wreathed in clouds of spooky white vapour, but as it dispersed I could see that the baking tray had come alive. A chocolate amoeba rippled and bubbled and pulsed and pullulated around it, like angry lava or a sulphur spring. It formed and reformed into different shapes. Brown pseudopodia swarmed outwards and then were swallowed up again. It reminded me of the T1000 robot reassembling towards the end of *Terminator 2*. A great piece of theatre. "That's terrific Jocky—"

"Aye, but it's not over yet. *Look!*"

The frenzy slowed slightly, and then suddenly the liquid was gone. Only a scattering of brown powder remained on the baking tray. It was as though none of what I had just witnessed had actually happened—as though I had dreamed it. I could imagine that that's how the children must have felt during the guided tour of Wonka's factory, and I knew it would have the same effect on my guests.

"Fantastic! Amazing!" I'd gone Wonka again, talking in exclamation marks. "I think we've got ourselves the basis for a chocolate waterfall," I told Jocky. "Now all we have to do is sort out a couple of things to serve alongside. We'll need a chocolate bar, of course. You can't have a Wonka Feast without a chocolate bar, and I've got an idea about that. Dahl loved wordplay, so let's have a pun of our own." Roald Dahl wrote a book called *The BFG*, and at the restaurant we serve a Black Forest Gâteau affectionately known as the BFG. "How about turning the gâteau into a kind of chocolate bar? And what about a golden ticket to go with it …?" ❧

Making chocolate water and a tank of super-cold liquid nitrogen.

MENU

Lickable Wallpaper

Caesar's Mushroom Purée

*Jellied Consommé of Mushrooms, Cream of Madeira,
Enoki Disguised as Fly Agaric, Truffle Butter,
Cep Brioche and a Very Deep Voice!*

Heston's Duck Orange

Duck and Celeriac Pastilles, Smoky Duck Salt 'n' Shake Crisps, Sucking Sweet 'n' Gravy Sauce in Edible Wrappers

Chocolate Unmixed by Waterfall

Chocolate Water and the BFG

Golden Ticket

"SAUSAGE ON A STICK" LICKABLE WALLPAPER

FOR THE SAUSAGE OIL BREADCRUMBS

50g butter
150g grapeseed oil
4 jumbo pork sausages
200g dried breadcrumbs

Melt the butter in a sauté pan with the grapeseed oil and fry the sausages over a high heat for 5–10 minutes until well caramelised.

Strain the oil through a sieve and reserve (discard the sausages).

Heat the sausage-infused oil to 150°C. Add the breadcrumbs and fry until golden brown.

Drain on kitchen paper and place in a dryer overnight to get rid of any excess oil.

FOR THE LICKABLE SAUSAGE MIX

175g sausage oil breadcrumbs (see above)
1g rosemary
9g pork stock cubes
2g chicken stock cubes
0.3g ground nutmeg
0.2g ground ginger
0.2g freshly ground white pepper
0.8g red cocoa colouring
1.2g black cocoa colouring

Blitz all of the ingredient together in a food processor and pass through a drum sieve. Place on kitchen paper in a dryer and dry overnight.

FOR THE WALLPAPER GEL BASE

100g brown chicken stock
16g strong beef stock
25g golden syrup
2.2g Worcestershire sauce
1g salt

Whisk the ingredients together thoroughly and weigh out 74g.

TO FINISH THE GEL

74g wallpaper gel base mixture (see above)
2g pectin jaune
2g caster sugar

In a small saucepan, bring the base mixture to 80°C. Mix the pectin and sugar together and add to the pan.

Bring the mixture to the boil while whisking, then remove from the heat and cool.

TO SERVE

Cut a stencil of a cocktail sausage out of a piece of thin rigid plastic material.

Brush the gel onto a wall using the stencil and a stencil brush.

Using a tea strainer, dust over the lickable sausage mix evenly. When it is dry, flatten with the back of a spatula and carefully lift off the stencil.

CAESAR'S MUSHROOM PURÉE

FOR THE MUSHROOM PURÉE
25g grapeseed oil
25g shallots, finely diced
570g Caesar's mushrooms, cleaned
40g mirin
600g dashi (see below)
80g white soy sauce

In a saucepan, heat the grapeseed oil over a low heat. Add the shallots and sweat them slowly until soft and richly caramelised.

Add the mushrooms and continue to cook over a medium-low heat until they are slightly caramelised on the outside.

Deglaze the pan with the mirin and begin to simmer over a medium heat.

Once the mirin has reduced enough to burn off the alcohol, add the dashi. Simmer over a medium heat until the liquid has reduced by two-thirds, then remove from the heat and add the white soy.

Transfer the mixture to a tall, cylindrical container and purée with a hand blender, checking the consistency and seasoning. At this point you can increase the seasoning if needed with more white soy.

Pass the purée through a drum sieve, using a plastic spatula to push it through.

Divide the purée between two PacoJet containers and freeze.

Run the containers through the PacoJet machine and proceed to the finishing steps.

TO FINISH THE PURÉE
6.7g leaf gelatine
355g mushroom purée (see above)

Soak the gelatine in cold water to cover.

Warm a little of the mushroom purée in a pan. Squeeze excess water from the gelatine, then add to the warm purée and stir until melted. Stir this back into the rest of the mushroom purée.

Add 30g of the mixture to each mushroom bowl. Cover and chill until needed.

FOR THE DASHI
15g rishiri kombu (kelp)
900g low-calcium mineral water
25g katsuo bushi (dried bonito flakes)

Wipe the kombu with a damp cloth and place in a pan with the mineral water. Heat to 60°C and hold at this temperature for 1 hour.

Remove the kombu from the water and discard. Increase the water temperature to 80°C. Turn off the heat and immediately add the katsuo bushi.

After 10 seconds, strain the stock through a sieve lined with damp muslin, allowing the stock to run through freely without pressing. Discard the solids and set the dashi aside to cool.

FOR THE SMOKED WATER
In a small stove-top smoker, burn some apple wood chips.

Fill a small ramekin with cold water and place in the smoker until lightly smoked (approximately 30 minutes).

FOR THE MUSHROOM STOCK
200g unsalted butter
1.5kg button mushrooms, rinsed
    and dried
400g East India Madeira
3kg water
15g thyme sprigs
6g black peppercorns

In a pressure cooker, melt the butter and cook the mushrooms over a medium heat until well caramelised. Add the Madeira and reduce the liquor to a syrup.

Pour in the water, then add the thyme and peppercorns, tied in a muslin bag. Bring to full pressure for 30 minutes.

Allow to de-pressurise, then strain the stock through a fine sieve and transfer to a clean pan. Bring to the boil and reduce down to 1 litre. Refrigerate until needed.

FOR THE VEGETABLE STOCK

400g unsalted butter

500g onions, finely sliced

500g leeks (white and pale green parts only), finely sliced

250g carrots, thinly sliced

375g Syrah red wine

225g water

Heat the butter in a saucepan over a medium heat until it is dark brown and nutty, to make beurre noisette. Strain through a fine sieve.

Heat 125g of the beurre noisette in a pressure cooker, add the vegetables and sweat until soft.

In a separate pan, bring the wine to the boil, flame off the alcohol and reduce to 250g.

Add the water and reduced wine to the vegetables. Put the lid on, bring to full pressure and cook for 1 hour.

Allow the pan to cool before removing the lid. Pass the stock through a sieve and incorporate the remaining beurre noisette with a hand-held blender. Refrigerate overnight.

Before using, remove the solidified fat and strain the stock through a fine sieve.

FOR THE MADEIRA REDUCTION

75g shallots, finely sliced

25g leeks (white and pale green parts only), finely sliced

2.5g garlic, finely sliced

375g East India Madeira

Combine all of the ingredients in a saucepan and place over a medium heat. Reduce to 250g (weight including vegetables). Pass through a fine sieve and reserve.

FOR THE COMBINED STOCKS AND ICE FILTRATION

1kg mushroom stock (see above)

300g vegetable stock (see above)

120g Madeira reduction (see above)

smoked water to taste (see above)

salt as needed

15g leaf gelatine, plus extra for finishing

Combine the cooled stocks, Madeira reduction and smoked water. Season with salt if needed.

Soak the gelatine in a little cold water. Warm 300g of the stock mixture to around 60°C. Remove the gelatine and shake off most of the water. Add to the warm stock and whisk to melt. Stir back into the remaining stock.

Pour the mixture into a large sous-vide bag, seal and freeze into a 2cm thick block.

Turn the frozen block onto a perforated tray lined with a double layer of muslin. Set this over a container to catch the liquid as it defrosts and place in the fridge to thaw very slowly for about 48 hours, until only the gelatine remains in the muslin.

Weigh the liquid after ice filtration. Weigh out 2% of that weight in leaf gelatine. Soak the gelatine in cold water. Warm some of the stock. Squeeze the gelatine to remove excess water, add to the warm stock and stir until melted. Pour back into the rest of the stock.

Set 60g of this jelly in each mushroom bowl on top of the 30g mushroom purée.

FOR THE MADEIRA AND SHERRY CREAM

150g East India Madeira

150g Solera sherry

65g double cream

salt

Combine the Madeira and sherry in a saucepan and bring to the boil over a medium heat. Reduce to a thick syrup.

Add the cream, season with salt and allow to cool.

Using a beaker with a spout, pour just enough of the cream over the top of the jelly in each serving bowl to cover it.

FOR THE PAINTED ENOKI MUSHROOMS

golden enoki mushrooms

carmine extract

50g white chocolate

2g food-grade titanium oxide

Cut each enoki, leaving a long stem (2cm).

Dip each cap into carmine extract. Stick a toothpick at an angle where the cap meets the stem. Stick the other end of the toothpick into a new, dry sponge and leave to dry in the fridge.

Meanwhile, melt the white chocolate with the titanium oxide. Using a toothpick, make dots on the red enoki caps.

Refrigerate until needed (best used within 1–2 hours).

FOR THE CEP BRIOCHE

375g strong bread flour
14g salt
20g dried cep powder
28g unrefined caster sugar
12g fresh yeast
108g warm milk (30°C)
150g cep purée
210g beaten eggs (at room temperature)
263g unsalted butter (at room temperature)

Sift the flour, salt, cep powder and sugar into a mixer with the paddle attachment fitted. Crumble the fresh yeast into the bowl.

Add the milk, cep purée and eggs and beat on speed 2 for 15 minutes. Spoon in the soft butter in stages and mix for 2 minutes or until all the butter is fully incorporated.

Place in a container and cover with clingfilm. Store in the fridge overnight.

To bake the brioche, preheat the oven to 190°C (fan). Divide some of the dough into 20g portions, roll into balls and place in conical piping nozzles; cover and allow to prove for 30 minutes. Divide the remaining dough into 30g portions, place in half-sphere moulds and allow to prove, covered, for 45 minutes.

Once the time has elapsed for the dough in the piping nozzles, bake these for 10 minutes.

In the meantime, cut a slit in the centre of the dough in the half-spheres.

Take the half-baked pieces out of the piping nozzles and place in the slit in the half-spheres. Bake for 20 minutes. Remove from the mould and place on a wire rack.

FOR THE PASTRY LEAVES

puff pastry
icing sugar
cep powder
groundnut oil

Roll out the puff pastry, using a rolling pin. Sprinkle both sides of the pastry with icing sugar and cep powder.

Continue rolling until the pastry is approximately 2mm thick. Using leaf shape cutters, cut out different shapes. Reserve in an airtight container until ready to serve.

Before serving, heat a sauté pan, oil lightly and place a leaf in the centre of the pan. Hold it down with a spatula until the underside is brown, then flip over and repeat the process until both sides are golden brown in colour.

Take the leaf out and place on the edge of a plate to dry; this will give shape to the leaf.

TO SERVE

dry ice pellets
oak moss
assembled mushroom jelly bowls (see above)
painted enoki mushrooms (see above)
crisp pastry leaves (see above)
cep brioche (see above)
oak moss essential oil
oak chip essential oil

Place the dry ice pellets in the bottom of each serving tray. Cover with a perforated lid, then place the moss over the top to fit securely in the tray.

Place one mushroom jelly bowl on top of the moss and insert the painted enoki mushrooms (10 per dish).

Place 3 pastry leaves on top of the moss and stand one of the brioche "mushrooms" up on the moss.

Just before serving, combine hot water with the oak moss and oak chip essential oils. Then, in front of the guests, pour over the moss (being careful not to get the pastry, jelly or moss wet) to release the forest floor vapour.

DUCK AND CELERIAC PASTILLES

FOR THE DUCK STOCK

75g duck fat
3.5kg duck bones
1.5kg onions, sliced
1.5kg carrots, sliced
15g star anise
1.1kg water

In a pressure cooker, heat the duck fat and brown the bones evenly over a medium–high heat. Remove and set aside.

Add the onions, carrots and star anise to the cooker and brown slowly over a medium heat until evenly caramelised.

Return the bones to the pressure cooker, cover with the water, seal and pressure-cook for 2 hours.

De-pressurise and remove the lid. Strain the liquid and return to the pan (discarding the solids). Reduce the liquid to 900g, then set aside to cool.

FOR THE BEEF STOCK

3.25kg beef bones
1kg oxtail, chopped into sections
grapeseed oil, for frying
3.25kg boneless shin of beef
1.5kg carrots, thinly sliced
1.5kg onions, thinly sliced
15g star anise
1.1kg red wine
6.4kg water

Preheat the oven to 190°C.

Combine the beef bones and the oxtail pieces in a roasting pan and roast until golden brown on all sides, turning regularly.

In the bottom of a pressure cooker over a high heat, heat a thin film of grapeseed oil. Brown the beef in batches, colouring deeply without burning.

Take out the meat and add the carrots and onions to the pan. Sauté the vegetables until soft and then add the star anise. Continue to sauté the vegetables until evenly coloured but not caramelised.

Add the red wine and flame off the alcohol. When the flames have died out and the wine has reduced by half, add the beef bones and the meat and cover with the water.

Put the lid on and bring to full pressure. Cook at full pressure for 2 hours.

De-pressurise and remove the lid. Strain the liquid and return it to the pan (discarding the solids). Reduce the liquid to 800g, then set aside to cool.

FOR THE DUCK SAUCE

900g duck stock (see above)
800g beef stock (see above)

Combine the stocks and whisk together.

Heat before serving to a glaze consistency.

FOR THE ORANGE ZEST POWDER

780g caster sugar
500g glucose
2.8kg water
12 oranges

Combine the sugar, glucose and water in a large saucepan and bring to the boil to make a syrup, then lower the heat.

Poke the oranges with a toothpick several times and place them in the syrup. Cover the oranges with a piece of muslin to keep them submerged and simmer over a low heat for 2–3 hours.

Remove the oranges from the syrup and freeze them overnight.

Zest the oranges with a microplane and let the zest dry in a warm, dry place.

FOR THE DUCK PASTILLES

50g salt
1kg water
2 skinless duck breasts
duck sauce (see above)
orange zest powder (see above)
sea salt

Add the 50g salt to the water and stir to dissolve, creating a brine. Chill thoroughly.

Lay the duck breasts on a board and remove the top layer that contains the sinew. Cut the duck breasts crosswise into strips.

Place the duck strips in the brine for 1 hour. Remove and drain.

Lay out pieces of clingfilm on a surface. Wrap single strips of duck breast in clingfilm, rolling them up tightly into cylinders and tightening down each side to keep the shape.

Place each roll in a sous-vide bag and seal under full pressure.

To serve, preheat a water bath to 56°C. Add the sealed duck strips and cook for 40 minutes. Lift out, unwrap the duck strips and slice into small rounds.

Glaze the duck with the duck sauce and dip in the orange zest powder to coat. Season with sea salt.

FOR THE CELERIAC PASTILLES

1 celeriac
400g butter, plus extra for searing
400g brown chicken stock
sea salt
100g fresh black truffle, finely chopped

Cut the celeriac into 1.5cm cubes. Place the celeriac pieces in 3 sous-vide bags, divide the butter amongst the bags and seal under full pressure.

Preheat a water bath to 84°C. Add the sealed celeriac and cook for 5½ hours or until soft.

Take out the sous-vide bags and allow to cool to room temperature, then chill in iced water.

Remove the celeriac from the bags and pat dry. Cut the celeriac into discs of a similar size and thickness to the duck pastilles.

To serve, sear the celeriac discs in foaming butter and add the brown chicken stock. Let the stock reduce to glaze the discs, then remove the celeriac and drain.

Season the glazed celeriac discs with sea salt and roll each one in chopped black truffle.

TO ASSEMBLE THE PASTILLE PACKAGES

duck pastilles (see above)
celeriac pastilles (see above)
sweet wrappers

Preheat the oven to 70°C. Place alternating pieces of duck and celeriac in the sweet wrapper and roll tight. Place in the oven for 5 minutes to get surface heat into the wrapper and then serve.

THE BFG AND GOLDEN TICKET

THE GOLDEN TICKET

about 500g cornflour
500g sugar
170g water
200g kirsch
grapeseed oil, for brushing

Place the cornflour in a baking tray (14×24cm and 2.5cm deep) in the dehydrator for 24 hours.

The next day, press the cornflour down and make sure it is completely flat. Using a small rectangular shape, about 1.5×5cm, press the cornflour to create a bar mould and set aside.

Place the sugar and water in a pan, dissolve and bring to 117°C. Add the kirsch, cover with a towel and allow to infuse for 5 minutes. Pass the syrup between 2 pans 5 times to mix well.

Using a pipette, drip the syrup into the indentations in the cornflour, then sprinkle more cornflour over the top. Place the tray back in the dehydrator at 45°C for at least 8 hours.

Once the bars have crystallised, using a soft brush, clean off the excess starch. Remove carefully using a small offset spatula and reserve in an airtight container.

Brush the bars with a little grapeseed oil and then wrap with edible gold leaf.

FOR THE BFG CHOCOLATE BAR MOULDS

750g dark chocolate (64% cocoa solids)

Temper the chocolate and line a perforated-style chocolate bar mould.

Fill the cavities to the brim with the chocolate, then knock the sides of the mould repeatedly with the back of a large spoon to remove any air bubbles. Invert the mould and drain the chocolate back into the working bowl. Repeat to make 6 chocolate bar moulds.

Using a scraper, scrape the surface of the mould clean, then place the mould upside down on a wire rack so that any excess liquid can drain out as the chocolate sets.

Once fully set, remove the bars and store in an airtight container in a cool, dry place.

FOR THE OLIVE OIL BISCUIT

450g butter
400g unrefined caster sugar
700g plain flour
12g salt
6g baking powder
2.5g vanilla seeds
180g egg yolks
150g extra virgin olive oil

In a mixer fitted with the paddle attachment, beat the butter and sugar until smooth, then incorporate all the dry ingredients, taking care not to overmix.

Add the egg yolks and olive oil and bring the dough together. Cover and leave to rest in the fridge overnight.

Preheat the oven to 150°C. Roll the dough between 2 pieces of baking parchment to a 2mm thickness and bake for 14 minutes.

While still warm, cut the biscuit to the dimensions of the moulds (i.e. the size they will be once cut and trimmed, using the perforations of the mould as the guide).

FOR THE CHERRY MOUSSE

10.5g leaf gelatine
220g cherry purée
110g egg whites
50g caster sugar
35g water
230g whipping cream

Soak the gelatine in cold water to cover. Heat the cherry purée in a small pan. Squeeze excess water from the gelatine, then add to the cherry purée and stir until melted. Leave to cool.

Whip the egg whites to soft peaks.

In a pan, dissolve the sugar in the water and heat to 120°C, then gradually whisk into the egg whites to make an Italian meringue.

Mix the purée into the meringue.

In a separate bowl, whip the cream to very soft peaks, then fold in the cherry mixture.

Pipe into the lined chocolate moulds (leaving enough room for the ganache) and chill to set.

FOR THE KIRSCH GANACHE

550g UHT cream
70g invert sugar
110g kirsch
3g salt
500g Amedei Chuao chocolate
    (70% cocoa solids), melted

Pour the cream into a pan. Add the invert sugar, kirsch and salt, and bring the mixture just to the boil.

Fold the cream mixture into the melted chocolate in 5 stages. Let the ganache cool down to 29°C.

Place 30x20cm bottomless, rectangular frames on a baking tray lined with baking parchment and pour in the ganache (550g in each). Leave overnight to fully set.

The next day, take off the frame with a hot knife. Leave at room temperature overnight.

Cut to the dimensions of the inside of the mould and freeze until solid. Place in the mould, pressing lightly into the cherry mousse.

FOR THE CHERRY PÂTE DE FRUIT

7.5g tartaric acid
7.5g water
350g caster sugar
13g pectin jaune
100g glucose syrup
500g cherry purée

Combine the tartaric acid and water in a small container and set aside.

Mix the sugar with the pectin and place in a pan with the glucose and cherry purée. Bring the mixture to the boil and reduce to 67° Brix.

Remove from the heat and add the tartaric acid solution. Divide the mixture between 2 PacoJet containers and allow to set.

Once set, blitz completely in the PacoJet machine and pass through a drum sieve.

Place in piping bags and pipe an even layer into the moulds across the ganache layer. Re-chill the filled moulds before proceeding to the next step.

FOR THE KIRSCH ICE CREAM

90g egg yolks
275g brown sugar
1kg milk
120g kirsch
635g soured cream

Whisk the egg yolks and brown sugar together in a bowl until light and creamy.

In a pan, heat the milk to 52°C. Gradually whisk it into the egg mixture.

Return the mixture to the pan and bring to 70°C, stirring constantly. Hold at this temperature for 10 minutes.

Strain through a fine sieve into a container set in a bowl of iced water and allow to cool.

Before churning, add the kirsch and soured cream to the base, mixing well to incorporate.

Churn in an ice-cream machine until -5°C. Cover and store in the freezer until needed.

TO ASSEMBLY, FINISH AND SERVE

olive oil biscuits (see above)
filled chocolate bar moulds (see above)
a little cherry purée
500g dark chocolate (70% cocoa solids),
    plus extra for shavings
200g cocoa butter
kirsch ice cream (see above)

Place the biscuits in the chocolate bar moulds, using the cherry purée to secure them.

Turn out the chocolate bars and heat a long slicing knife with a blowtorch. Slice the bars lengthwise, reserving only the centre sections (those pieces with 2 cut sides).

Chop the chocolate and cocoa butter and melt gently in a bain-marie. Pour into a paint spray gun and, working quickly, spray the cut sides evenly. Chill in the fridge prior to serving.

Run a small knife along a block of chocolate to make shavings.

Place the bars on a plate with a quenelle of ice cream. Finish with the chocolate shavings.

Place a golden ticket bar on top of each chocolate bar.

A Seventies Feast

OR THIS Feast I didn't have to raid the history books because I grew up in the 1970s, and the recipes could draw on my sense of the past. Nostalgia is important to me, particularly when it comes to cooking, because much of our enjoyment of food comes from the memories and associations that it triggers. Unfortunately, cuisine in Britain in the seventies was, frankly, awful. The home cook had to make do with a much less varied choice of produce: flaccid sliced white bread, spectacularly flavourless tomatoes and flabby overprocessed sausages. The only types of pasta widely available were spaghetti and macaroni, and olive oil could only be obtained from the chemist's, where it was sold as an earwax remover!

Nevertheless, this was my childhood, so I retain a huge affection for all kinds of dishes and foodstuffs that would hardly be considered gastronomic: butterscotch Angel Delight, Smash, Cresta ("It's frothy, man") and Corona ("Every bubble's passed its fizzical"), cheesecake, spag bol, prawn cocktail (which is still a secret vice of mine), cheese-and-pineapple sticks and, of course, loads of sweets and snacks—Hula Hoops, Marathon, Curly Wurly, Lyons Maid vanilla brick, pineapple Mivvi, Funny Faces, Lord Toffingham, Zoom...

The question was, could I take some of these things and turn them into something delicious, something that might transport my guests back to their childhood?

THE FRITTER AND THE SLIPPER

Spam, Spam, Spam, Spam
Hormel's new miracle meat in a can
Tastes fine, saves time
If you want something grand, ask for Spam

Spam jingle from the 1930s

There's a classic Monty Python sketch in which a typical Python couple (Mr Bun wears a narrow brown suit, trilby and Fair Isle sweater; Mrs Bun clutches her handbag tightly in front of her) are winched into a greasy-spoon café and ask about the menu. Among the choices are egg and Spam; egg, bacon and Spam; egg, bacon, sausage and Spam; Spam, egg, Spam, Spam, Bacon and Spam; Spam, Spam, Spam, baked beans, Spam and Spam; and lobster thermidor aux crevettes with a Mornay sauce garnished with truffle pâté, brandy, a fried egg and Spam. When Mrs Bun objects loudly that she doesn't want or like Spam, she's offered egg, bacon, Spam and sausage because that's not got much Spam in it. At which a point a bunch of Vikings at the corner table begin singing "Spam, Spam, Spam, Spam. Lovely Spam, wonderful Spam."

The scene is a piece of surreal madness—I've no idea why the Buns are winched in, nor what the Vikings are doing there—but it's spot-on about the ubiquity of Spam in the 1970s. When I was a kid, for school dinner we often had Spam fritters, usually accompanied by two gummy hemispheres of green-tinged mashed potato and peas like bullets or cabbage so soft that it squirted through the tines of the fork. I agreed with Mrs Bun: I didn't much like Spam either. But it was such an iconic symbol of 1970s grub that I felt I had to see if I could do something with it, and I was hoping I might find inspiration in *Spam: The Cookbook*.

Yes, incredible as it might seem, there exists a cookery book devoted entirely to Spam. Even more incredibly, its author is Marguerite Patten, a highly respected food writer. Leafing through the book, with its optimistic recipes for Spam scones and Chicken Cordon Bleu ("Spam's rich flavour makes it an ideal ingredient to use in stuffings for other

216

*Consulting the processed meat-lover's bible—*Spam: The Cookbook.

meats"), I began to suspect that Marguerite's enthusiasm was more
nostalgic than gastronomic. The first supplies of Spam came to Britain
from the US during World War II— they both enlivened the monotonous
wartime diet and helped boost a family's meat ration, which was limited
to the equivalent of two lamb chops per person per week. Under such
circumstances, anyone would develop a devotion to Spam and retain
fond memories of it. Patten had managed to work Spam into a number
of real seventies classics, like Spam pâté, Spam and pepper quiche and
Spam steaks in port wine. I was tempted to try out the Spam Porcupine,
in which cocktail sticks garnished with diced Spam, silverskin onions,
gherkins, pineapple chunks, avocado and glacé cherries are pushed

A master butcher discusses the meaty merits of the Spam Slipper.

into a head of cabbage. But in the end I settled for Spam Slippers, seduced as much by the name as by its culinary potential.

Of course, the camera crew weren't about to let me try this out in private, which is why I found myself at a stall in Oxford's Covered Market with a portable hob and oven and a neatly stacked pyramid of Spam's blue and yellow tins to show what I was up to. As I began to follow the recipe, halving and salting aubergines, then baking them and mashing the flesh, I would occasionally hear a passer-by say *"Spam!?"* under their breath, as though they couldn't quite believe it.

"Just push on," I told myself. I chopped up some onions and threw them in a pan with a little olive oil (I had decided I would ignore any objections of inauthenticity from blocked-ear sufferers of the 1970s), then added chopped garlic and a couple of skinned and chopped tomatoes and let it all soften and mingle before mixing in the aubergine pulp, paprika, fresh coriander, salt and pepper and, of course, finely chopped Spam.

I spooned the mixture back into the aubergine skins (keeping the green stalk on *had* made them look a little like pointy Turkish slippers), sprinkled grated cheese and breadcrumbs on top, and returned them to the oven for fifteen minutes. The result looked very much like the kind of thing that appeared in Cordon Bleu magazines of the period: a vaguely Greek-looking filling for vegetables perhaps. To me it tasted mainly of the herbs. I went in search of people to try out the dish.

My first customer had to be the old man in a thick fleece hat and bulky waterproof coat who'd been steadfastly waiting for a taste. "Delicious!" he asserted. "I like the aubergine. Good Mediterranean flavours. Excellent on a cold day like today."

"What about the Spam?"

"To me that tastes good too. But then isn't most mass-marketed pork reconstituted these days, so it's hard to tell the difference."

I moved onto a woman who, it turned out, was predestined to like the recipe. "I *love* Spam," she told me. "And so does my partner."

"What do you think of this?"

She put the thin slice in her mouth. "Is that aubergine? I'm not usually a fan of aubergine, but that's very nice, even though I can't really taste the Spam in there."

"How would you normally choose to eat Spam, then?"

"We have it in sandwiches. Or my partner does Spam fritters."

"Boy, you truly are a fan. Well, what about my dish? Would he go for it? Would he swap his fritter for a slipper?"

"Do you know, I reckon he just might!"

There were a few people who disagreed with the old man and the Spam-lover. One woman looked horrified at the idea of eating the dish and would only do so after I assured her that I'd tried it and it was okay. Her verdict was: "Inoffensive—that's the best you can say about it.

It's never going to replace *melanzane parmigiano*." However, most were quite happy to eat it, including several of the market's master butchers, whom you'd expect to be a bit scathing about processed meat, and the local community policeman, whom you'd expect to be reasonably honest. Most of them, however, said that they hardly noticed that Spam was an ingredient and I wondered if this was why the recipe had won approval.

I also realised that most of the recipes in *Spam: The Cookbook* seemed designed to hide the presence of the meat, which was hardly an approach that I could adopt for a Feast celebrating the 1970s. If Spam was to be included, it had somehow to be the star of the show.

SUPERSPAM

Maybe the way forward was to take Spam's basic components and replace them with better versions. First of all I checked out the list of ingredients on the side of the tin. Then I began by chopping up four different types of meat: free-range pork shoulder, two sorts of prosciutto cotto and some Spanish pata negra ham, which comes from acorn-fed pigs and is, without doubt, one of the finest (and most expensive) cured hams in the world.

These all went into a stainless-steel mixing bowl along with a little salt—I was stinting here because the pata negra also has a fair amount of salt—and some polyphosphates to help bind the meat-mix into a frankfurter-like emulsion. I then passed the mixture through a grinder and a food processor to give it a Spam-like smoothness. The tin's list mentioned water, but I decided to add chicken stock to the food processor instead, to give more richness and body.

The mixture swiftly amalgamated to a slippery paste that could be smeared against the side of the processor bowl. This was the sort of texture I was looking for—a kind of meat purée. I added plenty of freshly ground black pepper and a little powdered ginger, which works wonders for pork sausages, so I saw no reason why it wouldn't add something here, too. I smelled the mix. To my nose it already seemed better than the stuff out of a tin, but the real test would be once it was cooked. Spam is heated in its can in a pressurised environment, so I aimed to do the same. I put the purée in a Kilner jar in a pressure cooker and left it to cook for half an hour.

I couldn't at first place the smell that hit me as I lifted the pressure cooker's lid thirty minutes later. Then I got it—boloney—and hoped fervently that it wasn't a sign that all this research would turn out to be a load of old boloney. My assistant Otto's comment that it had "the aroma of a hot dog at the ballpark" didn't fill me with confidence either, but in fact the delicate texture and flavours were so good I began to wonder whether I couldn't develop it separately as a filling for tortellini. It had worked much better than I had expected, which was a relief, but it left me with a new question. How could I serve it in a way that was as unmistakably seventies as flared trousers and the Ford Cortina?

ICED CANAPES I: ROCKET SCIENCE

The appetisers for my Feasts had a lot of work to do. Not only did they have to whet the appetite, get the saliva going and set the standard for what was to follow, they also had to be instantly recognisable as belonging to a particular period and transport my guests back to that time. For the Seventies Feast I couldn't think of a better way to begin than with my favourite childhood lolly—Zoom, the rocket-shaped, three-coloured water ice on a stick that turned your tongue a funny colour. Just looking at it reminded me of long hot summer holidays and chaotic cricket games with my mates in Hyde Park. I was sure it would trigger memories for my guests, too.

Of course, there was no point in simply making a Zoom: that would hardly be surprising (except for the fact that it was being served in completely the wrong place in the meal). Besides, I wanted to bring to the experience a very childlike pleasure-in-the-unexpected, so I decided to give my guests what looked like a Zoom, with its layers of lime, lemon and strawberry, but turned out to have the flavours of

Preparing the apple and celery stripes of my savoury Zoom.

a 1970s party classic—Waldorf salad. I commissioned a miniature rocket-shaped mould and then began to consider which ingredients in the salad should represent the three stripes. I reckoned juiced red apples with the skin on would make a good stand-in for strawberry, particularly if I added some beetroot juice to get the kind of garish colour kids like.

One of the challenges with savoury lollies is keeping the sweetness in check—if there was too much sugar my guests' brains would flip into dessert mode, and the confusion would ruin the appetiser. The apple layer would need the addition of some acid to cut the sweetness, probably malic acid, which is present in apples and softer than citric acid. For the green layer, on the other hand, I was thinking of using celery, so there wouldn't be the problem of sweetness, though I'd need to incorporate something fruity, such as grapes, to temper celery's saltiness, and if I was going to get a nice brash colouring in this stripe, I would almost certainly have to add some chlorophyll (an extract from plant leaves).

For the final layer, I wanted to use walnuts because they're such a distinctive feature of the Waldorf salad. I roasted a handful, put them in milk, let them infuse for a while, then blitzed and strained the liquid and tasted the result. It definitely had the nutty note I was looking for. Excitedly, I began to build my savoury Zoom, pouring into the mould first the walnut milk and letting it freeze, then the juiced apple and flat wooden stick and letting that freeze, and then the celery juice. It was a slow process, but eventually it was ready.

It looked great—the tiny size was really enchanting—and it tasted great, too. The lolly captured the flavours of a Waldorf salad, and the controlled sweetness meant the experience was wonderful rather than weird. It might need a few adjustments, but my first iced canapé was a success. Now I had to find a couple of others to go with it. I started looking for suitable candidates among the lollies I remembered: Captain Rainbow? Star Wars? Red Devil? Totem Pole? Jelly Terror? Rev? Orange Quench? Smashers? Mr Merlin's Magic Purple Potion? Cola Rola? King Kong?…

THE POT FACTORY

The taxi driver reached the outskirts of the Welsh town of Crumlin and wound his way through the streets of a housing estate. I was beginning to think we'd come to the wrong place when suddenly I found myself facing a large, grey, hangar-like building fronted by a large sign with the words POT NOODLE surrounded by that familiar brash red-and-yellow starburst—the factory where the snack has been made ever since it first appeared in 1979.

I'd come here because when I was a kid I found it really exciting to be able to pour hot water into a pot to produce, as if by magic, a meal. (The original owners, Golden Wonder, had taken the idea from Japanese cuisine and there was simply nothing else like it in Britain at the time.) I hoped to make my own retro version of Pot Noodle and perhaps use it as a vehicle for another mini-obsession of mine: edible packaging. At the Fat Duck I already served Apple Pie Caramels in cellophane wrappers that could be eaten along with the sweet, and I had been playing around with ideas for edible drinks bottles and soup packets. Maybe this was an opportunity to develop some of these further.

The factory's health and safety procedure was stringent and it felt like entering a nuclear zone. After putting on thick-soled protective shoes, blue overjacket, dayglo gilet, miniature ear-defenders and a hairnet, I removed my watch and swapped my pen for one that would pass through the metal detector, then followed the detailed instructions for washing my hands using taps that were operated by the elbow, after which I pushed through the double doors with Stephen Lewis, my guide for the day, and stepped onto the factory floor.

It soon became evident why we needed ear-defenders. Bulky steel machines moved the pots through the various parts of the filling process, hissing and clanking and clattering as they did so. Forklifts raced around the building, sirens blaring, to be answered by periodic wails from some other piece of technology. The air smelled of tomato soup and flour, and this, coupled with sirens' insistent calls, produced an almost hypnotic state. In their blue overalls and hairnets, the workers looked unreal and almost Oompa-Loompa-like.

Hot noodles for Pot Noodles.

"Let me take you through the Pot Noodle process," said Stephen loudly, bringing me back to business. "Most people think this is just an assembly line but in fact the noodles are made from scratch. We mix flour, water, salt and firming agents—potassium carbonate and sodium carbonate—to create a pasta dough. Then we put it through this machine." He waved his hand at a sort of wire-meshed cage that housed a series of spinning rollers. "It's a lot bigger than a home pasta machine but it does the same job, rolling the dough to a very thin sheet and then feeding it over a grooved cylinder that cuts it into noodles."

We walked to the end of the machine and, sure enough, fat squiggles of dough emerged and shimmied along a conveyor belt. "Now they are

The Pot Noodle factory gets a new inspector.

dropped into a steamer to cook," Stephen explained, pointing to the stainless-steel steamer with the shape and dimensions of an old-fashioned locomotive. Vapour gusted out of various outlets. Once again we walked to the far end of the machine. The noodles were now yellow and had drooped and flattened, giving the conveyor belt a shagpile appearance. (Very seventies!) The belt ascended steeply to where a line of nozzles washed away excess starch, and by the time the noodles dropped into view again they were in little grey tubs.

"Now comes the frying," Stephen shouted over the machinery. It was proving hard to film amid all the noise. "Some of the water molecules in the noodles get replaced by oil molecules."

226

"Yes, I see. That'll give the noodles texture. A bit of bite." They came out of the fryer tangled into compact, pot-shaped lumps and gave off that characteristic fried aroma you get in Chinese takeaways.

"Now all they need is a stint in the cooler and they're ready. Here, try the end product before it goes in the pot," said Stephen, handing over a lump. I nibbled a few of the broken, brittle strands. They had a nicely savoury flavour, like breadsticks, which definitely gave Pot Noodle a lot of its character. But what about the other ingredients?

"Has the Pot Noodle recipe changed much over time?"

"Not really. We've brought out all kinds of different versions over the years—with rice rather than noodles, or with fish. We've done a casserole. We've even done desserts like Apple and Blackberry. Basically, if it can be put in a pot, we've done it. But the Chicken and Mushroom Pot Noodle—which is still the biggest seller—has pretty much stayed the same. We add less salt now, that's all."

"Thanks for the potted history, Stephen. Can you tell me what goes into the Chicken and Mushroom Pot Noodle?"

"Got it here all ready for you, Heston." He took me over to a work surface covered with plastic tubs containing pale-coloured powders. "Mushrooms, sweetcorn, chives," he explained, spooning an amount of each into a mixing bowl. "Each of these is freeze-dried."

"I find people are often dismissive of freeze-drying," I said. "But it's a good method of preserving flavour. Better in many ways than a process that involves heat, such as canning, which destroys some of the freshness and often gives the ingredients a cooked aspect."

"Absolutely," Stephen agreed. "A herb and spice mix goes in too."

"Of course. That would give the noodles colour and flavour. Where's the chicken?"

"Actually, it's not chicken but soy protein."

"What? Even in the seventies?"

"Yep. Right from the start. Okay, we need to add some flour to the bowl and some maltodextrin."

"The low-sweetness sugar? That's proved a very useful ingredient for me. I've used it to make all sorts of savoury ices—sardine-on-toast sorbet, that kind of thing. For a long time I dreamed of using it to make savoury candyfloss, but it didn't work out."

"Savoury candyfloss?" Stephen replied. I couldn't tell whether he was bemused by the idea or trying to work out whether he could put it in a pot. The coarse powder in the bowl was turmeric yellow, flecked with green from the chives, until I stirred in the salt, which paled down the mixture. "That's it," Stephen said. "That's what goes in the pot."

I ate a spoonful of the powder. It had a salty, savoury taste that reminded me above all of crisps. Where did this leave me in terms of recipe development for my Feast? I wasn't sure. But maybe I'd found a couple of raw ingredients that I could work with.

ICED CANAPES II: A TWISTER WITH A TWIST

... Haunted House? Dalek's Death Ray? Crime Squad? Bionic? Space 1999? Orange Maid? Lolly Gobble Choc Bomb?... There were so many lollies I could choose from to make my savoury appetisers.

Or were there? Each of my three appetisers needed to have an appearance so distinctive that my guests would instantly recognise it. And each had to contrast with the other two in terms of appearance and flavour. And they had to have colours that could be replicated with savoury ingredients, and that corresponded with some sort of savoury starter. And the whole thing had to work in a frozen format.

Very few lollies managed to meet all the criteria, but Twister's green and cream swirls and reddish centre reminded me of that 1970s hors d'oeuvre—smoked salmon and avocado with a blob of horseradish. I reckoned it'd be easy enough to turn one into the other: trim some salmon fillet into a long, thin baton and wrap it tightly in clingfilm to give it a cylindrical shape, then push a stick into it. Pipe alternate lines of avocado mousse and horseradish cream next to each other on a sheet of clingfilm, then put them in the fridge to set. Unwrap the salmon cylinder, place it on top of the stripes, wrap the clingfilm around, then carefully peel it off, leaving the cream and green lines curved round the salmon. Seal the join of the stripes with a warmed palette knife.

A batch of savoury Twisters.

PLAYAWAY

As I've said, for me the best thing about Pot Noodle was that magical hot-water-induced transformation. I wanted to create a dish that gave my guests a similar thrill of the unexpected. I'd read somewhere that Play-Doh is edible (which made sense: after all, kids are bound to put it in their mouths), so I decided to begin by trying to make Play-Doh noodles, hoping that working with kids' stuff might give me an idea for how to induce a childlike sense of wonderment in my guests.

Once again I had with me a portable hob, but this time I wasn't in a market but on the first floor of Hamleys toyshop. Before me, a crowd of children had already gathered and were scrutinising my every move. So far, they didn't look impressed. I willed the stockpot to boil more quickly, prised the lid off a tub of pale green Play-Doh and got a big hit of that unmistakable odour—perfumed and rubbery all at the same time. I pulled off a large chunk, rubbed it between finger and thumb to make a narrow cylinder, and pushed it into the extruder.

Pasta is made by forcing dough through shaped dies (the best versions use bronze dies that impart a wonderful texture; others use nylon dies that produce something smooth and bland). Fashioning Play-Doh involved exactly the same process, except that my extruder was a four-inch-high model of a wide-eyed baby with a pattern of little holes in his head. I pressed down the lever and thin snakes of Play-Doh began to sprout from the baby's bald bonce, provoking laughter from the kids and giving him a swiftly changing range of hairstyles—skinhead, flat-top, bob, afro, shaggy perm, hippy. I upended the baby, ran a knife across his locks so that they dropped into the pan of now-boiling water, and let them cook for half a minute before draining them and adding soy sauce for flavouring (and also as a little nod to Pot Noodle, which sometimes comes with its own packet of soy).

I put the noodles in my mouth and spat them out almost at once, to more laughter. "That is truly unpleasant. Not even soy sauce can rescue those noodles." The texture was bizarre—slimy and slithery—and the taste appalling. They were incredibly salty. On the side of the tub I noticed a warning: NOTICE TO PARENTS: CONTAINS WHEAT.

What better way to make Play-Doh pasta than by extruding from a baby's head?

Perhaps it should also say TASTES HORRIBLE! Play-Doh might be non-toxic, but no one should actually eat it. "Kids, *don't* try this at home."

It seemed unlikely that they would. In fact they were getting restless. Clearly they had expected to see more than a chef cooking food for thirty seconds and then spitting it out. I hurried on to the second part of my demonstration—Play Dough.

The internet is full of websites that give a recipe for Play Dough. It's offered as a cheap way of making a version of Play-Doh but, since it's basically pasta dough, it suited my purpose perfectly. I grabbed hold of a plastic cup from a toy cooking set and started measuring equal quantities of flour and water into a tiny mixing bowl. To this

I added some cream of tartar and a drop or two of red food colouring to get a kind of raspberry gloop. This was more like it; a couple of children who'd been on the verge of leaving crowded in closer.

The small plastic spatula wasn't up to the mixing process and promptly Uri Gellered into a U. I scooped the mix onto a floured board and began kneading. Given that I had to push this through the head of a wide-eyed baby rather than a bronze pasta dye, the dough had to be very loose. I added some olive oil and worked it until I had what I hoped was the right consistency, let it rest as long as I thought my audience would tolerate, then extruded it into the pan. A couple of minutes later I asked: "Who wants to eat some Play Dough pasta?"

"*Meeeee*," chorused the kids, their faces alight with a mixture of curiosity and excitement at the prospect of doing something ridiculous. As wide-eyed, in fact, as Baby Extruderhead. I spooned the noodles into a little yellow plastic frying pan and offered them round.

"They look like big pink worms," observed one boy, giggling as he tried to manoeuvre the strands onto his fork. "But it tastes like ordinary pasta!" said a dark-haired girl in a white parka. The boy next to her ate his portion, nodded solemnly as though lost in the possibilities of this new foodstuff, then thrust out his plate for more. "Is your name Oliver, by any chance?" I teased. I moved on down the line and met with the same response throughout. Everyone seemed to like the noodles, and everyone seemed surprised by this. Somehow I had to pull off a similar surprise for the guests at my Feast, but it was going to take more than a kids' playset to do it.

TRIFLING WITH THE PIC 'N' MIX

When I was a child, the Pic 'n' Mix counter was always exciting, not because the sweets were particularly great (I found them way too sweet and I was keener on chocolate—Freddo Frog, the Pink Panther bar, Caramac), but because of the total freedom to choose whatever you liked. Kids I knew would fantasise about taking this even further—instead of a cardboard carton they'd fill a big pot with the stuff, and they'd do so *for free*! And now here I was, in perhaps the most famous toyshop in the world, doing exactly that.

Pic 'n' Mix was such an iconic feature of childhood in the 1970s and still has such an emotive power over anyone who grew up in the period that I felt I had to find a way of introducing it to the Feast in some form. I'd decided to start by trying to make a trifle using only Pic 'n' Mix. A daft idea perhaps, but one that I hoped would work a bit like jazz improvisation and take me somewhere interesting.

Glow Worms, Turtles, Cable Bites, Kola Cubes, Midget Gems, Giant Spiders, Octopuses, Fried Eggs, Baby Gobstoppers, Dolly Mixture, Vanilla Fudge... I hadn't eaten any of these for years, yet even the names on the bank of little plastic drawers made me nostalgic. I nibbled the top of a Milk Bottle. Oddly, there was a hint of oak in there. What was *that* doing in a child's sweet? I flipped open the next drawer and bit the head off a shocking pink Foam Shrimp. It was even more grainy and synthetic-tasting than I remembered but I enjoyed the way it made me feel like a kid again, and how it triggered old memories. I tried a Foam Banana. Despite being a different colour, name and shape, it tasted exactly like the shrimp, but maybe it had a place in my trifle. As a kid I liked bananas mashed with a little brown sugar and served with lots of custard—so why not add Foam Bananas to the custard layer?

I had found my first ingredient. I was up and running. The Toasted Teacakes caught my eye. They turned out to be surprisingly edible, with a nice coconut flavour that'd go with banana. In the pot they went.

As well as a custard layer, the trifle needed a jelly layer. I chose Wine Gums over Octopuses because they seemed more acidic and I needed to counteract the cloying sugariness of most of what was on offer. (I had noticed Hamleys was selling small yellow drums of the unbelievably sour sweets called Toxic Waste and had decided that, in an emergency, I'd dump a load of them into the mix.) I had no idea what setting agent the retailers used to set the gums, but I had to work fast if I wanted my jelly to set in time for me to try the trifle out on customers before the store closed. I set aside my pot of Pic 'n' Mix and

Picking from the Pic 'n' Mix to make a very sweet trifle.

put three scoops of Wine Gums into a pan. (Ideally, they'd have all been one colour, so that I didn't end up with the murky brown you get if you mix lots of colours together, but there wasn't time for careful selection). I put the pan on the hob, poured in some hot water and began to stir vigorously.

Nothing happened. A weird cherryade aroma filled the air but the gums stayed stubbornly separate. Whatever setting agent had been used, it was heat-resistant. A quick sprint around the sweets section scanning ingredients lists revealed that Haribo Strawberries were made with gelatine so into the pan they went instead, with the juice from a tin of raspberries. It melted. I tasted. Very, very sweet. But at least I'd got my first layer. I poured it into a bowl, pressed in sponge fingers, and into the fridge it went to set while I got the custard going.

I poured 600ml double cream into the pan, threw in a scoop or two of Foam Bananas, a handful of Toasted Teacakes and then heated and stirred. The mixture took on the intense bright yellow of the Bananas, giving it a highly unnatural appearance. I put a spoonful in my mouth and got a hit of warm liquid banana that reminded me of something. Nesquik? No—Angel Delight! It was lumpy and I had no sieve to hand, but it seemed quite 1970s to have lumpy custard so I emptied it on top of my jelly layer and sent the bowl off for another fridge session. When it came back I sprayed whipped cream on top in dainty little blobs and, for a final seventies touch, scattered over chocolate sprinkles. It looked artificial enough to be from the period, but how did it taste? To me it was faithful to my childhood memories. "That is synthetic and sweet and not at all enjoyable," I told the camera crew as I reluctantly set off to find people to try it, "and I bet you no one likes it."

I lost the bet. Everyone else thought it tasted really good. One young woman even exclaimed, "Lordy—It's like the trifle of my dreams has returned." I thanked her, but in despair. "I just don't get it," I said. "If people really like this, then the world is truly mixed-up. Pic 'n' Mixed-up." Still, while I might worry about the nation's tastebuds, this was good news for my Feast. If Pic 'n' Mix worked its magic here, I'd find a way of getting it to work its magic on my guests too.

USING MY NOODLE

Sometimes the tiniest detail turns out to be the catalyst for a recipe (my Snail Porridge, for example, sprang from a mistranslation on a Chinese menu). With the Pot Noodle-themed dish for my Feast, inspiration came from the little sachet of soy sauce that the factory put in some of its pots.

The sachet was a reminder that Pot Noodle was originally inspired by Japanese cuisine, and I realised that a surefire way to bring some gastronomic character to my version was to return the dish to its roots. Dashi—the Japanese stock made from gently cooking kelp and then briefly infusing dried bonito flakes in the liquor—works well as the foundation for a dish because it's packed full of the "fifth taste", umami. Dashi, then, could be my recipe base, and I'd introduce other Japanese elements to it, as well as some of the usual Pot Noodle ingredients—an East-meets-West of freeze-dried spring onions, sesame seeds and dried kombu, plus freeze-dried sweetcorn and peas. I had a picture of a bowl containing a neat coil of Asian noodles, surrounded by cubes of mushroom, chicken and dainty green herb leaves, over which the dashi could be poured to make a broth.

This was sure to be delicious, but it was hardly astounding. I really wanted my guests to enjoy the kind of excitement I'd had when I first ate Pot Noodle as a kid—the magic of hot water creating a soup—and began to cast around for ideas. In Hamleys I had said that it would take more than a kid's playset to spring that kind of surprise, yet what I eventually came up with wasn't that far off, and kept faith with the oriental logic of the dish. There's an old-fashioned Japanese implement for making noodles called a tokoroten-tsuki. It's basically a long rectangular box with mesh over one end, and open at the other. A long fat strip of gelled dashi is inserted in the open end and then a kind of long-handled, square-headed mallet is pushed into the opening, forcing the gel out through the mesh to become noodles.

Along with the bowl of cubed mushrooms and coiled noodles, I could give each guest a tokoroten-tsuki, a beaker of hot water and a teapot. They'd be encouraged to make their own noodles, extruding

Filling edible packets with freeze-dried veg for melting in my Pot Noodle.

Pushing gelatine-set dashi through a tokoroten-tsuki, a Japanese noodle extruder.

them into the teapot. This would be fun, I reckoned, but there'd be another surprise in store. Rather than make the noodles with a heat-resistant gel like agar-agar, I'd use gelatine, which would dissolve as the water was poured on. The noodles would appear to vanish and be replaced by the dashi.

And that's when the little soy sauce sachet gave me a second idea. I could put my East-West freeze-dried dashi flavourings into little edible-cellophane packets in a plastic pot. The guests would pour their noodles-turned-dashi into their very own Pot Noodle to create the soup that would then be poured into the bowl of chicken, noodles and mushrooms.

TAKING PIC ’N’ MIX TO THE MAX

I hoped to get my guests as excited by Pic ’n’ Mix as they would have been as kids. It was a tall order, but I had reckoned I could do it by constructing a GIGANTIC Flying Saucer. At the TV company’s set-design warehouse I’d enthusiastically melted three thousand normal-sized Flying Saucers in water, ready to make one big one. Now I stared down at a brightly coloured mulch that refused to dry, like a primary school papier mâché project gone wrong. *Effort: A. Attainment: E.*

But then I began to wonder whether I was overthinking this anyway. I hadn’t particularly liked Pic ’n’ Mix as a kid, yet just seeing and eating the sweets in Hamleys, after a gap of thirty years, had been both fun and nostalgic. Why shouldn’t my guests feel the same? And why shouldn’t I serve them a selection of my own versions of Pic ’n’ Mix? They could look totally authentic; the surprise would be that they would taste absolutely fantastic—full of complex, unexpected, grown-up flavours.

Once I’d got the idea, some of the sweets proved easy to do. After all, many of the Pic ’n’ Mix are a triumph of form rather than content. Mice, cola bottles, bananas—we delight to the fact that they look like particular things. I commissioned shrimp moulds and filled them with a mixture of vanilla ice cream and rhubarb sorbet (giving my guests a 2-for-1 Pic ’n’ Mix—a Foam Shrimp *plus* a Rhubarb-and-Custard). After they’d been frozen and sprayed with a combination of white chocolate, pink colouring and cocoa butter to give a suede-like finish, they looked absolutely spot-on.

As did the Fried Eggs I developed, which proved even easier to prepare, so long as you had a Dewar flask of liquid nitrogen to hand. From a visual point of view a Fried Egg is just a blob of yellow on top of a misshapen oval of something white. All I had to do was take something like fromage blanc and place it in a wok that had been made seriously cold by placing it over a bowl of liquid nitrogen for a while. The cold would gradually set the fromage blanc, after which I could dollop on mango purée (which has exactly the orangey-yellow of an egg yolk) and let that set.

Spooning mango purée onto nitro-set fromage blanc to create a Fried Egg.

I began to think about getting a 2-for-1 Pic 'n' Mix in here as well, maybe caramelising a small disc of brioche, then trimming the edges to turn it into a Toasted Teacake. The Fried Egg could, of course, be served on top.

I was beginning to wonder, too, whether I could put the Fat Duck's newly acquired sugar-blowing skills to good use. For the Fairy Tale Feast, I'd employed the technique to create red-and-green apples. Their delicate blown-sugar "skin" had shattered perfectly in the mouth to let through all the texture and flavour of the boar's heart parfait. The round shape and glossy sheen of a blown sugar ball would look exactly like a Gobstopper, particularly if it was given the kind of garish

Flocking a Foam Shrimp.

in-yer-face colour that attracts children. When my guests bit in, the crunchy shell could give way to... what? I figured I would pipe into the shell a filling of fromage blanc set with gelatine and flavoured with ingredients that were fragrant or a bit acidic. Orange flower water was a definite candidate, possibly mixed with bergamot to add a perfumed Earl Grey characteristic. I could see a place here, too, for finger limes, a citrus fruit from Australia that looks like a browned chipolata but its pulp has a nice crunch and a real citric sharpness that makes you shiver. And I wondered whether I might be able to spring a little surprise as well—add a bit of Space Dust to the mix in the Gobstopper perhaps, just to get my guests' eyes to widen like a kid's...

ICED CANAPES III: A FEAST FOR A FEAST

Waldorf salad, smoked salmon and avocado… Another standard starter of the 1970s was chicken liver pâté. If I put it in a flattish, tongue-shaped mould, froze it, dipped it in gelatine plus something that would produce a chocolate-like sheen (maybe a mix of fig compote and port?), then sprinkled it with lightly caramelised almonds, wouldn't it look like a Wall's Feast?

TRUFFLED, STUFFED AND BATTERED

I had continued developing my deluxe version of Spam, which now consisted of twice-ground pork back fat and shoulder mixed with pata negra and a filler made of bread and cashew nuts. Sausage-makers often add ice cubes to the meat mixture to keep it cold (which prevents microbial activity and preserves the freshness of the ingredients), but I realised I could use the technique for the purposes of luxury as well as hygiene, so I froze cubes of truffle juice and added them to the grinder along with the meat.

I hadn't originally intended to produce something with such an expensive list of ingredients—a tin of it would have cost easily more than £100—but I have to admit I was amused by the idea of taking a convenience food and turning it into an indulgence. So I added one final extravagant ingredient: half a litre of mixed port, white port, Madeira and brandy reduced right down to a single tablespoon of the most complex and super-concentrated sauce imaginable. The mother of all reductions!

Making Spam Slippers in Oxford had convinced me that there was little to be gained from disguising the meat as something else. I had decided instead to give my guests a taste of my school life by serving them fritters (although the ones I'd had at school didn't come to the table encased in a lovely light tempura batter sprinkled with Japanese breadcrumbs for extra crunch). And I wanted to garnish the fritters with all the things I remembered from the dinner hall, such as the peas and lumpy gravy. The peas could be cooked delicately, puréed and

A savoury Feast lolly and the truffled pea filling for my fritter.

Dipping the Spam fritter into a Japanese tempura batter.

then stuffed inside the fritter itself, perhaps with a little chopped black truffle, but I also wanted the plate to contain something that resembled the hemispherical scoop of mash that, for me, was the biggest memory-trigger of 1970s school dinners.

The problem was that school-dinner mash was scoopable because it had been cooked to the point where it was more like wallpaper paste than potato. I needed to find a way of shaping a smooth, buttery potato purée, and wondered whether coating it around another ingredient would help it hold together. Puzzling over dilemmas like this sometimes gives rise to other ideas. I reasoned that if I fashioned cabbage into a ball, wrapped it in clingfilm, steamed it for three to four minutes

Cookery school—the set for a Seventies Feast inspired by my childhood.

—rather than the dinner ladies' boil-to-mush approach—and then wrapped the purée around the cabbage, I could both solve my potato problem and introduce another of my school-dinner memories.

I tried a simple version and it worked. So long as it continued to work once I had added a few other flavourings to the cabbage (onion, pancetta, a little chilli, maybe some sauerkraut for freshness and acidity), my dish was ready apart from the gravy, and I already had a great idea for how to serve that—in a taper-necked milk bottle with a silver foil top, just like we used to have at school. As I got on with the business of developing gourmet lumps for my gravy, I found myself quietly chanting, "Thatcher, Thatcher, milk snatcher." ❉

247

MENU

✻

Mr Softee's Special Savoury Lollies

*Waldorf Salad Zoom, Chicken Liver Parfait Feast,
Smoked Salmon and Avocado Twister*

✻

Posh Pot Noodle

*Agar Noodles, Chicken Thighs, Button Mushrooms and
Dashi Broth, Edible East-meets-West Sachets:
Freeze-dried Sweetcorn and Peas; and Freeze-dried
Spring Onions, Sesame Seeds and Salted Kombu*

✻

❅

School Dinner

*Spam Fritter with Pea, Cabbage and Black Truffle Centre,
Cabbage and Mash Scoop, Lumpy Bone Marrow Gravy*

❅

Pic 'n' Mix Deluxe

*Rhubarb & Custard Foam Shrimp, Gobstopper,
Pine Sherbet Fountain,
Nitro-fried Egg on a Toasted Teacake*

Smell of a Sweetshop on a Flying Saucer

❅

WALDORF SALAD ZOOM

FOR THE WALNUT LAYER
250g shelled walnuts
300g whole milk

Preheat the oven to 180°C.

Place the walnuts on a tray and roast in the oven for 8–10 minutes until lightly browned.

Place the hot walnuts in the cold milk and allow to infuse in the fridge for 2 hours.

Using a hand blender, lightly break up the walnuts and then pass through a fine-meshed sieve, reserving the milk.

Pour 2g of the walnut milk inside each rocket mould with an ice-lolly stick in the centre. Allow to freeze until solid.

FOR THE APPLE LAYER
1kg Cox's apples
0.05g malic acid
0.75g beetroot juice

Remove the cores from the apples and push them through a juicer.

Strain the liquid through a fine-meshed sieve and weigh out 160g of juice (the apple juice should register 35° Brix; if it is lower, then add fructose to resolve as needed).

Combine the apple juice with the malic acid and beetroot juice.

Take the frozen rocket moulds out of the freezer and add 5g of the apple mixture to each one to create a second layer.

Put the moulds back into the freezer and allow to freeze completely before adding the last layer.

FOR THE CELERY LAYER
1 head of celery, washed
1 bunch of green grapes
0.2g chlorophyll extract

Juice the celery and then the grapes in the juicer, straining the liquid into separate containers.

Weigh out 50g of celery juice and 30g of the grape juice and combine the two, then add the chlorophyll.

Take the frozen moulds out of the freezer and pour 8g of juice into each of them for the final layer.

Allow to freeze completely, then remove from the mould when ready to serve.

POSH POT NOODLE

FOR THE DASHI BROTH
15g rishiri kombu (kelp)
1.5kg low-calcium mineral water
60g katsuo bushi (dried bonito flakes)

Wipe the kombu with a damp cloth, then place it in a pan with the water and heat to 60°C. Hold at this temperature for 1 hour.

Remove and discard the kombu. Raise the temperature of the water to 80°C. Turn off the heat and immediately add the katsuo bushi.

After 10 seconds, strain the stock through a sieve lined with damp muslin, allowing the stock to run through freely without pressing. Discard the solids and allow the stock to cool.

FOR THE GELATINE-SET DASHI
500g dashi broth (see above)
white soy sauce
25g leaf gelatine

Season the dashi with the white soy sauce to taste. Add the gelatine and allow it to soften, then heat the mixture gently to melt the gelatine.

Pour into a rectangular container, place in the fridge and leave until set.

Cut the set mixture into strips that fit into a torokoten tsuki (Japanese noodle cutting machine) and reserve until needed.

FOR THE AGAR-SET DASHI NOODLES

500g dashi broth (see above)
10g agar agar
35g tamari soy sauce

In a Thermomix, blend the dashi on medium speed, bringing the temperature up to 100°C.

Add the agar agar and blend for 2 minutes. Turn off the heat, add the tamari and quickly pour into a container. Allow to set.

Cut the set mixture into strips that fit into the torokoten tsuki and extrude into noodles. Reserve until needed.

FOR THE EDIBLE SACHETS

200g water
3g leaf gelatine
freeze-dried peas
freeze-dried corn
toasted white sesame seeds
salted kombu (Fujiko Kombu), finely
   chopped
freeze-dried spring onion

Combine the water and the gelatine in a saucepan and allow the gelatine to soften. Bring the water to the boil, stirring continuously to melt the gelatine.

Using a pipette, deposit 6g of this solution into individual Petri dishes (9cm in diameter) and swirl the liquid to evenly coat the bottom. Tap the dishes to break any air bubbles.

Place the Petri dishes on racks and cover lightly with parchment to prevent any dust from settling onto the films while they dry.

Dry the films for 20–25 hours in a warm room, or until the films are completely dry and can be peeled off the Petri dishes. Before proceeding, cut the wrappers into squares using thin, sharp scissors.

Using a heat-sealing bar, place two wrappers together evenly and seal on three sides. Spoon in a mixture of the peas, corn, sesame seeds, salted kombu and spring onions and seal the final side. Reserve until needed.

TO SERVE

dashi broth (see above)
agar-set dashi noodles (see above)
edible sachets (see above)
gelatine-set dashi (see above)

Preheat the oven to 75°C.

Heat a little dashi to 70°C in a pan, add the agar noodles and warm through.

Place the warm noodles into ring moulds on a baking tray and cover with heat-resistant clingfilm. Place in the preheated oven for 10 minutes.

After 10 minutes, transfer a ring of noodles to each serving bowl. Place the edible sachet in individual jugs and place 6 teapots over tea-lights to keep warm.

A torokoten tsuki is given to each guest with the dashi gel inside and the guests extrude the noodles into their teapots. When the noodles have melted, the hot liquid is poured over the edible sachets.

When the sachets have melted and the vegetables are soft and rehydrated, the contents of the jug are poured over the agar noodles to complete the dish.

"SPAM" FRITTERS

FOR THE JOSELITO PASTE
100g shallots, finely diced
3g garlic, crushed
20g olive oil
185g milk
75g double cream
90g brioche crumbs
450g Joselito ham, diced
150g toasted cashew nuts, ground

Sweat the shallots and garlic in the olive oil until translucent.

Add the milk and cream and bring to the boil. Add the brioche crumbs and stir until the liquid thickens, then remove from the heat and leave to cool.

When cool, add the diced ham and ground cashew nuts and mix thoroughly. Cover and chill in the fridge.

In the meantime, place the components of the grinder, including the 8mm and 3mm grinder plates, in the freezer to chill.

Grind the chilled mixture through the cold 8mm grinder plate into a bowl set over ice. Repeat through a 3mm grinder plate and reserve the paste in the fridge.

FOR THE PORK BASE
225g diced pork shoulder
170g diced pork back fat

Chill the components of the grinder, including the 8mm grinding plate, in the freezer. Semi-freeze the pork shoulder and fat.

Using the 8mm grinding plate, grind the diced shoulder and fat into a bowl set over ice. Reserve in the fridge until required.

FOR THE ALCOHOL REDUCTION
100g shallots, thinly sliced
3g garlic, crushed
15g thyme sprigs
150g Madeira
150g ruby port
75g white port
50g brandy

Combine all the ingredients for the alcohol reduction in a container and leave to infuse in the fridge for 24 hours.

In a pan, bring the mixture to the boil and reduce to a thick syrup (approximately 75g), stirring occasionally. Allow the mixture to cool and reserve.

FOR THE "SPAM" SHEETS
200g pork base (see above)
40g frozen truffle juice, broken into small pieces
4g salt
1g nutrifos
0.7g Prague powder
17g alcohol reduction (see above)
100g Joselito paste (see above)

Chill the components of the grinder, including the 3mm grinder plate, in the freezer.

Mix the cold pork base with the frozen truffle juice, salt, nutrifos and Prague powder and grind through the chilled 3mm plate into a bowl set over ice.

Add the alcohol reduction and Joselito paste and mix lightly. Place in a mixer fitted with a paddle attachment and mix until well combined (about 10–15 seconds). Place in the fridge until completely cold.

Roll out the mixture between two sheets of parchment to a 5mm thickness and freeze on baking trays.

FOR THE PEA PURÉE
500g frozen Birds Eye peas

Defrost the frozen peas on several layers of kitchen paper. Blot off as much moisture as possible while the peas defrost.

While the peas are still very cold, blend them to a purée in a food processor and pass through a fine sieve to remove the skins.

Quickly blend the peas again and pour into a PacoJet container. Freeze until solid.

Using the PacoJet machine, blitz the frozen pea purée again, holding down the air-release valve to prevent the mixture from becoming foamy. Re-freeze the pea purée. Repeat this process again, then reserve in the fridge.

FOR THE "SPAM" FRITTER

20g foie gras
60g pea purée (see above)
90g peeled frozen Birds Eye peas
15g black truffle, finely chopped
10g Savoy cabbage, finely shredded, sautéed in butter and cooled
salt and freshly ground black pepper
"Spam" sheets (see above)

Preheat a water bath to 60°C. Put the foie gras into a sous-vide bag and seal at medium pressure. Immerse in the water bath and cook for 1 hour. Remove the bag and allow to cool.

Dice the foie gras and fold into the pea purée with the peeled peas, black truffle and sautéed cabbage. Season with salt and pepper.

From the frozen sheets of "Spam", cut two 7 x 11cm rectangles (the base and lid); two 11 x 5mm strips (the sides); and two 6cm x 5mm strips (the top and bottom). Peel off the parchment and reserve in the freezer on a tray.

Take a square of parchment large enough to fit the "Spam" base and lay the base on it. Then position the bottom, sides and top on the fritter base and push down lightly, creating a recess.

Place 40g of the pea, foie gras and truffle mixture inside each fritter and spread evenly in the recess. Take the second "Spam" rectangle (the lid) and place on top, flush with all edges and press down to seal. Smooth any gaps or ridges with a small palette knife and return to a tray in the freezer until required.

TO SERVE

100g plain flour, plus extra for dredging
100g cornflour
6g salt
2g bicarbonate of soda
210g cold water
grapeseed or groundnut oil, for deep-frying
"Spam" fritters (see above)
50g Japanese panko breadcrumbs

In a mixing bowl set over ice, gently stir together the flour, cornflour, salt, bicarbonate of soda and water until just combined (being careful not to overmix; leave the mixture a little lumpy).

Heat the oil in a deep-fat fryer to 190°C. Preheat the oven to 150°C.

Deep-fry the "Spam" fritters one at a time: dredge the frozen fritter in flour and shake off the excess. Dip the fritter into the batter and coat completely before lifting out. Sprinkle the Japanese breadcrumbs around the top and sides, but not the bottom.

Gently place the fritter in the deep-fat fryer, shaking the basket gently so the fritter does not stick to the bottom. Cook until golden brown, then lift out and place on a wire rack. Repeat with the rest. Place the rack in the oven until the "Spam" filling reaches 55°C internally.

Remove from the oven and flash the fritter through the fryer for a final crisp up. Drain on kitchen paper before serving, with scoops of mashed potato and lumpy gravy.

RHUBARB & CUSTARD FOAM SHRIMPS

FOR THE CUSTARD ICE CREAM

 1kg milk
 100g egg yolks
 180g refined caster sugar
 650g tinned custard

In a pan, heat the milk over a medium heat until it reaches a temperature of 52°C. In the meantime, using a hand blender, blitz the egg yolks and sugar together until the mixture is light and creamy.

Once the milk has reached the temperature, add a little of it to the egg and sugar mixture in order to temper the eggs.

Return the mixture to the pan, combine with the rest of the milk and whisk continuously until the mixture reaches 70°C. Hold it at this temperature for 10 minutes, whisking from time to time.

Strain the mixture into a bowl set over ice to cool quickly.

Before churning, weigh out 800g of the ice-cream base and place in a bowl. Add the tinned custard to it and blitz using a hand blender until evenly blended.

In an ice-cream machine, churn the mixture until it reaches a temperature of -5°C.

Transfer the ice cream to a chilled container, cover and place in the freezer until required.

FOR THE RHUBARB SORBET

 1.6kg rhubarb, cut into 3cm pieces
 380g fructose
 320g grenadine
 fresh rhubarb juice

Put the rhubarb, fructose and grenadine in a pan and bring to the boil. Reduce until the liquid reaches 42° Brix.

Blitz the mixture with a hand blender and pass the purée through a fine-meshed sieve; allow to cool completely.

Before churning, add fresh rhubarb juice to the purée until it reaches 22° Brix. Pour the mixture into PacoJet containers and freeze completely.

In an ice-cream machine, churn until the mixture reaches a temperature of -5°C. Transfer the sorbet to a chilled container, cover and place in the freezer until required.

FOR THE RHUBARB PÂTE DE FRUIT

 500g rhubarb purée
 100g glucose
 350g sugar
 13g pectin
 7.5g malic acid
 7.5g water

Place the rhubarb purée and glucose in a pan. Mix the sugar and pectin in a bowl, then add to the pan and bring up to a simmer. Continue to heat until the temperature reaches 106°C, stirring continuously.

Dissolve the malic acid in the water. Take the pan off the heat and then stir in the malic acid solution.

Pour the mixture into a PacoJet container. Allow the mixture to cool and set.

Run through the PacoJet machine and reserve until required.

FOR THE PINK CHOCOLATE SPRAY

 400g cocoa butter
 red food colouring
 800g white chocolate

In a small pan, melt 75g of the cocoa butter. Once melted, add red food colouring to make an intense red paste.

Put the white chocolate and remaining cocoa butter in a bowl and place over a pan of simmering water to melt, stirring with a spatula from time to time.

Begin to add some of the red paste to the melted chocolate and cocoa butter until it becomes pink in colour.

Place the coloured chocolate back in the bowl over the pan of simmering water until ready to serve.

TO SERVE
custard ice cream (see above)
rhubarb sorbet (see above)
pink chocolate spray (see above)
rhubarb pâte de fruit (see above)

Put the ice cream and sorbet into separate piping bags fitted with medium nozzles.

Oil a plastic shrimp-shaped mould, then pipe the rhubarb sorbet in the bottom. Place the mould in the freezer for 10 minutes.

Take the mould out of the freezer and pipe the ice cream on top of the sorbet to form a second layer, scraping the top of the mould in order to obtain a flat surface. Return to the freezer for 1 hour.

Fill a shallow bowl with warm water. Take one of the shrimp moulds out of the freezer and briefly place it in the warm water to loosen the shrimp-shaped ice cream from the sides of the mould.

Remove each shrimp in this way and return them to the freezer for 1 hour.

In the meantime, fill a paint-spraying gun with the warm pink chocolate.

One by one, spray the shrimps with the melted pink chocolate until the entire surface is covered; place them back in the freezer as soon as they are sprayed.

When ready to serve, place a small amount of the rhubarb pâte de fruit on a plate and place a frozen shrimp on top.

"NITRO-FRIED EGG"

FOR THE "EGG WHITE"
150g hanged fromage blanc
10g icing sugar
90g lychee purée
5 drops lychee essential oil

Combine the ingredients together in a bowl, mix thoroughly and reserve in the fridge.

FOR THE "EGG YOLK"
300g water
6 leaves gelatine
1kg mango purée

Pour the water into a pan and bring up to a simmer.

In the meantime, soften the gelatine in cold water. Squeeze the excess water from the gelatine leaves, then add them to the simmering water. Stir to dissolve the gelatine.

Take the pan off the heat and allow the liquid to cool slightly before adding it to the mango purée. Blitz together using a hand blender.

Cover with clingfilm and place in the fridge until ready to assemble.

FOR THE VANILLA SALT
5g vanilla powder
60g Welsh salt

Blitz the ingredients together in a food processor and reserve.

TO ASSEMBLE
"egg white" (see above)
"egg yolk" (see above)
vanilla salt (see above)

Half-fill a polystyrene box with liquid nitrogen.

Place a flat metal tray on top and allow it to freeze for 3 minutes.

Using a small ladle, pour the "egg white" mixture onto the frozen tray and allow to spread, so that it resembles the white part of a fried egg.

Using a spoon, pour the "egg yolk" mixture in the centre of the white, to resemble the yolk. Allow to set.

Using a spatula, remove the "fried egg" from the tray and place on a plate in the fridge until ready to serve.

An Eighties Feast

LIKE THE Regency era, the 1980s was a time of excess and extravagance. The comedian Harry Enfield created a character who waved a fistful of notes in our faces while triumphantly bellowing, "LOADSAMONEY!" It became the catchphrase for the age. We earned more and spent more. Home ownership went up by twenty-five per cent, supermarket product lines doubled and wealth trebled (except for the lowest-paid, whose income went down significantly. The 1980s were—again like the Regency era—a time of social injustice that led to the Miners' Strike, the Brixton and Toxteth riots, and the poll tax riots. Unemployment reached three million.)

We also wanted more—faster food, longer opening hours, tougher workouts, wider shoulders, bigger hair. The voracious social climate made this a decade of fads: Rubik's cube, aerobics, New Romantics, breakdancing, rolled jacket sleeves in the style of *Miami Vice* (the must-see show), spandex, spritzers, power lunches. Naturally, food became as much of a commodity as everything else. New restaurants opened and experimented clumsily with nouvelle cuisine. People suddenly had fierce opinions about brands of mineral water or boasted about how they'd "discovered" sun-dried tomatoes. It's not surprising that the eighties saw the birth of the Foodie.

How did we manage to live this lifestyle and feed all these new appetites? Technology. The first mobile phones went on sale, although they were the size of a brick and cost £3,000. Homes gained microwaves for quick cooking, and video players and Atari games consoles for a quick fix of entertainment. The Sony Walkman allowed us to listen to music while doing other things. The answerphone allowed us to be in while we were out. Technology helped us to multitask, which was the only way to get through the fast-paced decade, so I wanted to build my Feast around this brave new world of gizmos and gadgets.

BOLLY AND THE BLUE NUN

"Greed… is good," declared Gordon Gekko, the slick-suited, slick-haired, conscience-free financial whizz-kid in *Wall Street*, and yuppies bought into his philosophy. Sales of Champagne went from ten million bottles in 1983 to twenty million in 1989, and plenty of it was guzzled by City traders who would celebrate a successful day by popping the cork of a bottle of Bollinger, Krug or Dom Perignon. Of course, such extravagance couldn't last. The financial boom was followed by a bust—the Black Monday crash of 19 October 1987, when the Dow Jones industrial average dropped massively and £50 billion was wiped off share values. It seemed appropriate that the appetiser for my Feast involved Champagne, but since in 2010 we were in the middle of another fiscal crisis, it also seemed appropriate to make it a credit-crunch bubbly. And I'd got a great idea for how to do this using a very eighties piece of kit: the SodaStream.

The SodaStream is basically a device that forces carbon dioxide gas into a liquid. Take the specially designed bottle, fill it with water and concentrated syrup, slot it into the machine, hit the button and *psssssssssssssssssssssStSHOOM!* You've got yourself a fizzy drink. As you can imagine, when these first became popular in the eighties, they seemed very glamorous and high-tech, and kids whose parents had got one couldn't resist showing it off to their mates. (Although, as far as I can remember, the performance was often a real let-down because the SodaStream had run out of gas. We would crowd around as the button was pressed. Instead of the much-anticipated high-pressure

Faking bubbly with a SodaStream in the City.

Ready to get a City boy to take the Blue Nun taste test.

explosive hiss, the machine would give out a feeble belch and we'd be left faking enthusiasm for a cup of dodgy flat cordial.) Now I was hoping to take an inexpensive white wine—the early eighties classic, Blue Nun—give it the SodaStream treatment, and see if modern-day moneymen could tell the difference between that and Champagne.

The place to do this was, of course, the City. I had set up a table in front of the Lloyd's Building, with its "exposed services as ornamental order" (architectspeak for "the plumbing is on the outside"). As glass lifts rocketed up and down the outside of the surrounding skyscrapers, I opened a bottle of Blue Nun and took a little swig. It tasted okay and even had the smell of sparkling wine—sweet and sort of fruity. "This is going to be good," I told the camera. "To be honest, I had my doubts about whether it would work, but now I reckon it just might. So let's get busy with the fizzy." I charged the SodaStream, filled the special bottle with Blue Nun, fed it into the slot, pressed the button, got the hiss and tasted the result. It was sweeter and less creamy than Champagne, but it was definitely close enough that, if you weren't in the know, you might well be fooled into thinking it was the real thing, or at least Prosecco or something like that.

I lined up glasses of fake fizz and true Champagne and went in search of someone to take the Taste Test. My first guinea pig wore tailored dark overcoat, crisp checked shirt and red polka-dot tie. "Which of these is Champagne?" I challenged him, and he guessed right. Maybe I was fooling myself, maybe this wasn't going to work after all. "What do you think the other one was?"

"Oh, I don't know. A nice sparkling wine?"

"Actually, it's Blue Nun that's been SodaStreamed."

"Well, I would never have guessed that!"

Maybe my little experiment could still come good. I approached a man in tailored grey overcoat, blue shirt and pink polka-dot tie. "Hello. Can you tell me which of these is Champagne?"

He took a slurp of each, considered and opted for the Nun.

"I'm sorry, but in fact it's the other one that's the real Champagne. Can you guess what this one is?"

"Oh, I don't know. Spumante? Cava?"

"What if I were to tell you that it's Blue Nun that has been put through a SodaStream?"

"I'd be amazed because I hate Blue Nun."

About a third of the people I asked thought that the Blue Nun was Champagne, and even those who guessed right had no idea what was in the other glass. They all thought it was a perfectly acceptable sparkling wine. This was a great start to the development of my starter. I hoped I could incorporate the SodaStream in the service of a dish, which would definitely give the meal an eighties feel, and could be a lot of fun, too.

HOW TO NOBBLE A LOBSTER

In the 1980s it wasn't only drink that involved a lot of showing off. The money-mad culture with its expense-account lunches offered equal opportunities for some serious culinary one-upmanship. I wanted to capture that grandstanding by including something suitably pricy in my Feast, like lobster. However, on its own a luxurious lobster recipe didn't scream eighties to me; I needed something else to make it recognisably of its time. So I trawled through contemporary cookbooks until I found the perfect candidate—the microwave oven.

The 1980s saw the social structure and economy of the country change: many more women entered the workforce. Many more people lived alone because they were divorced or living longer or just because they chose to; in the financial sector, work hours went up massively. To help cope with this, people began to rely on appliances like the microwave. Although commercial microwave ovens first appeared in America in the 1950s, take-up of the invention was slow—partly, I suspect, because of that widespread and weirdly selective fear of technology that causes people to dismiss the culinary potential of centrifuges and water baths and rotary evaporators, even though their kitchens are full of equally complicated devices such as refrigerators and fan-assisted ovens and food processors.

When microwave ovens began to appear in British homes, there were all kinds of rumours: if you didn't follow the correct procedures it would explode, or if you stood in front of the glass-panelled door while it was on, microwaves would cook your internal organs. These fears were due to a lack of understanding about the science involved: even now many people believe that microwaves cook from the inside out. In fact the oven uses microwaves (which, like radio waves, are waves of electromagnetic radiation) to produce an electric field that reverses direction billions of times a second. Since the water molecules in food behave like electric magnets and line up with the direction of a magnetic field—like a compass-needle seeking north—they end up constantly flipping and colliding with their neighbours, and the energy of this produces heat. A great way of demonstrating this is to make an ice tumbler by freezing a cup of water and hollowing out the centre, then filling it with water and putting it in the microwave. The water will boil before the tumbler melts—not because microwaves cook from the inside out but because the water molecules in the ice, trapped as they are in a rigid crystal latticework, can't easily flip back and forth.

Despite the misperceptions, by the mid-eighties microwave ovens were a feature in many households and microwave cookbooks appeared, cashing in on the new enthusiasm. In one of these I found a recipe for Lobster Thermidor. This seemed such an eighties clash of the classical and the brashly modern that I felt I had to try it out.

So I chopped onions and sliced button mushrooms, mixed them with butter, slid the bowl into the chamber, shut the glass-panelled door and hit the buttons for 2 minutes on FULL POWER, then removed the bowl, stirred and returned for 1 minute on FULL POWER.

I stirred in flour, seasoned "to taste". (An odd instruction that: at this point the mixture tasted of raw flour and onion. Salt and pepper wouldn't make much difference.) Gave it 1 minute on FULL POWER.

Gradually whisked in chicken stock and cream, then 2 minutes on MEDIUM POWER.

Removed the bowl, stirred and returned for another 2 minutes on MEDIUM POWER.

Separated an egg. Added a little of the hot mixture to the yolk (adding too much hot liquid all at once would have curdled the egg), then poured it back in the bowl, added some sherry and stirred. Back in the microwave for 3 minutes on MEDIUM POWER.

Removed cooked lobster from its shell. Flaked it and added it to the bowl. Gave it 3 minutes on FULL POWER. Rearranged. A final 2 minutes on FULL POWER.

Spooned the mixture into the lobster-shell halves and sprinkled it with grated Cheddar cheese and Parmesan. At this point, the recipe directed the cook to put the shells under the grill, but after taking the dish in and out of the microwave eight times, it seemed a bit faithless to forsake the machine at the final furlong. I whacked the mixture back in for a few minutes on FULL POWER.

I took out the finished dish and thankfully closed the microwave door for the last time. The result was a bit cheesy (in all senses) and a bit gloopy, though that was down to the amount of flour used, which could be adjusted. The main problem was that, as I expected, the lobster was obliterated. One of the problems with the microwave oven is that, since it works by agitating water molecules, ingredients with different water contents will cook at different rates. Cooking times, therefore, involve a lot of compromise, and that doesn't suit delicate items like lobster.

For me, though, the least practical aspect of the recipe was the fact that, in the end, it was barely quicker than cooking the whole thing from scratch, and the constant shuttling of the bowl in and out of the microwave meant I was stuck in the kitchen and unable to do anything else. So much for labour-saving! The recipe was indeed very eighties— in the sense that it was a triumph of style over content.

SLUSH YUPPIE

"It's arrived," Jocky told me on the phone. I left my office, walked down the narrow corridor to the Fat Duck lab and pushed open the door. The delivery was a five-foot-high, stainless-steel cuboid. At either side of it, a clear plastic tube extended upwards, like an antenna. Across the front was a shelf with six named dispensers: *Crushin' Cola, Snappy Strawberry, Sunshine Orange, Rip-roarin' Raspberry, Lickin' Lemon, Very Cherry*. Above, a giant model polystyrene foam cup printed with a picture of a dog in a blue woolly hat and jumper revolved endlessly. The Slush Puppie machine.

Just catching sight of it took me back to the eighties, and I figured it might do the same to my guests. My idea was to create a savoury Slush Puppie, so I poured the base mix into the machine and left it to freeze while I searched out some contenders for the flavouring. A couple of hours later I had a work surface full of tins and jars of pesto, baby beetroots, mulligatawny, French onion soup, whole gherkins, mustard, sweet 'n' sour sauce and pickled onions ready to try out.

A new Slush range: Totally Truffle, Blindin' Beetroot and Top Tomato.

First, though, I wanted to taste the original ingredients—for the first time in twenty-five years—so I pushed the handle on the machine to get a squirt of slushy ice, then pressed the plunger on a dispenser to get a shot of Rip-roarin' Raspberry, which for some reason was blue. "Looks like toilet cleaner," offered Jocky.

"That's a very synthetic flavour," I told the camera. "But I like the refreshing feel of the little bits of ice and the smoothness of them. If it was a bit less sweet, it could be nice." I tried Snappy Strawberry and got a similar tidal wave of sweetness. "Urgh! It's like a liquid version of Pic 'n' Mix. That's going to be the biggest problem—countering the sugary element in the base mixture."

Lush Puppie—the Beetroot & Sherry Vinegar Savoury Slush.

Nonetheless, I squirted out more slush, added a little cream of tomato soup and took a sip. At the start it was okay: the iciness brought a bit of welcome freshness, but eventually the sweetness took over and it became sickly. As I was tasting, Jocky had strained a jar of sweet 'n' sour sauce. He handed over a slushy cup of it. "That's just strange," was all I could say.

"Aye, it was sweet already. Now it's gone too far. Now it could be marketed as Very Sweet 'n' Sour Sauce."

"But if we cut down the sugar, we might lose the smoothness of the ice granules."

"Here's the next, Heston. French onion soup."

I tasted—and grimaced. Jocky just laughed. This wasn't working. Clearly I'd have to change my tactics or give up on the Puppie. I had noticed that the syrups in the dispensers were very acidic, and now I could see why: they had to balance the unbelievable sweetness of the base mix. So I'd have to focus on savoury ingredients that had a sufficiently acidic character to hold their own—pickled onions, perhaps, or gherkins or baby beetroots—and maybe even concentrate that acidity further by putting them in The Rocket.

AN ARTIST OF THE FLOATING WORLD

Over time, many scientific and technological innovations first developed for space exploration have found more mainstream applications. We have NASA to thank for cordless power tools, invisible dental braces, foam mattresses that "remember" your shape, water filters and shoe insoles that absorb impact and give more spring (which shows that the first moon landing was, in the most literal way, a leap for mankind). In the eighties I remember the first "space foods" going on sale: familiar foodstuffs that had been freeze-dried and sealed in silver foil packages. They looked convincingly like the kind of thing that might be found in the kitchen of a Skylab-style space station, and were guaranteed to grab the imagination of any teenage boy. I wondered whether I could provide my guests with a freeze-dried dessert and, as a tribute to the space programme's hand in developing the technology, make it float above the table, as though gravity-free. So I went to Reading University's Department of Food Bioscience to find out.

The room that housed the freeze-dryers was a vast and airy space with drainage grilles running the length of the floor on both sides and a succession of machines that looked as though they had been designed by W. Heath Robinson—a labyrinth of pipes and gauges and tubing and silvery lagging. Every so often a placard fixed to a wall or machine identified the process to which a particular set of buttons and dials was devoted: *Swept Surface Heat Exchanger*; *Multi-Functional Process Plant*; *Direct and Indirect Steam Injection*. By contrast, the freeze-dryer to which Dr Mike Lewis led me was an undramatic red metal column topped by something that looked a lot like a microwave.

"The freeze-dryer relies on a process called sublimation: the change from solid to vapour without passing through the liquid state," Mike explained. "We put a thin slice of Viennetta in the machine like this," he slid in a wedge of layered vanilla ice cream and chocolate and closed the double doors. "Then we switch on the vacuum." He pressed some buttons, setting off a faint but steady sucking sound. "The heat-plate melts the ice but, because there's no pressure in the chamber, it becomes a gas rather than a liquid. And because very little heat is used, there's very little shrinkage and the flavours are preserved."

I gazed in through the glass window set into the freeze-dryer door. After a minute the Viennetta looked more like soufflé and began rising and falling, almost as though breathing. "I had no idea it was so quick. I guess that as the pressure goes down, the water evaporates and the air released expands, making the food go up and down like that."

Mike nodded. "And as the water evaporates the temperature goes down until it freezes. Although you see a very noticeable alteration early on, the full drying process takes about twenty-four hours to complete. But it's intriguing to see what has already happened."

He opened the chamber and handed me the Viennetta. It looked fluffy with a texture like meringue. "Interesting," I said. "It's basically a frozen foam, but as all the water is gone, it isn't cold to the touch."

"Well, if you think that's interesting, Heston, have a look at this," Mike said, opening the door of a metallic-blue Stokes freeze-dryer and passing over a foil tray in which there lay a dark brown slab with a sort of fractal patterning across the surface, like ice on a windscreen. "Freeze-dried tea."

I pinched off a little and put it on my tongue. Almost immediately my mouth was flooded with impossibly bitter tannins, as if I had just taken a slurp of very stewed tea. "Cor that's strong!"

"Yes, with all the liquid driven off, it's extremely concentrated. Here are some freeze-dried tomatoes."

"That's strange." The appearance was altered—they'd taken on an attractive pastel orange colour and felt very light and airy and delicate. Part of the fruit was meringue-like, other parts not frozen at all. And it was cold—somewhere between fridge and freezer cold. Freeze-drying had changed it into something quite different. "Mike, this is fascinating, but what I really need to find out is whether freeze-drying can help me make food fly. You said the drying process takes twenty-four hours, so I'm hoping that you've already got some Viennetta that you prepared earlier, so we can test it out with these." I brandished a hairdryer and a motorised pedicure set.

He looked dubious about my low-tech approach but went off to a storage area and returned with a foil tray. The twenty-four-hour transformation was remarkable: the Viennetta was now unbelievably light, almost like a powder that was stuck together. It seemed very fragile. "There's no way that's going to float," I told Mike. "It's too delicate. It'll either blow away or the blast of air will destroy it." To prove my point, I picked off a chunk, held it over the hairdryer and pressed the switch, flipping it into the air and out of sight behind a steel table.

We tried out other freeze-dried ingredients—raspberries, chocolate fudge cake, banoffee pie—but nothing worked. Even the raspberries simply shot off into the distance when air was trained on them. One of the problems was that we had ended up with a hairdryer that didn't have a cold-air option, and the ingredients melted almost as soon as

I put them in position. After half an hour dripping chocolate had shorted out two hairdryers, and the work table was a chaotic jumble of sugar granules, cake smears, scissors, melted plastic, pumice-stones, kitchen towel and discarded wrappers. Puffballs of banoffee pie rolled around the surface like tumbleweed.

We were, however, no nearer a result, and the director was getting frustrated. "Look, I know this works. I've seen it done. I'll show you. Sarah?" Jay looked around for our assistant producer who, ever the problem-solver, was already on the balls of her feet, ready to run off in search of whatever was needed. "Please get us a packet of Maltesers. And a box of straws. And we need a new hairdryer. One that can do cold air as well as hot."

As soon as she returned, Jay cut off a small piece of straw, put one end in his mouth, tilted his chin upwards, held the Malteser between thumb and forefinger just above the other end, then let go and blew through the straw at the same time. The Malteser hovered in the slipstream a centimetre or so above the straw, eddying this way and that. "See?" he said, when the Malteser finally spun out of control and fell to the floor.

We went at it with a new determination. The keys to successful flight stimulation, we decided, were a spherical shape and a narrowly focused stream of air. Mike tracked down a small plastic funnel that could be placed over the hairdryer while I began sanding nuggets of freeze-dried food into neatly streamlined balls with the nail-buffer attachment. Eventually, we were ready for a second go. I put the funnel over the nozzle of the new hairdryer and gripped them both tightly in one hand. With the other, I held the freeze-dried ball above the pointy end of the funnel and turned on the hairdryer. The ball bobbed and danced and rotated, perfectly suspended in mid-air.

Intoxicated with success after so many failed attempts I did it over and over, saying, "Look! It floats! I've made floating food," like a little kid. It wasn't exactly space-age, admittedly—I'd have to get a lot more technical if I was going to serve a whole weightless dessert—but it was a really exciting start.

SUPERSTRINGS

In the mid-eighties there was great upheaval in the world of theoretical physics when scientists suggested that the behaviour of elementary particles could be explained by String Theory. The theory argued that electrons and quarks are not point-like and shapeless but in fact more like loops of string whose movement and vibration is what identifies them as particular particles. Several versions of the theory required a world not of four dimensions—height, width, depth and time—but ten, eleven or even twenty-six.

Fortunately, twenty-five years on, my own string theory was a lot simpler. I reckoned that if I carefully melted the right form of cheese in a fondue pan, I could create something ultra-stringy that would give my guests some fun and remind them of the experience of eating a toastie—the way that the cheese would stretch and stretch, forcing the eater to hold the toastie at arm's length in a desperate bid to detach the yellow umbilical strings from either their mouth or the sandwich.

In the Fat Duck lab, Jocky and I had got a fondue set and a number of cheeses I thought might work: Emmental, Gruyère, Comté, Cheddar, Jarlsberg and Cheesestrings (with a name like that, I *had* to test its potential). I felt that the key to stringiness might be kneading the cheese, which would stretch and align and strengthen the proteins, much as it does in breadmaking, but decided I'd better seek confirmation for this from Harold McGee's *On Food & Cooking*.

When the book was first published (in 1984, appropriately enough), it revolutionised the way I thought about cooking, encouraging me to question everything, and to apply a scientific logic and rigour to my exploration of recipes, ingredients and techniques. It lucidly outlines the nature and behaviour of ingredients and explains the science behind cooking practices, covering everything from the character of yak milk to why it's difficult to make jelly with fresh pineapple. If any kitchen reference book was going to explore the factors that contribute to cheese's stringiness, it would be Harold's.

Sure enough the book told me that stringiness was the result of calcium causing casein molecules to crosslink to form long rope-like

"No pain, no gain"—my fondue undergoes a few stretching exercises.

fibres. Harold warned me off well-aged grating cheeses, such as Parmesan (ripening enzymes attack casein, preventing it from forming fibres), and those with a high acid, fat, moisture or salt content. He identified the melting point as the moment when cheese was at its stringiest. So I put some Emmental in a pan, heated it up and then began teasing out a strand, but not quickly enough for Jocky, who loves this kind of hands-on stuff and grabbed the end off me and pulled. The cheese extended a good metre before snapping. "It gets brittle as it cools," he said. "Maybe we can add in something that'd help strengthen it—cornstarch? Citrate?"

Stefan melted some Emmental in a water bath to emulsify it and we began stretching it out on the lab floor alongside a tape measure. "2.8 metres," said Jocky. Keen to reach the three-metre mark, we melted more cheese and enlisted more chefs to gently tease out the strings and keep them from breaking. "Three-and-a-half metres and still going!" Jocky shouted. "Four metres from one cheese string! It's like a skipping rope. Is there a world record for cheese stretching?"

"Bound to be," I told him. "Probably as part of the Gastrolympics. Let's try those Cheesestrings because it seems to me that, since they've probably already had a vigorous kneading from industrial machines, they might well have the strength to stretch without snapping."

Stefan bunged an unopened packet in the water bath for a few minutes, then we pulled it, straight out of the packet, at head height, from one end of the lab to the other, with everybody cheering on the cheese as it extended to the far wall. "*Yessss*! That's gotta be more than five metres!" Jocky cried. "We need more room. Let's go outside."

We clattered downstairs and out into the Fat Duck car park, press-ganging whoever we encountered along the way—chefs, office staff, TV researchers—to join us in an attempt at the world's longest cheese string. But either we'd got lucky indoors or we'd reached the limits of our cheese manipulation skills because this time we couldn't manage anything near five metres. There was a moment's excitement when Jocky decided that gravity might be the answer and began stretching a cheese string by whirling it round his head like a lasso, scattering chefs in all directions, but this too proved short-lived. Suddenly everybody came to their senses, realised how disproportionately excited they'd got about stretching a piece of cheese and we all shuffled back upstairs, a little embarrassed.

A LOBSTERCINO FOR GORDON GEKKO

I had waved goodbye to the idea of microwaving a lobster, but there was another piece of technology that I was keen to try out—the filter coffee machine. This had been all the rage in the 1980s, and as I ransacked my memories for contemporary gadgets that might help create my Feast (and perhaps even feature in its service), I began to think that the filter machine could be well suited to the job. After all, it's basically a reservoir, a filter and a hotplate, all things that are used in cuisine, and the steady drip-drip-drip of water through ground coffee and into the glass jug is a form of infusion, a cooking technique that I often use to produce very subtle flavours.

My idea was to place lobster bisque in the water reservoir and a variety of fairly delicate herbs in the filter-holder. As the bisque made its way through the machine it would hopefully take on all the fragrance and freshness of the herbs, after which I'd pour it into an espresso cup and spoon on some foam to create a Lobstercino—the ultimate eighties concoction. I could imagine Gordon Gekko endorsing it. *Lunch? Lunch is for wimps. I just get a Lobstercino to go.* The more I thought about it, the more I liked the idea, particularly after I remembered that in the 1980s one of my heroes, the French chef Alain Chapel, invented *bouillon de champignons de printemps comme un cappuccino*—a mushroom soup frothed in the manner of a cappuccino.

So I got hold of a very eighties filter coffee machine in gleaming white plastic and travelled down to the harbour at Whitstable in Kent, where I would be sure to find some extremely fresh lobster for the experiment, and maybe a lobster-lover or two to try it out. At Wee Willie Winkle's café in the corner of the fishmarket, I tried to ignore the seen-it-all-before stares of the fishmongers while I blanched a

Is lunch for wimps? Checking out the potential of the Lobstercino.

lobster for one minute—long enough to firm the meat on the outside without cooking the middle—then removed the shell, chopped the flesh and placed it in the glass jug. Small handfuls of chopped herbs— parsley, chervil, chives and a little tarragon—went straight into the conical mesh filter-holder (without any filter paper), along with some matchsticks of fresh ginger. I poured strained lobster bisque into the reservoir, flicked the on switch and crouched down beside the counter to keep an eye on the soup's progress.

The machine started making throaty gurgling noises and a steady stream of thick orange liquid began to fill the jug, quickly submerging the lobster pieces. I was hoping that since the flesh was heated solely

283

TEA - £1.00
HOT CH
COFFEE - £1.50
LOBSTER CAPPUCC
Check all appliances are switched off.
After Saturday shift top up fryers.
After Sunday shift leave fryers, Roy will clean them.
Empty and clean chip warmer.
Clear trays from glass food warmer and clean inside & out.
Clean and clear table between display and coffee machine.
Clean coffee machine and steam WAND this must be done as milk kills.
Clean s/s milk jug as well.
Store milk in fridge, check sell by date. Give to main kitchen if needed.
Turn off GAS and clean main griddle & rack empty fat drain.
Clean and wash soup kettles.
Wash all utensils and replace them back in WWW kitchen.
Wash all s/s tables.
Sweep behind and out front.
Saturday re- stock for Sunday.
Sunday clean kitchen out of all food items.
Replace all black bags, and remove rubbish to back yard.
Check all equipment is switched off.
Ensure Roy has refilled fryers BEFORE YOU SWITCH THEM
Chemex
Wipes

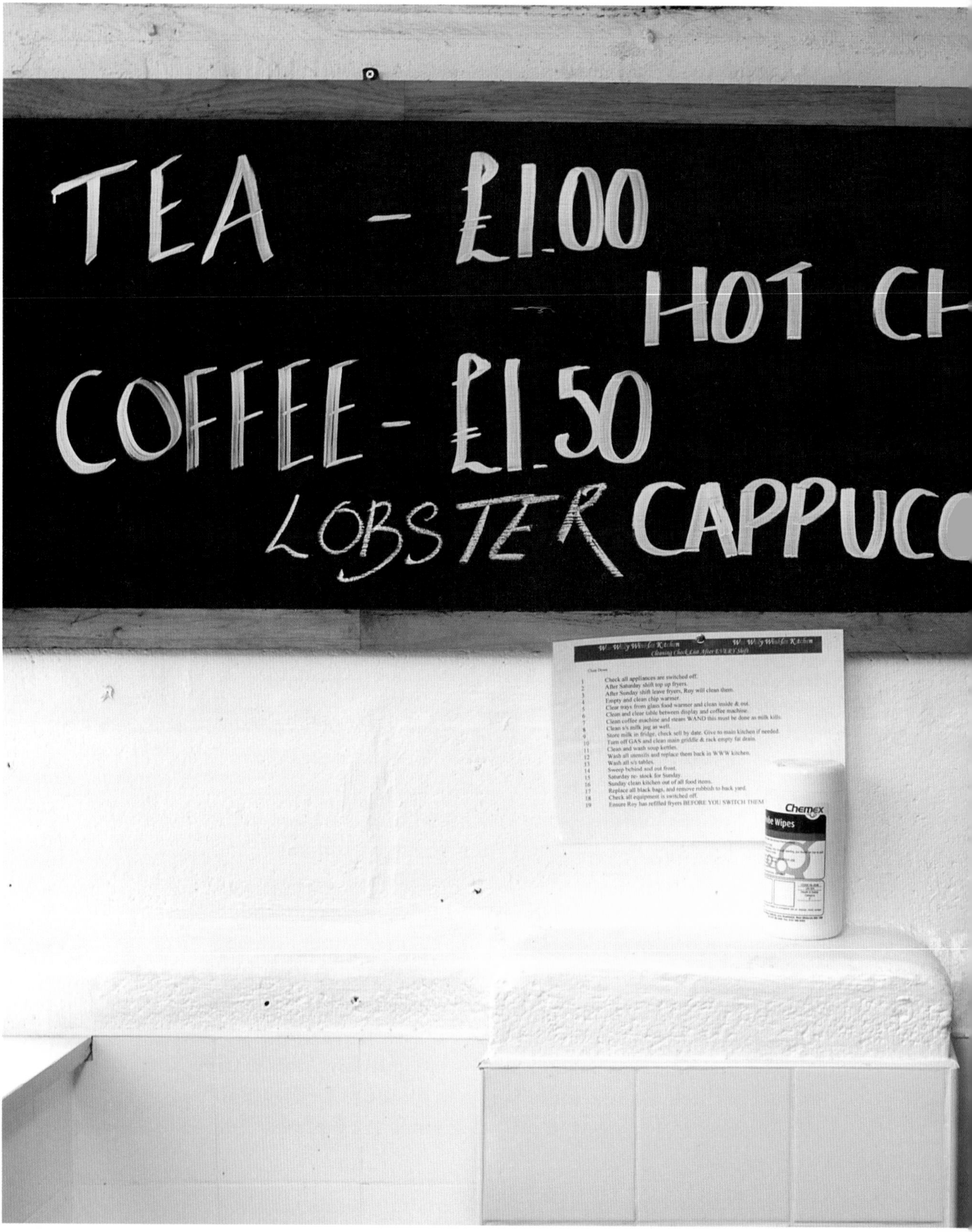

by means of the liquid now covering it, overcooking would be avoided. Already there was a delightfully rich, fishy smell and the aroma of tarragon and ginger. I was impatient to open the jug and taste it to see if those herbs had actually flavoured the bisque, but I knew I had to let the liquid run its course.

Finally it was ready. I put some morsels of lobster meat in the bottom of the espresso cup and poured in the bisque. Since I had sieved the liquid to make sure that it passed easily through the machine, it was possibly a bit thin, but very refined nonetheless. I poured a little more of the bisque into a container with some milk, Aerolatted it to a froth and spooned it on top. As a finishing touch, I sprinkled on little freeze-dried granules of lobster bisque (because the juxtaposition of different textures of the same ingredient—grated raw apple on a tarte Tatin, for example—can really heighten the flavours), and then I took my first taste of the Lobstercino.

It had a lovely velvety texture and the herbs really had infused into the liquid, making it fresh and fragrant and lively and light. The lobster pieces were perfectly cooked. I drank every last drop. I hadn't expected much from my coffee-filter technique and the fact that it had surpassed my expectations so spectacularly made me want to celebrate. I went in search of the SodaStream and a bottle of Blue Nun.

TURNING JAPANESE

It's not surprising that sushi started to become a feature of British cuisine in the 1980s. It was expensive, healthy, stylish and compact— the perfect finger food—and City types began serving it at business shindigs. So it seemed to me the perfect way to open my Feast, particularly because I had thought of a terrific way of presenting it. "LOOK AT MY WAD!" had been another of Harry Enfield's catchphrases as he waved loadsamoney in your face, and I was going to give each of my guests what looked like a great big wedge of cash, secured by a money clip, and then invite them to eat it all up. Not a sushi roll—a sushi bankroll.

LOOK AT MY WAD!—the sushi money wedge goes public.

Recalling the eighties: sake, SodaStream, massive mobile.

I reckoned it could be done by preparing sushi rice in the traditional way—cooking it for fifteen minutes, then adding in flavourings and seasonings (dried egg yolk, dried bonito flakes, wasabi, nori, kombu, sesame seeds, soy sauce and a salty-sweet, five-day-fermented seaweed vinegar to give the characteristic sour note)—and then flattening small palmfuls into a wedge shape. Smear other flavourings on top, such as fromage blanc for freshness, horseradish for a bit of a kick and fish roe for that delightful burst-in-the-mouth texture, and then wrap around the rice a sheet of green nori seaweed followed by a sheet of rice paper printed to look like a banknote, and it would look like a pretty convincing stash of cash.

And how about a bit of bubbly to go with it—the reward for a hard day spent getting that money in the first place? Why not give sake the SodaStream treatment and serve that to my guests as well?

FAD GADGET

I wanted to make the ultimate cheese toastie and had experimented with all sorts of fancy breads and unusual fillings. I had even built the mother of all toastie makers—loads of machines rigged up together to create one giant one—to bring a bit of theatre to the service. But this didn't get me any nearer to solving the key dilemma of toastie-making: how do you get a lovely crisp, browned exterior without overcooking the filling? And since I had decided on a filling of Comté, Gruyère, softened onions, Extremadura ham, braised suckling pig belly and sliced black truffles—the classic ham 'n' cheese toastie but with a luxury upgrade—it really needed delicate handling.

In the past I've often solved this kind of dilemma by cooking the ingredients separately and then putting them together. The Fat Duck's Lasagne of Langoustine is done like this, as is the Fish Pie that features in *Further Adventures in Search of Perfection*. I saw no reason why I couldn't do the same here.

So I cut a triangular piece of foam from a kitchen sponge, wrapped it in clingfilm and inserted it between the two triangular pieces of bread that would go in the toastie-maker, then placed my sponge-filled bread in the machine and closed it.

Ten minutes later I opened the lid. It had worked! The bread was nicely browned but, when I ran a knife around the seam, I opened it out to find I had a perfectly shaped casing for my cheese and ham filling. I would have to fine-tune some of the details, like how I was going to reseal the seams on the bread, but basically I could cook the toast to just the right level of colour and crispness and then add the filling and give it a final touch of heat to warm it through.

Now all I had to do was find the right flavours for the savoury Slush Puppie that would accompany my turbo-charged toastie.

THE ONLY WAY IS UP

Since Maltesers had proved to be the breakthrough at Reading, when I was trying to make food float, it seemed wise to make something similar for my Feast, so that at least one of my desserts was guaranteed to get off the ground. I would, I decided, make chocolate hemispheres in a mould and fill them with freeze-dried eighties flavours: raspberry pieces, ground mascarpone and yoghurt powder could make a plausible raspberry cheesecake, for example, and maybe freeze-dried banana and passionfruit would simulate banoffee pie. Once I'd painted the edge of the filled hemisphere with melted chocolate and placed another hemisphere on top, it would look just like a big Malteser. I'd have to find a more reliable method of making them float than a cut-off drinking straw, but I was sure the TV set designers would come up with something good for that.

But what would I serve alongside this? Some form of Eton Mess in a white chocolate moon? A tiramisu because, although it was invented in Italy in the 1970s, it took off in Britain in a big way in the eighties? (Which wasn't surprising, really. After all, the eighties was the decade of the dinner party and tiramisu is perfect party fodder—showy, exotic, easy to prepare and laced with enough chocolate, cream and booze to get any gathering going.)

I definitely wanted to get Campari in somewhere, in some form, because of the TV advertisements for it in the seventies: "Were you truly wafted here from paradise?" asks the white-suited toff. "Nah, Luton airport," replies Lorraine Chase. The ads so perfectly anticipated the kind of aspirational values that dominated the eighties, it almost seemed as though they had been the catalyst for them.

I began thinking about a spin on Campari & soda—a sugar syrup made with plenty of orange juice and zest plus pectin to thicken it. If I made this, then added whipped egg whites to give it an airiness, plus some Campari and Prosecco, I could put the mixture in a siphon to create an incredibly light foam. In storage somewhere at the Fat Duck I knew I had a set of moulds for making ice globes that could be used as drinking vessels: I'd bought them years ago because I liked the idea,

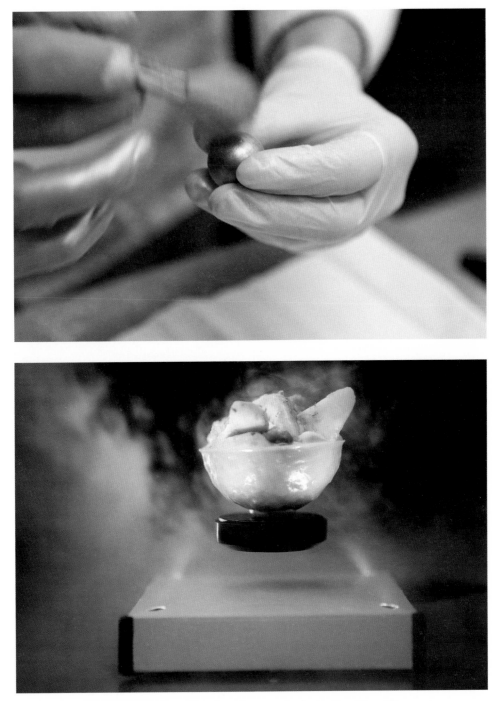

A glitzed-up banoffee chocolate and a levitating Eton Mess.

Wafted here from paradise—Campari & soda foam in a globe of ice.

but had never found an opportunity to use them. They would be the ideal way to serve my Campari foam cocktail, with a hollowed-out vanilla pod as a drinking straw.

A picture for the presentation of the dish was forming in my mind. I wondered about serving the tiramisu as a cocktail too, and somehow getting the drinks to float above the table. I had heard of a catering company that sold something clever to do with magnets. Apparently you got a baseplate that, when it was switched on, created a magnetic field, and then a disc could be made to hover above it, upon which food could be placed. I reckoned it might be what I was looking for.

Maybe the whole idea was going to fly, after all.

ROCK LOBSTER

The Lobstercino had worked so well that I felt I had to include it in my Feast, and pretty much in the form that I'd tried it out in, with a lobster stock in the reservoir of a coffee machine and the herbs in the filter. The only change would be to use roasted bones (and possibly caramel colouring or squid ink) to make the stock, so that it was darker and more coffee-like. Ideally, I'd like my guests to think they were getting a coffee right up to the point where they smelled the aroma coming from the cup and took their first sip. And maybe I could reinforce this illusion by using gelatine to set a thin layer of milk at the very bottom of the cup. My guests would pour some "black coffee" from the pot and it would turn pale brown before their eyes.

This got me thinking about creating a power lunch that even Gordon Gekko would sit down to eat—something suitably luxurious and look-at-me. Gradually an idea took shape. There would have to be more lobster, of course: perhaps tails cooked gently in a water bath, then fried quickly in lobster-infused oil and bottarga (dried roe of grey mullet) to give a nutty note. And there would have to be carbs—my triple-cooked chips recipe would fit the bill (first simmered for a soft fluffy interior, then fried to allow oil to penetrate the cracks and fissures and give some crunch, then fried again to get a lovely golden-brown exterior)—but they would have to be done in a more eighties format. Maybe a potato waffle?

For the garnish I wanted to serve baked beans, but done in a way that would pass muster at a big-league bean-counter's business lunch. They could be cooked in a pressure cooker with tomato juice so that they had a nice unblemished skin and a smooth, creamy centre, and then warmed in a pan with other luxurious ingredients—rich, sweet tomato fondue; cherry tomatoes pressure-cooked with the seeds and all the pulp for a full-on umami taste; olive oil infused with tomatoes and roasted lobster shell; and perhaps a little lobster flesh from the claws, added at the last minute so that it didn't overcook.

I reckoned it'd work on Gordon Gekko. One taste of this and he'd be rewriting his famous speech so it began: "Greedy is good…" 🔲

MENU

❖

Sushi Money Wedge
Nori, Sushi Rice, Horseradish Fromage Blanc, Ricepaper Banknote

Sake SodaStream Bubbly

❖

Cheese & Ham Toastie
Comté, Gruyère, Extremadura Ham,
Braised Suckling Pig Belly,
Sliced Black Truffle, Lardo

Stringy Cheese Fondue

Savoury Slush Puppies:
Tomato & Basil; Truffle; Beetroot & Sherry Vinegar

❖

Power Lunch

*"Lobstercino", Boil-in-the-bag, Bottarga-basted Lobster,
Triple-cooked Potato Waffle, Lobster Baked Beans*

Skylab Desserts

*Floating Chocolate Balls,
Campari & Soda Cocktail in an Ice-planet Glass, Tiramisu,
Banana Eton Mess served on a Floating Half-moon*

SUSHI MONEY WEDGE

FOR THE SUSHI-ZU
80g "red" rice vinegar (yusen)
70g refined caster sugar
25g sea salt
8 x 8cm square kombu

Place the rice vinegar, sugar and salt in a bowl and whisk until dissolved.

Once dissolved, add the kombu square and store in an airtight container in the fridge for at least 4 days before using.

FOR THE TROUT ROE
400g sake
50g fresh trout roe
100g mirin
100g soy sauce
1 sudachi (a type of Japanese lime)

Pour half of the sake into a small bowl. Add the trout roe to the bowl of sake and gently separate the individual eggs. Using tweezers or chopsticks, remove any empty egg sacs that float to the surface.

Strain the roe, wash the bowl thoroughly with water, and pour the second half of the sake into the bowl. Add the roe to the sake and rinse a second time to remove the impurities from the exterior of the roe.

Drain the eggs and discard the sake. Combine the mirin and soy sauce in a small container. Finely grate a quarter of the sudachi using a microplane and add to the mixture. When the roe has completely drained, add to the mixture and marinate for 2 hours in the fridge before serving.

FOR THE HORSERADISH FROMAGE BLANC
20g freshly grated horseradish
100g fromage blanc
1g salt

Place all the ingredients in a bowl and whisk thoroughly to combine. Cover and keep in the fridge until required.

FOR THE SUSHI RICE
500g sushi rice
450g water
sushi-zu (see above)
30g roasted sesame seeds (iri goma)
30g noritama furikake "Marumiya"
20g otonano furikake katsuo "Nagatanien"
20g honkatsuo furikake "Marumuya"
20g natto furikake
15g "thin mouth" soy sauce (kuchi shoyu)

Wash the rice thoroughly in a bowl of cold water, changing the water 6–8 times until it becomes clear.

Return the rice to the bowl and soak in fresh cold water for 30 minutes.

Drain the rice well and place in a rice cooker with the 450g water. Close the lid and cook until the rice is tender. Once cooked, allow to remain on the "keep warm" setting for 10–20 minutes before using, to evenly distribute the moisture.

Transfer the rice to a cedar tub (hangiri), which has been prepared by wiping with cold water and set onto a scale that has been tared to zero.

Measure out 10% of the weight of the rice in sushi-zu and begin folding it into the rice using a wooden paddle. Gently cut and turn the rice to evenly distribute the sushi-zu, while using a hand-held fan or paddle to cool the rice during the process.

When the rice is cooled to body temperature, cover with a towel that has been moistened with warm water.

When ready to serve, fold the sesame seeds and remaining ingredients into the rice.

TO FORM THE SUSHI
100g ice-cold water
10g sushi-zu (see above)
roasted nori (seaweed) sheets
sushi rice (see above)
horseradish fromage blanc (see above)
trout roe (see above)
counterfeit money rice paper

Place the water and sushi-zu in a bowl and mix well; use this liquid to moisten your hands for forming the sushi.

Cut the nori in the shape of the counterfeit money rice paper (7.8×14.5 cm).

On a sushi mat (maki-su), place a sheet of nori that has been trimmed to size.

Wetting your hands in the water and sushi-zu, form a small ball of the prepared rice, then flatten it, forming a square shape about 1cm thick and the size of half a £20 note (7.25×7.8 cm).

Spread a thin layer of the horseradish fromage blanc on top of the rice and place the trout roe on top to cover the entire surface. Place this on the bottom half of the nori and fold the nori in half to enclose the filling.

Place the sushi inside the counterfeit money rice paper and hold together with a money clip.

FOR THE FIZZY SAKE
Jumai Daiginjo Sake, chilled

Place the sake in a soda siphon to two-thirds of the capacity. Charge and refrigerate for 30 minutes before using to build pressure.

To serve, siphon into chilled glasses and serve immediately.

CHEESE & HAM TOASTIE

FOR THE SANDWICH SHELL

The sandwich is made in two separate halves (the triangles) and not as a square. You will also need a new kitchen sponge (2cm thick).

2 sheets of brik pastry (feuille de brick)
4 slices of medium sliced white bread, crusts removed
100g very soft butter

Open a sandwich toaster and measure the sides of the small recess of the triangle (the deepest part) which should be approximately 8 x 8.5 x 12cm. Cut the new kitchen sponge into two pieces of this size and shape and wrap each one in clingfilm. Poke holes in the clingfilm and set aside.

Cut 4 pieces of brik pastry into triangles of the same size and set aside.

Next, measure the surrounding triangle around the recess in the sandwich machine which should be approximately 10.5 x 12 x 16cm. Cut 4 triangles of bread to this size; discard the remaining bread.

To form the shells, brush the soft butter onto the outsides of two bread triangles, making sure that they are in line with each other when sandwiched together with the butter on the outside. Place a triangle of brik pastry on the buttered side of each bread triangle and brush more butter over the top of the pastry. Place a sponge triangle in between the two slices of bread as if it were the filling.

Place into a hot sandwich machine, close and cook until golden. Remove, leave to cool and cut carefully along two of the three sides to open the toastie and to remove the sponge. The shell is ready to fill.

FOR THE ONION COMPOTE

45g butter
375g baby onions, halved and thinly sliced
5g garlic, crushed
4 thyme sprigs
20g Madeira
25g double cream
salt and freshly ground black pepper
70g bacon lardons, cooked until crisp and cooled
20g black truffle, chopped

Melt the butter in a pan. Add the sliced onions, garlic and thyme and cook slowly for 10–15 minutes until softened but not coloured.

Add the Madeira and cook for 1 minute, then stir in the cream and cook for a further minute. Season with salt and pepper.

Remove the thyme sprigs and blend half of the onion mixture using a hand blender until smooth. Pass through a fine sieve and stir back into the rest of the cooked onions.

Add the lardons and truffle and leave to cool.

FOR THE CHEESE FONDUE SLICES

450g Gruyère cheese
450g Comté cheese
14g cornflour
500g white wine
20g lemon juice
30g sherry, infused with garlic and thyme sprigs
5g mustard powder
pinch of ground cloves

Grate both of the cheeses and toss with the cornflour.

In a small pan, bring the wine and lemon juice to the boil. Sprinkle in the grated cheeses and cornflour mix, whisking constantly to encourage the cheeses to melt.

When the mixture is smooth and creamy, add the sherry, mustard powder and cloves. Keeping the mixture below boiling point, continue to whisk until the fondue thickens and becomes stringy.

For the cheese slices, pour the fondue into a deep bread tin lined with clingfilm. Cover the surface of the cheese with more clingfilm. Put into the fridge until firm.

Unwrap and cut the fondue into 3mm slices to fit the toastie.

TO BUILD THE TOASTIES

Per triangle:

tomato ketchup

7 thin slices of peeled button mushroom

15g onion compote (see above)

25g pata negra ham, thinly sliced

15g cooked streaky bacon, diced

20g cooked suckling pig belly, sliced

4 slices of black truffle

1 slice of cheese fondue, 3mm thick (see above)

1 triangle of lardo, 1mm thick (the size of the brik pastry)

very soft butter

3 strips of brik pastry 3cm wide (one 10.5cm long; one 12cm long; one 16cm long)

Open the toastie shells and brush a thin coating of tomato ketchup onto each of the internal sides of the shell, then lay the mushroom slices on one side of the shell.

Place the onion compote on top of the mushrooms, spreading it evenly.

Follow with the ham, bacon and belly pork, then the truffle and the cheese slice and, finally, the lardo.

Fold the lid over, brush the outside of the closed toastie with the soft butter and then place the strips of brik pastry one by one on the respective sides, covering the gaps between the top and bottom of the toastie, and making sure that there is an even amount of pastry either side of the gaps.

Smooth over and hold it closed, then repeat with the other sides; brush the pastry with butter again. The toastie should now be closed.

Place in a preheated toasted sandwich maker and cook for 2–3 minutes until the fresh pastry is golden and the filling is warm inside.

SAVOURY SLUSH PUPPIES

FOR THE SYRUP
10kg water
250g refined caster sugar
2kg maltodextrin IT-19
50g glycerine

Place all the ingredients in a large pan, whisk to dissolve and pour into the slush machine; turn the machine to the freeze setting and leave to churn for at least 4 hours.

When serving, pour 100g of slush into a cup with the suggested quantity of one of the following syrups.

FOR THE TRUFFLE SYRUP
1.12kg truffle juice
0.5g white truffle oil
1g olive oil
1g salt

Put the truffle juice into a rotary evaporator (Rocket) and reduce to 400g.

To serve, take 25g of the truffle juice and mix with the olive oil and salt.

Mix well and serve with 100g of the frozen syrup for a truffle slush.

FOR THE BEETROOT & SHERRY VINEGAR SLUSH
1.8kg beetroot juice
3.5g salt
38g sherry vinegar
16.5g balsamic vinegar

Put the beetroot juice into a rotary evaporator (Rocket) and reduce to a 50° Brix syrup.

Combine 180g of the reduced beetroot juice with the salt and vinegars. Mix well.

Serve 12g of the beetroot mix with 100g of frozen syrup for a beetroot slush.

FOR THE TOMATO & BASIL SLUSH
1.8kg red peppers, cored and seeded
2.9kg cherry tomatoes
16g salt
400g cucumber
0.6g cayenne pepper
4 garlic cloves, peeled
3g coriander seeds, crushed
30g sherry vinegar
25g olive oil
2 basil leaves, chopped as finely
   as possible

In a blender, purée the red peppers, cherry tomatoes, salt, cucumber, cayenne pepper and garlic cloves until smooth. Transfer to a bowl, add the crushed coriander seeds and refrigerate for 12 hours.

Pass the mixture through a Superbag, place in a rotary evaporator (Rocket) and reduce by three-quarters.

Add the sherry vinegar and olive oil and blitz with a hand blender to combine.

To serve, put the finely chopped basil leaves into the bottom of a cup and add 12g of the mix with 100g of the frozen slush syrup.

"LOBSTERCINO"

FOR THE LOBSTER STOCK
3.6kg lobster shells and broken claws
grapeseed or groundnut oil, for frying
720g Noilly Prat
1kg onions, thinly sliced
1kg carrots, thinly sliced
100g celery, thinly sliced
300g button mushrooms
10g garlic, thinly sliced
400g plum tomatoes, roughly chopped
500g lobster juices, reserved from
   de-shelling the tails and claws
50g fresh root ginger, peeled and sliced

In a 12-litre pressure cooker, fry the lobster
shells and claws in a little oil for several
minutes. Add the Noilly Prat and reduce to
a syrup. Remove the mixture from the pan and
set aside. Return the pan to the heat.

Add the onions, carrots, celery, mushrooms
and garlic and sauté over a high heat for
10 minutes. Add the tomatoes, lobster shell
mixture and lobster juices. Pour in enough
water to cover.

Put the lid on and cook under pressure for
2 hours. Remove from the heat, allow to cool,
then de-pressurise and remove the lid. Strain
the contents of the pan through a fine-meshed
strainer. Return the liquid to a clean pan and
reduce by two-thirds.

Remove from the heat and add the ginger.
Allow to infuse for 20 minutes and then strain.
Cool and reserve.

FOR THE LOBSTER FOAM
150g lobster stock (see above)
350g double cream
salt

In a pan, combine the lobster stock and
cream and heat until the mixture reaches
a temperature of 80°C. Season with salt and
pour into a siphon canister.

Prepare the siphon with 2 charges and store
in a 65°C water bath until required.

FOR THE MILK GEL
3.5g leaf gelatine
150g skimmed milk

Soak the gelatine in cold water to cover.

Heat the milk in a saucepan to 80°C and
remove from the heat. Squeeze excess water
from the gelatine, then add to the hot milk
and stir until melted.

Place 20g of the milk mixture into the
bottom of each cappuccino cup and place in
the fridge to set.

FOR THE "CHOCOLATE POWDER"
50g fresh ground coffee
25g vanilla seeds, dried to a powder

Combine the ground coffee and the vanilla
powder and place in a Rubik's Cube pepper
mill for service.

TO SERVE
lobster stock (see above), heated
salt and freshly ground pepper
chervil tops
tarragon leaves
cappuccino cups with set milk gel
  (see above)
lobster foam in a siphon (see above)
"chocolate powder" (see above)

Season the lobster stock with salt and pepper
and pour into the reservoir of a filter-coffee
machine. Place the herbs in the section where
the coffee grounds are normally held.

In front of the guests, turn on the coffee
machine; the stock will heat up and pass
through the herbs for a fresh infusion.

Pour the infused liquid into the individual
cappuccino cups and allow the gel to melt to
make white coffee.

Siphon the lobster foam onto the top for
a cappuccino effect.

Grind the coffee and vanilla powder over the
surface to finish.

TIRAMISU

FOR THE DARK CHOCOLATE DISCS

250g dark chocolate

Temper the chocolate in a tempering machine or by hand and spread thinly and evenly on acetate sheets.

As the chocolate begins to set at room temperature, cut with round cutters to 4 different sizes to fit into martini glasses at different levels.

Store in an airtight container for the assembly.

FOR THE TIRAMISU MIXTURE

60g pasteurised egg yolks
80g pasteurised egg whites
75g refined caster sugar
300g mascarpone cheese
200g whipping cream
540g marsala
Pavesini (sponge fingers)
80g instant coffee

Whisk the egg yolks and whites together with the sugar until thick and creamy. Add the mascarpone and whisk together.

In a separate bowl, whip the cream with 40g of the marsala to soft peaks. Fold into the mascarpone mixture in 3 stages.

Lay the Pavesini in a shallow dish. Mix the coffee with the remaining marsala, stirring to dissolve. Spoon the mixture over the Pavesini until the biscuits are fully soaked. Keep the tiramisu mixture and soaked biscuits separate until ready to assemble.

TO ASSEMBLE

soaked Pavesini fingers (see tiramisu, above)
dark chocolate discs (see above)
tiramisu mixture (see above)
cocoa powder, for dusting

Place a layer of soaked Pavesini fingers in the bottom of each martini glass. Place a disc of chocolate on top. Spoon some tiramisu mixture over the chocolate and lay another disc of chocolate on top. Press down evenly.

Repeat these layers, finishing with a layer of mascarpone on top. Use a metal spatula to level the mixture flush with the rim of the glass.

Cool in the fridge for at least 8 hours. Dust the surface with cocoa powder before serving.

CAMPARI & SODA COCKTAIL

500g mandarin purée
500g blood orange purée
110g refined caster sugar
12g yellow pectin
zest of 4 oranges
75g egg whites
80g fresh blood orange juice
1g malic acid
0.3g salt
70g Prosecco
50g Campari

In a saucepan, heat the mandarin and blood orange purées.

Combine the sugar and pectin in a bowl, then whisk into the warm purées. Heat for 1 minute, whisking constantly, then remove from the heat.

Add the orange zest and allow the mixture to cool. Strain the mixture and weigh out 370g.

Combine this mixture with the egg whites, blood orange juice, malic acid, salt, Prosecco and Campari and whisk together. Pour into a soda siphon and add the charges.

Place the siphon in the fridge for at least 30 minutes before serving, to build up the gas.

When ready to serve, siphon into iced cups and serve immediately.

Acknowledgements

Firstly I'd like to thank all of the people who generously shared their expertise and resources with me: Miss Hope and Mr Greenwood; Steve Howard, Tim Slatter and all the crew at The Cake Store; Karl-Josef Fuchs and Lutz and his fellow-hunters; Carl Peters and everyone at Biopharm Leeches (UK); Tony the butcher, for providing the goose blood; Gail Leonard and Youness and Faycal, who looked after me so well in Fes; Omar and Abd-el Aziz; Mike Richardson; Venetia Phillips, Lisa Marie Russo and Deirdre Traynor; Alexandru, Codruta, Adi and Gheorghe and his family in Transylvania; Fergus Drennan; Fay MacDonald and Sam Wilson; the team at Waterlands and the team at Currys in Fulham; Sarah Robson; Gillian Milner; Anthony Scala and his colleagues at the London Glassblowing Workshop; Pete Fareham, James Sizer and everyone at Breville for running with a crazy idea; Stephen Lewis and the workers at the Pot Noodle factory; Lulu Gwynne at Betty Blythe's; Zoe Fletcher and the burlesque girls; Mark P. Campbell and the team at Hamleys; Peter Bennet and Elizabeth Wright at Wee Willie Winkle's in Whitstable; Professor John Morris and Adina J. Henson at the Department of Physiology, Anatomy and Genetics, Oxford University; Dr Mike Lewis and Professor Don Mottram at Reading University; Franck Tournel at Le Petit Canard in Paris; and everyone in Bagnolo, especially Graziella, Moreno, Massimo, Lucia, Egino, Signor Sensi, Leonardo, Fabio, Sabrina and Enyo.

Secondly I'd like to thank the team at Optomen TV, especially Jay Taylor, Tim Whitwell, Patrick Furlong, Russell Edwards, Sarah Veevers, Charlotte White, Emma Magee and Melany Hunt, and also David Weare, Matt Hunter and Giles Thompson for their incredible set designs.

I'd also like to thank everyone who helped create this book against the odds: my literary agent, Zoë Waldie; my agent, Jonny Dawes; my PR agent, Monica Brown; my commissioning editor, Richard Atkinson, and the rest of the team at Bloomsbury: Natalie Hunt, Xa Shaw Stewart and Penny Edwards. Thanks must also go to Rachel Calder at the Sayle Literary Agency and Nathaniel and Bronwen Jones for reading drafts of the manuscript; Janet Illsley for editing the text with great sensitivity and intelligence; Sally Somers for reading the proofs and Hilary Bird for preparing the index. Peter Dawson and Tom Lane did a wonderful job of creating a suitably magical design for the whole thing, and I'm grateful to Andy Sewell for once more capturing such a great set of photographs on the hoof.

I'm indebted to my PA, Deborah Chalcroft, for organising my insane filming schedule in a way that made it survivable; Pascal Cariss for his brilliant way with words and inimitable sense of humour; Camilla Stoddart for shepherding the manuscript through the publishing process at the Fat Duck end so that it arrived at Bloomsbury buff rather than duff; and all the waiters who provided such a superlative service and made sure it all went without a hitch on the day: Eric Doerr, Esher Williams, Simon King, Julien Gardin, Simone Bohner, Thomas Aragones, Arnaud Lamboley, Remi Cousin, Nicolas Boise and Fanny Houlette.

Finally I have to thank all the chefs for making these feasts as memorable as possible: Jocky Petrie, Kyle Connaughton, Stefan Cosser, Otto Romer, Matt Gojevic, Natalie Phanphensophon, Ida Garphagen, Jonny Spilling, Evelyn Wu and Andrea Soldini. They have worked harder than anyone could possibly imagine to make it all work. To say it couldn't have happened without them is an understatement.

Index

To Zanna, Jack, Jessie and Joy—the A Team

HESTON'S FEASTS IS AN OPTOMEN TELEVISION PRODUCTION
FOR CHANNEL 4

First published in 2010

Project editor: Janet Illsley
Designer: Peter Dawson, www.gradedesign.com
Photographer: Andy Sewell, www.andysewell.com
Illustrator: Tom Lane, www.gingermonkeydesign.com
Indexer: Hilary Bird

Bloomsbury Publishing Plc, 36 Soho Square, London W1D 3QY
Bloomsbury USA, 175 Fifth Avenue, New York, NY 10010
Bloomsbury Publishing, London, New York and Berlin

A CIP catalogue record for this book is available from the British Library.
Cataloging-in-Publication Data is available from the Library of Congress.

UK ISBN 978 1 4088 0860 3
US ISBN 978 1 60819 369 1
Special edition ISBN 978 1 4088 1320 1

10 9 8 7 6 5 4 3 2 1

Printed and bound in Italy by Graphicom

This book is typeset in Paperback, a typeface family from the foundry House Industries. Designed
by John Downer, Paperback is a resurrection of the practice of designing different typefaces for use
at specific sizes for specific usages, allowing the family to prosper in a wide range of situations.
This process of mastering has largely fallen by the wayside since the demise of cut metal type.

Mixed Sources
Product group from well-managed
forests, controlled sources and
recycled wood or fibre
www.fsc.org   Cert no. CQ-COC-000015
©1996 Forest Stewardship Council
FSC

www.bloomsbury.com/hestonblumenthal
www.bloomsburyusa.com